Amada's Blessings from the Peyote Gardens of South Texas

Amada's Blessings *from the* Peyote Gardens *of* South Texas

Stacy B. Schaefer

University of New Mexico Press | Albuquerque

© 2015 by the University of New Mexico Press
All rights reserved. Published 2015
Printed in the United States of America
First Paperback Edition, 2015

Library of Congress Cataloging-in-Publication Data
Schaefer, Stacy B., 1956–
  Amada's blessings from the peyote gardens of South Texas / Stacy B. Schaefer.
    pages cm
  Includes bibliographical references and index.
  ISBN 978-0-8263-5621-5 (paperback) — ISBN 978-0-8263-5622-2 (electronic)
  1. Cardenas, Amada. 2. Mexican American women—Biography. 3. Mexican Americans—Social life and customs. 4. Mexican Americans—Religion. 5. Peyotism. 6. Native American Church of North America. I. Title.
  E184.M5S322 2015
  305.48'86872073—dc23

                                    2015004415

Cover photo: Close-up of Amada making a peyote chief, 1995. Courtesy of Stacy B. Schaefer.
Designed by Lila Sanchez
Composed in Adobe Garamond Pro
Display type is Bernhard Modern

This book is dedicated to the memory and legacy of Amada and Claudio Cardenas Sr., to their son Claudio Cardenas Jr. and his family, and to all the people I was so fortunate to meet along the path to and from the peyote gardens.

And to the future of the gardens. Long may the peyote flourish in its native lands and continue to open the hearts of those who listen to its song.

Contents

Acknowledgments		ix
Introduction	Feliz Cumpleaños, Amada	1
Chapter 1	Beginnings: The Land of the Peyote Gardens and Los Ojuelos	17
Chapter 2	The Peyote Trade	31
Chapter 3	Mirando City and the Peyote Business	51
Chapter 4	Tepees on the Landscape: The Cardenases and the Native American Church	91
Chapter 5	The Mustang Plains: Amada's Place in the '60s and '70s	111
Chapter 6	Amada's Home: A Worldly Place	137
Chapter 7	Saint, Mom, and Grandma on Sacred Peyote Grounds	165
Chapter 8	Amada's Love	201
Conclusion	Amada's Legacy	223
Appendix	Legal Documents and Landmark Charters of Incorporation in Native American Church History	235
Notes		245
References		275
Index		287

Illustrations follow pages 76 and 153

Acknowledgments

Writing this book has provided me with profound insights into the beauty that humanity is capable of expressing. Amada manifested this beauty in her character and reflected the divine nature of the world.

I am eternally grateful to have known Amada as a friend and a mentor, and I feel extremely fortunate to have shared moments of life with her and to have seen how her presence has positively influenced so many people in a kind and charitable way—in the peyote way. The experiences I have had with Amada and at Amada's home began the life-changing journey I have taken that led to the research and writing of this book. Along the way many people have generously contributed their time, their thoughts, and their friendship.

First and foremost, I want to thank the members of Amada's family whom I had the pleasure and honor to know. I feel blessed to have been accepted as a family member. I send a heartfelt thanks to Amada's son, Claudio Jr., for his friendship and generosity, for his patience and willingness to answer so many of my questions, and for sharing with me important information, documents, photographs, and even a part of his and his family's history, to make this book possible. I always looked forward to seeing Claudio, Joanne, the granddaughters, and whomever of the kids visited with Amada. I also have fond memories of the few times that Claudio accompanied Jim, Bear, and me for a day in Nuevo Laredo to rendezvous with members of my Huichol family. Many warm thanks go out to Claudio's wife, Joanne; their children, Alan, Cheryl, and Vicki; Amada's sister Andrea, whom Amada and I would visit in Laredo, and her niece, Gloria; Geraldine, another of Amada's nieces in Laredo; Amada's brother, Juan Guerra, and family; and the Guadiano members of Amada's family from Benavides and San Antonio, who would also visit. Nora Martinez, her husband, Isidro, and children, Gracie and Abel, and Gracie's husband, James, became Amada's family in their home in the latter part of her life. They, too, shared their home, meals, friendship, hospitality, and the spice of Tejano life with me. Until she had to return to Monterrey, shortly after which she passed away, Nora's *tía* (Aunt) Ana had a quiet but supportive presence at Amada's house. I would also like to recognize Nora's mother, the late Teresa Johnson, who brought her spunk and laughter to the ambiance at Amada's. I appreciate the phone calls she would make to me at Amada's house to check in when Amada was unable to come to the phone.

My dear husband, Jim, whom Amada also adored, has been my sincere, loving, and supportive compañero, sharing in our visits with Amada in South Texas along with the many other worlds we travel together. I feel so fortunate for his editorial flair through the numerous versions of the book manuscript and for the map. I am beholden to John Byram and the staff at the University of New Mexico Press for recognizing the importance of telling Amada's story and for their expertise and professionalism in manifesting this labor of love into book form. Many thanks go out especially to Jessica Knauss for her care and meticulous editing skills; Lila Sanchez for the beautiful cover design, which truly captures Amada's essence; Beth Hadas for her summarizing craft; as well as to James Ayers, Marie Switzer Landau, and Maya Allen-Gallegos. I am also grateful to Norma Cantú and the anonymous reviewer for the time and thought they put toward contributing many germane comments and suggestions that further strengthened the content and quality of this book.

The wonders of synchronicity have been key in my meeting Amada and the many people and experiences that have unfolded as a result. I wish to thank Sheila and Tom Pozorski, who, early in my tenure at University of Texas–Pan American (UT–PA, now University of Texas Rio Grande Valley [UTRGV]), gave me the newspaper feature about peyote dealers from the

McAllen Monitor that spurred me to learn more, and who have been genuinely supportive of this project. I am grateful to Amando Reyna and the Reyna family, the peyote dealers in Rio Grande City who first told me of Amada and encouraged me to visit her. I am also thankful to the other peyote dealers I got to know—Salvador Johnson and his wife, Vicenta, who have warmly greeted and extended to me their big Tejano hospitality; Mauro Morales, always a gentleman and kind person; and Miguel Rodriguez, who could make anyone laugh with his sense of humor. Jody Patterson from the Department of Public Safety has been helpful in providing information about the peyote trade.

In Laredo, I wish to acknowledge Cathy Kazen and the late Jackie Geissler, and her husband Richard, for their friendships and hospitality. Rosie and Ricardo de Anda were most gracious in inviting Amada and me to the festive Tejano events they held at their house in Laredo. Jose Moreno from Special Collections at the Laredo Public Library was extremely helpful in locating information and references for this book. I applaud his efforts and those of the Texas Historical Commission in working to recognize Amada and the important role she and Claudio Sr. had in the cultural history of the area and beyond. I am thankful to Carolyn Boyd and the Shumla Staff in West Texas for the hospitality they extended and for the brainstorming sessions we have had at the White Shaman's Cave and other impressive ancient rock art sites.

My gratitude to Gary and Debbie Perez is immeasurable. They gave me their friendship and included me in social networks, and they do so much in Amada's memory to maintain her place and continue the peyote traditions there. Thanks to Gary for his creative ideas, the wisdom he has imparted, and his wildly amusing sense of humor. I would like to recognize Cristala for introducing the Perezes' kids, Autumn and Cameron, to Amada, and for connecting me with Gary and Debbie in 2004. I will always remember my first visit with the Perez family, which took place at the San Antonio Missions followed by a meal at Elvia Cristan's family restaurant in San Antonio. Little did any of us know at that time the vital role Gary and Debbie Perez would take in keeping Amada's place open and her wishes vibrantly alive. Special thanks go out to Donna and Will Dozier for their efforts and the contributions they make to Amada's home.

Also top on my list of acknowledgements are Jerry and Linda Patchen. I remember my first prayer meeting at Amada's, sitting in the tepee next to Jerry Patchen and Anthony Davis, both of whom were active participants. I appreciate their help in teaching me proper etiquette for conducting myself in the meeting. I will always treasure the friendship the Patchens and their family, especially Michelle, extended to me. I have the utmost appreciation for all that Jerry and Linda have shared with me, starting with sending me a copy of George Morgan's dissertation, and their visits at Amada's, at their house in Houston, and at the "Plants, Shamanism and Altered States of Consciousness" conference held in Lérida, near Barcelona, Spain. Linda and Jerry lovingly dedicated themselves for many years to visiting and helping Amada as well as many others who made the long journey to her place and to the peyote gardens. Their hearts and deeds have also contributed greatly to this book and its story.

Thanks go out to Patti Hamrick for the sleepovers we had at Amada's and the companionship, kindness, and love she shared with Amada, and to Barry "Bear" Hamrick for all the heartfelt care he showered upon Amada and everyone around, as well as his contributions to helping my Huichol family. Many thanks go out to Coahuiltecans Manuel Kuhautli Vásquez and José Zepeda for sharing their stories with me and for honoring Amada in the ways they do.

I will always be grateful to Melvin George and his family for honoring Amada, and upon her request, graciously allowing me to attend the February meetings that Melvin ran, and for the patience and sincerity with which his family taught me the Native American Church ways as they had learned them from relatives at their family's fireplace. I am especially appreciative to Alden Naranjo and Juanita Nelson for all the love and care they gave to Amada and the annual meetings. I also wish to recognize the following people I came to know because of their visits over the years for Amada's birthday and the February meetings for all they have given of themselves for Amada: the late Bertha Grove; Everett D'Wolf; Jasper Gómez; Peter Templeton; Lillian and the late Jerry Etcitty; my dear friend Elva and her husband, the late James Yazzie; the late Anthony Davis; Wilbur and Melissa Goodblanket; Archie Hoffman; Nellie and the late Danny Sandoval; Sandy Hacquez; and Helen Walker. I also wish to thank Tom and Loretta Cook and Beatrice Weasel Bear for kindly sharing their thoughts and their home with Jim and me in Chadron, Nebraska. I am grateful to the late Ron Weedon, curator of the George Morgan Memorial Collection at Chadron State College, for allowing me access to Morgan's archive and for sharing with me stories that further confirmed for me how extraordinary this man was.

During my tenure at the UT–PA, there were a number of people who were supportive of me and who contributed in a variety of ways to this research. I offer many kind thoughts and thanks to Mark and Diana Glazer; Juanita Garza; Rudy Rocha; the late Irene Ledesma and the memory of her smiling personality; Raul Solís; Genáro Gonzalez; Isreal Cuellar; Dahlia and Arnie Guerra; Servando Hinojosa, who along with his father, Servando Sr., joined in the ceremonies and celebrations at Amada's place; George and Virgina Gause and Farzaneh Razzaghi for their library expertise; Marly Moran; and Sheldon Weisfeld. I am thankful to my students while I was a professor at UT–PA; they also played an important role in mentoring me in understanding and integrating local Tejano culture and history into my awareness of the meaning and importance of place. All of these people have taught me much about South Texas and its vibrant culture. I feel that through the years I lived and experienced Tejano culture, I have enculturated many aspects of its essence into my sense of who I am today.

At California State University, Chico, I wish to thank the Anthropology Department faculty, staff, and students for their support and genuine interest in the project that has been so much of a part of my life over the years. Special thanks go out to Nette Martinez, Frank Bayham, and Ginger Farr; graduate students Elizabeth Kallenbach, Chris Ruiz, Marlo Eakes, Matt Meyers, Niles Reynolds and Robert Stevens; and to former graduate students Traci Van Deest and Carrie Brown, who helped transcribe a number of the interview tapes. I most sincerely want to thank former Provost Scott McNall and his wife, Sally, as well as Susan Place, former Dean of the Graduate School, International and Interdisciplinary Studies, for their unwavering enthusiasm for my research. My gratitude also goes out to Byron Jackson, former Dean of the College of Behavioral and Social Sciences (BSS), who bestowed upon me the honor of being a distinguished speaker for the College of BSS Faculty Colloquium Lecture Series in December 2004; to Deb Besnard and Heather McCafferty from the Merriam Library for the many hours they spent scanning my slides and fine-tuning the digital images; and to Claudine Franquet of the Technology and Learning Program, who masterfully edited the video footage and photographs that Jim and I shot of Amada's one hundredth birthday celebration.

Many of my friends and colleagues outside of these two universities have also shared their interest and enthusiasm and given me encouragement for this project. I am grateful to geographers Darrel McDonald and Clarissa Kimber; Bonnie Glass Coffin and the students, faculty, and staff who hosted me in Logan, Utah, during my lectures sponsored by the Museum of Anthropology and the Department of Sociology, Social Work, and Anthropology at Utah State University; Lydia Nakashima Degarrod for inviting me to give several guest lectures at the California College of the Arts; and Manolo and Donna Torres for their friendship, their invitation to speak at Florida International University in Miami, and their visit to South Texas. The Cactus Conferences at Frogwood Lodge and Retreat Center in Boonville, California, have always provided exciting and lively inspiration and have served as a think tank for me as I further developed this book. Thanks so very much to Keeper Trout; Geoffrey Pomerantz; Seabrook Leaf; Martin Terry; Ted, Janica, Ann, and the late Sasha Shulgin; Tania and Greg Manning; David Theodoropoulos; Sherry Calkins; Ben Kamm; Bia Labate; and Kevin Feeney. I also wish to express my gratitude to my dear colleagues Jonathon Ott, Rob Montgomery, Brent Blosser, Doug Sharon, and the late Ted Anderson for sharing their ideas and traveling with me through the South Texas brushland when I lived in McAllen.

I feel especially privileged to have had the opportunity to interview Amada about her life. On my third visit to her home in Mirando City on November 27, 1993, she graciously consented to be interviewed. She agreed to a second interview at her home on February 2, 1997. On both occasions she shared intimate vignettes of her life, which I captured on cassette tape, pausing the recorder occasionally because of phone calls she received or visitors who arrived at the house. She was certainly popular and many people wanted to spend time visiting with her.

It was a pleasure to converse with many more individuals for this book. Each one enthusiastically agreed to be interviewed, often responding with a resounding "yes" or "absolutely." With so many people who cared about Amada, and she for them, it was not possible to speak with everyone due to distance and time constraints. I was able to interview a number of people whom I regularly saw at Amada's house or whom she would tell me about. Nora Martinez also played a crucial role in helping me connect with Amada's friends and family in Mirando City, Laredo, and Alice, Texas. I feel confident that the sentiments expressed by the people I spoke with are also held by many others. The thoughts and feelings expressed by people that were captured in the raw footage of the interviews Susan Maynard, Aida Franco, and crew carried out are further testament to the profound influence Amada had on people from so many walks of life. I am very grateful to Susan for sharing them with me.

In addition to my interviews with Amada, all but eight of the additional interviews for this book were conducted during my sabbatical in 2004 and the summer of 2005, when Amada was still with us. The interview with Margaret Behan and Linda D'Wolf took place in 1997; the interviews with Melvin George, Claudio Cardenas Jr., and Silvester and Anthony Davis took place in 2000. My interviews with Gary Perez and Alan Cardenas were conducted in 2011, several years after Amada had passed on. I wish to thank the following individuals for participating in these interviews, presented in alphabetical order:

Geri Arviso, Margaret Behan, Alan Cardenas, Claudio Cardenas, Loretta Afraid of Bear-Cook, Elvia Cristan, Linda D'Wolf, Anthony Davis, Maria Esquivel, Lillian and Jerry Etcitty, Jackie and Richard Geissler, Melvin George, Bertha Grove, Juan Guerra, Patti and Bear Hamrick, Catalina Inocencio, Salvador Johnson and his mother, Teresa Johnson, Guadalupe Lira, Margarito Lopez, Nora Martinez, Darrel McDonald, Raquel Mendieta, Mauro Morales, Alden Naranjo, Gloria Sanchez Palacios, Jerry Patchen, Gary Perez, Florinda Sheeran, Manuel Vásquez, Beatrice Weasel Bear, and José Zepeda.

Information I gathered that was pertinent to this book comes from the following museums, libraries, and archives: the Southwest Museum of the American Indian (now part of the Autry National Center), Los Angeles, California; the Graduate Library at UCLA, Los Angeles, California; the Republic of the Rio Grande Museum, Laredo, Texas; the Webb County Historical Foundation, Laredo, Texas; the Laredo Public Library Special Collections, Laredo, Texas; the shrine and museum of renowned curandero don Pedrito Jaramillo, Falfurrias, Texas; the shrine for the Virgin of San Juan, San Juan, Texas; the University of Texas–Pan American Library Special Collections, Edinburg, Texas; the private photo archive of Mrs. Linda Patchen, Houston, Texas; the George Morgan Memorial Collection archives, Chadron State College, Chadron, Nebraska.

The research for this project was made possible from the award of sabbaticals in spring 2004 and over the academic year 2010–2011 and various Strategic Performance Grants from the College of BSS at California State University, Chico. This book was made possible in large part by financial assistance from the Ruth Landes Memorial Research Fund, a program of the Reed Foundation. Dr. Landes's research has also inspired the writing of this book. Her pioneering works on Mexican Americans of Texas (1965), the Objiwa of Ontario and Minnesota (1937; 1938; 1968a), the Potawatomi of Kansas (1970), and the Mystic Lake Sioux (1968b), are intertwined with Amada's story, as some members of these tribes were members of the Native American Church and obtained peyote from local dealers in South Texas in the same area where Amada lived and worked in the peyote trade.

The following works by Ruth Landes influenced my anthropological approach throughout my time with Amada and her extended family.

1937 Ojibwa Sociology. New York: Columbia University Press.
1938 The Ojibwa Woman. New York: Columbia University Press.
1965 Latin Americans of the Southwest. St. Louis: Webster Division, McGraw Hill.
1968a Ojibwa Religion and Midewiwin. Madison: University of Wisconsin Press.
1968b The Mystic Lake Sioux: Sociology of the Mdewakantonwan Sioux. Madison: University of Wisconsin Press.
1970 The Prairie Potawatomi: Tradition and Ritual in the Twentieth Century. Madison: University of Wisconsin Press.

Many of the people in this book have last names of Spanish ancestry. I have included accent marks in these names only in cases in which an individual customarily uses them. Based on my questions to people living or born and raised in the borderlands of South Texas, many prefer not to use these accent marks.

Introduction

Feliz Cumpleaños, Amada

The name "Amada" is derived from the Spanish verb *amar* (to love), and means "beloved," "adored," or "dear one." Amada is all of these, an extraordinary woman filled with love from the time she was born in Rancho los Ojuelos in the heart of the peyote gardens of South Texas.

One Hundred Years of Life

"*Feliz cumpleaños* (happy birthday), Amada," the enthusiastic crowd shouted. Amada wore a dazzling rhinestone-studded tiara upon her soft, freshly styled hair. Under the bright lights of the Mirando City Civic Center, her white hair carried a hint of lavender, her favorite color. She sat in the place of honor, as poised as any queen would be. She was a tiny woman, but she had a magnetic presence that sparkled brightly. The day was October 26, 2004, and it was Amada Cardenas's one hundredth birthday. She had become a centenarian, an extraordinary accomplishment for anyone, and Amada was not just anyone. She was known and cherished near and far by a wide circle of people from many walks of life; a sampling of the thousands of people whose life she graced was present for this event. Amada's kin were there from Mirando City, Laredo, McAllen, Alice, San Antonio, and Houston to honor her and rejoice with her on this memorable day. Like so many others from that region, their origins were rooted in generations of Tejano families who were the first settlers to inhabit Texas under Spanish rule in place of the indigenous inhabitants who had fled or succumbed to Spanish domination. Her son

Claudio and his family, who had lived in Minnesota for many years, sat with Amada at the table of honor. Nora, her attentive caregiver who had become as good as her daughter, was close by Amada's side.

Across the United States and beyond, she was known as "Mom" and "Grandma" by countless American Indians who practiced the peyote religion of the Native American Church (NAC). Representatives from generations of Indian families who had known her and were dear friends were present, along with officers from the NAC chapters of Oklahoma, North America, Navajoland, and others. Coahuiltecans, Chicanos from South Texas who had reclaimed their Indian roots, had come to honor Amada, as did a number of non-Indians, whites—better known in Texas as Anglos— who hailed from various places in the nation. My husband, Jim, and I were some of those Anglos who were passionately committed to being here for this electrifying birthday celebration. You see, I had counted myself among the extraordinarily fortunate ones who knew Amada as a mom, a grandma, a mentor, and a friend, ever since that day that I bravely showed up on the doorstep of her home in Mirando City, Texas, in 1993. But before digressing to explain how I came to meet with Amada on that warm February day in South Texas, allow me to further describe her birthday celebration, the people who gathered, and the events that took place to honor this extraordinary woman—a living legend who found her way into the hearts of admirers from so many facets of her life.

From the Civic Center and throughout the town, the sights and sounds of birthday good cheer were evident; the Center is not far from Amada's property on the outskirts of Mirando City, a place she called home beginning in the 1940s. Amada Cardenas never lived more than two miles away from the small community of Rancho los Ojuelos (ranch of the little springs), where she was born in 1904. Now practically a ghost town, with a historical marker along the edge of Farm to Market Road 649, it was once an oasis of abundant spring waters within the thorny scrub brush of the present-day Texas borderland with the Mexican state of Tamaulipas. It was most likely the birthplace of the peyote trade and the *peyoteros*, the people who harvested, traded, and sold peyote in the United States (Morgan 1976:61, 136). Some of the older Tejanos who were present at the birthday celebration knew Amada from way back in the early days in Los Ojuelos, as they call it. Margarito Lopez, an old vaquero, knew Amada when she was young and helped her father, Esiquio Sanchez, dry peyote to sell to the Indians who came through. Margarito also recalls when Amada married her one-and-only sweetheart, Claudio Cardenas, and the two worked in the peyote trade, making it their lifelong passion. They were committed to helping Native Americans obtain this humble, spineless, vision-producing cactus that was and is the sacrament of the NAC.

Amada's niece, Gloria Sanchez Palacios, stood by the table of honor taking pictures and beaming at her aunt, her mother's oldest sister; she was overcome with emotion to see her aunt reach such a distinguished old age, unlike her less fortunate siblings, including Gloria's mother. Gloria had fond memories of growing up with Amada and Claudio Sr., who acted as her second parents and helped raise her and her older cousin Claudio Jr. Longtime residents of Mirando City from the time it was a booming oil town were also at Amada's birthday party, such as Raquel Mendieta and her husband Oscar; Maria Esquivel; and Guadalupe Lira, the mother of Amada's godson Juan. Catalina Inocencio and her husband, Oscar, made a point to come to this gala event; they had last seen Amada when they recently came to her home to deliver the *hostia* (holy wafer) from the local Catholic church, so that Amada, as she eagerly requested, could take Communion even if she could not make it to Sunday mass. Florinda Sheeran, dressed in a Texas-style cowboy hat and high-stepping boots, stood tall, looking on proudly at her friend, remembering years ago when Amada employed her sons to harvest peyote and bring these dust-gray, cut cactus tops to Amada's house, where she would dry them and sell them to the Indians. Also in attendance was Teresa Johnson, the mother of Nora, Amada's caregiver. Every so often, Mrs. Johnson would break into gay laughter, perhaps remembering times past when she was young and would go picnic at Los Ojuelos and flirt, like many of the girls did, with Amada's brother, who was now long gone. Nora's brother, Salvador Johnson, came to pay his special respects to Amada, his elder and mentor in the peyote trade, as did Mauro Morales and Miguel Rodriguez, both federally licensed peyote dealers from Rio Grande City, further south along the border.

In keeping with Tejano tradition, the first event to mark Amada's one hundredth birthday had been a mass in her honor at St. Agnes Catholic Church a few blocks away. No longer able to walk from years of degenerative arthritis in her knees, Amada sat regally in her wheelchair as she was helped up to the altar and anointed with holy water by the attending priest. This was a ritual she knew well, because for many years she had bestowed her own blessings with sacred water and prayers upon all of her visitors when they were leaving her house. As Amada was wheeled down the aisle to exit the church, her half brothers Juan and Jorge Guerra and her half sister Beatrice posed for photographs around her wheelchair. Cathy Kazen knelt by Amada's side for another photograph; she was the niece of Judge E. James Kazen of Laredo, who had ruled in favor of the NAC and Amada's efforts to continue to provide them with peyote for religious purposes. Many other adoring friends and family followed in line to have their picture taken with Amada. This, too, was a ritual that was endlessly repeated with visitors to her home. Everyone wanted to have a picture taken with Amada—personal family members, American Indian families, Anglos, and even foreign visitors from Japan, South America, and other faraway places. I think sometimes these visitors hoped that their picture with Amada would bring good memories and good luck, as if they could carry some of her soul and her blessings home with them.

From the church, the number of guests multiplied as they entered the Civic Center where the *gran pachanga* (big bash) was to take place. Once guests took their places at the festively decorated tables, the middle of the room became the central focus. Amada, flanked by her family, focused her gaze as she peered over the table at her two young friends, *danzantes* (Aztec dancers) in costumes. Manuel Vásquez, a Coahuiltecan from near San Antonio, wore a decorated loincloth and an ornate feathered headdress, while his companion, Lupe Ibarra from El Paso, wore a more subdued but elegant feathered headband and a cotton tunic. The scent of burning copal and sage incense filled the air as they prayed and blessed a representative peyote "button" and, with feather fans, sent their fragrant smoke-filled prayers to Amada. Manuel beat a handheld drum as they moved gracefully across the floor in dynamic choreographed steps, rattling with the special seedpods (*Thevetia*) strung together and tied around their ankles. Amada nodded her head to the beat, indicating she approved of and enjoyed this pageantry in her honor.

The energy was tangible. Just like the sparkling reflections that shone around the room from the tiara that Amada wore, the atmosphere at the party was charged with virtual *chispas* (sparks) in the air.

After the meal of barbecued brisket, beans, chiles, and tortillas, a DJ appeared on stage. He orchestrated a multicolored pulsating light show and sirens, and norteño music crashed out of a wall of speakers. Then out stepped the mariachis, the quintessential classic Mexican combo so necessary to serenade special occasions from Mexico City to South Texas. They were dressed in the typical attire: form-fitting black and silver-studded charro outfits with wide-brimmed hats. They played violins, trumpets, a classical guitar, a high-pitched five-string guitar, and a large acoustic bass. The day before, I had met one of the musicians; he was a Laredo police officer by day and a mariachi crooner by night.

The tenor singers blended their voices in harmony as they sang traditional mariachi songs to Amada. During musical interludes in their songs, they yelled out the *grito mexicano* (Mexican shout), a trilled "aaayyyy" that was so contagious that many of the guests joined in. Amada beamed with joyous nostalgia for the Tejano culture that runs deep down to the core of her being. People in the audience spontaneously rose from their metal folding chairs and started dancing in the center of the room. Nora wheeled Amada out to join them. Her friend Florinda Sheeran danced with Amada, pushing her wheelchair to the steps of the beat, while Amada swayed side to side in her chair, moving her arms to the rhythm. A loud cheer erupted when people saw her dancing. Then it was time for the cake and the traditional Mexican birthday song, "Las mañanitas," beautifully played and sung by the mariachis.

As the birthday party at the Civic Center drew to a close, another celebration was about to begin: a birthday meeting in the tradition of the NAC. During this celebration, participants gather all night in a sacred space, often a tepee, and under the guidance of the roadman, a religious specialist, partake of the sacred peyote cactus as they sing and offer good thoughts in prayer for the birthday honoree. Beyond the metal gates at the entrance to Amada's place—which were topped with the words "Native American Church, Spiritual Residence, Hope, Love, Faith, Charity" and the silhouette of a tepee—stood a real tepee erected in the customary place between the hogan, the picnic area, and Amada's house. Inside the tepee, special red sand had been carefully sculpted on the ground into a crescent moon–shaped altar, upon which the chief—a large, specially dried, and consecrated peyote—would be placed to guide the meeting that night in

Amada's honor. Jasper Gomez, from Taos Pueblo, had laid the sacred firewood in place and was kindling the fire. Peter Templeton, who had driven down with Jasper from Taos, also helped with preparations for the meeting. Jerry Etcitty, a Navajo from Aztec, New Mexico, was the roadman; he would run Amada's birthday meeting. His wife, Lillian, would be the "water woman"—the one who brought in the cool morning water, which she would bless with her tobacco-smoke-filled prayers for Amada. Melvin George, from the Yuchi tribe in Oklahoma, who had known Amada and her late husband, Claudio, for many years past, would "carry cedar"—be in charge of this traditional Native incense—in the meeting.

Jerry Patchen, a prominent lawyer from Houston, his wife, Linda, and their daughter, Michelle, Amada's dear friends since the 1970s, would be attending. So would "Junior" Naranjo, a Ute Indian from Colorado who had been coming to Amada's home with his family since he was a young boy and who usually ran the traditional Friday meeting at her place in February over Washington's birthday weekend. His wife, Juanita, accompanied him. Darrel McDonald, a geography professor from Nacogdoches, Texas, was there to show his respect for Amada, whom he met in the early 1980s by way of his professor and mentor, George Morgan. Barry ("Bear") Hamrick, a massage therapist from Austin, who with Patti, his former wife, had met Amada in the early 1990s, would also join in the tepee meeting. The midday meal that he was preparing for the next day was already slowly simmering in the makeshift kitchen he had set up on her property. The tepee would be filled with many more who wanted to share their profound sentiments for this diminutive woman with an enormous heart. The peyote tea had been brewed and the dried and fresh peyote had been procured for this special meeting in Amada's honor.

As the sun sank low in the west, the participants, many in traditional red-and-black or dark-blue clothing, lined up respectfully with their seating blankets outside the closed flap of the tepee until they were invited in. The line wound inside, clockwise, and everyone packed into a spot to stay respectfully sitting or kneeling until the next morning. Throughout the night, heartfelt prayers were poured out to the Creator God for this remarkable woman. Reverent singing of traditional songs, accompanied by the fervent sound of the gourd rattle and the body-penetrating beat of the water drum, resonated throughout her property and beyond. In the morning, Amada was wheeled into the tepee, accompanied by her son, Claudio Jr.; his wife, Jo Anne; Amada's grandson Alan and his two girls, Allison and Alexandra; and Amada's granddaughters Cheryl and Vicki and their children, Rachael, Nicole, Kelsey, and Tiana. Another lavishly decorated birthday cake for this celebration was placed on a blanket on the ground at Amada's feet behind the crescent moon altar. The roadman for the meeting, Jerry Etcitty, sprinkled dried cedar on the hot coals from the night's fire, now carefully shaped into the form of the sacred water bird. With his eagle feather, he fanned the fragrant smoke toward Amada and all around her body and then above her cake. He did the same for all of her family members, all the while speaking warm, happy words in his native Navajo tongue for Amada and her family's health and well-being.

Afterward a big meal was served outside on the picnic tables in the middle of Amada's property, under a veranda where one could seek refuge from the South Texas sun. I was there for all of it, savoring and embracing every moment of Amada's gala one hundredth birthday celebration.

By this point I had become much more of a part of all of these goings-on, a participant rather than an impartially distant ethnographer, immersing myself in the worlds that revolved around Amada and her life. I no longer took lengthy field notes as in earlier times, though I continued to document my experiences in photos when appropriate.

I can recall many of these experiences in still pictures and video clips of Amada and events and visits at her home. I also perceive these experiences as images conjured up from people's animated stories of their memories of Amada. Of all the touching images that I carry with me, I will always remember in a special way the first time that I met Amada.

Meeting Amada

I had waited almost a year for this moment. My mission: to meet Mrs. Amada Cardenas, famous among local Tejanos from Rio Grande City to Laredo as the first federally licensed peyote dealer. Now I was on the porch of her modest wood house, white with light blue trim, on the edge of Mirando City in South Texas brush country, where a colorful miniature wood painting of the Virgen de Guadalupe hung from the door.

To the right of the door, firmly nailed to the wall, was a metal plaque with an image of Jesus announcing, *"Bendiga este hogar de Sr. y Señora Claudio Cardenas"* (Bless this home of Mr. and Mrs. Claudio Cardenas). Several Native American women and a man were seated on the porch in white plastic chairs, carrying on a conversation that turned to chuckles and laughter, their heads often looking straight ahead toward the paved road some one hundred feet away. In the corner of the porch, to one side of the visitors, was a huge plastic pot overflowing with large, healthy peyote plants. Parked outside the property along the road and on the hard-packed soil within were a collection of vehicles with license plates from neighboring states and other states across the United States.

I stood on the porch, poised, with my student Marly Moran, who was originally from Brazil and now attended the University of Texas–Pan American (UTPA), at my side. Taking a deep breath, I tapped on the frame of the screen door of Mrs. Cardenas's house, anticipating her response, all the while feeling awkward and uncertain of my uninvited arrival, as well as vaguely uneasy about having brought Marly along. My thoughts were racing: *She isn't going to be thrilled to see a gringa here—no, "Anglo" is the word they use in these parts. She'll be even less welcoming to an anthropologist, let alone one who brings her student along.*

Just then, a grandmotherly voice with the lilt of a Mexican Spanish accent called from inside the house, "Come in, come on in, the door's open." As I opened the door and entered the house, my eyes fell upon the amazing myriad of decorations and photos of people on the walls, each one with a story to tell. My gaze continued straight to the table, where sat a charming older woman, small but of solid build; she must have been less than five feet tall when standing. Her kindly face was framed by silvery-white hair worn short with stylish waves given to her by nature. Through her thick, sturdy, pink-framed glasses, she beamed at Marly and me. "Welcome," she said. "Come on in, sit down. You must have come a long way. You must be tired. Would you like some coffee? Let me get you a cup. Do you take sugar and cream?" My mouth almost dropped open in amazement, and I instantly started to feel more at ease being here at Mrs. Cardenas's place. An American Indian couple sat at the table with her, one on either side. They introduced themselves by name and tribal affiliation, Cheyennes from Oklahoma. The man wore a cap that read

"Native American Church" on the front and was decorated with pins that indicated he was a proud military veteran.

Mrs. Cardenas was asking the couple if they had found some peyote to buy. They said they hadn't yet. She then rose from her seat, and, with a slight limp, went to the wall where her phone hung, reviewed the names and phone numbers on a handwritten list taped on the wall with the words "Peyote Dealers" at the top, and dialed the number next to one of the names on the list, Salvador Johnson, the local dealer in Mirando City. After a brief conversation on the line, Amada said she would send them over and returned the receiver to its resting place in the cradle of the phone. She shuffled back to her seat and told the couple, "Salvador Johnson has peyote; he says you can go pick it up."

This prompted the woman to state proudly, "My father was very active in keeping peyote legal for the Native American Church. In the forties he went to Washington, DC, to lobby so that Church members could use this sacrament."

The man said, "I'm sixty-eight, and I've been coming here since I was eight years old when my father would take me."

Amada piped up, "I'm eighty-eight."

The man continued, "Amada is always hospitable and, well, like family. Everyone calls her Mom because she's everyone's mom."

Amada asked us to sign our names in the large guest book that she kept close-by on the entry table, something she asked of all of her visitors. I later learned that Amada's guest book was a tradition she had maintained since she and her husband became peyote dealers in the 1930s. It was an honor to add my name to the information accumulated over the decades. After a pleasantly engaging visit with Amada, she told us to come the following weekend in February for the annual prayer meetings held over Washington's birthday weekend.

Elated, we returned the next weekend and found even more people at her place. A tepee had been set up on the grounds, and there was to be a prayer meeting that night, Friday, followed by a second on Saturday. Amada asked "Junior" Naranjo, the roadman for the Friday meeting, to take us into the tepee and explain the meaning of the prayer meeting and give us an overview of what went on there. She asked the roadman for Saturday night, Melvin George, to allow us to attend the meeting he would be running. He graciously agreed because Amada had requested it, and his family took seriously Amada's request for them to teach us the importance of a prayer meeting as well as the protocol and its meaning and how to behave. I am forever grateful that Amada made this possible for us and am equally thankful to these roadmen and their families for teaching me vital lessons in the NAC's ways of hope, love, faith, and charity. From that time forward, I have attended over two dozen meetings, all of them on the grounds of Amada's home.[1]

I quickly realized that Amada's place was on holy ground and was part of the greater Peyote Gardens where NAC members make pilgrimages, often from far away, to pray and purchase peyote to take home. It was a haven, where one could rest and feel safe from the thick dry prickly shrubs that characterize the regional landscape, a refuge from the unforgiving heat, a place where people from across the United States, and some from other countries, converged for healing and spiritual introspection, a place where all felt welcome. Amada made all of this possible. Here, on the borderlands with Mexico, where *corridos*, *cumbias*, and Texas country music flooded the airwaves and where Mexican Spanish and Tex-Mex were the predominant languages, American English served as the *lingua franca* for communication among the visitors from near and far.

Fortunately, when I was younger, I lived in Mexico for more than three years with a Mexican family that I still consider my second family, so I was fluent in Spanish and felt quite comfortable within Mexican culture. I was also familiar with peyote and its importance to the Huichol Indians of Mexico, with whom I have conducted long-term ethnographic fieldwork. The Huichol people have revered this vision-producing plant since ancient times and annually made pilgrimages to the sacred peyote land of Wirikuta in the Mexican state of San Luis Potosí, and I had participated in several such pilgrimages. I was also becoming acquainted with and gaining fluency in the unique Tejano culture that flourishes in South Texas, where I relocated to take a tenure-track position in anthropology at UTPA shortly after I completed my PhD in anthropology at UCLA.[2]

During the spring 1992 semester, my second at UTPA, my colleagues, Shelia and Tom Pozorski, had placed in my office mailbox an article from the newspaper about the peyote dealers in Rio Grande City, a town forty-five minutes away from my home in McAllen, Texas. This piqued my curiosity. I knew about peyote on the Mexican side of the border and about Huichol peyote traditions, but until reading this article I had no idea that I was living near one of only two areas in the continental United States (both in Texas) that were the native habitat for peyote. I also knew virtually nothing about the peyote religion of the NAC. I decided to pursue this subject further and asked students in my anthropology classes if any of them knew any dealers. One student approached me after class and told me her cousin was a dealer in Rio Grande City. She gave me his name, Amando Reyna, and his contact information, and she said she would tell him in advance about me. I called him a few days later and he agreed to let me visit his family's home the following weekend. Amando's father, Roque Reyna, had long been a peyote dealer in Rio Grande City, but he had since retired, and Amando had taken over the family business. He shared with me the workings of the peyote trade and explained the official paperwork through the Federal Drug Enforcement Administration (DEA) and the Texas Department of Public Safety (DPS) that was needed to acquire a peyote distributor's license, as well as the policies and procedures required by these agencies to legally sell peyote to members of the NAC. Over time, Amando also introduced me to other peyote dealers in Rio Grande City. From the onset, he told me about Mrs. Cardenas and highly encouraged me to meet her because I would learn far more about the peyote trade and the NAC from her, and a visit to her home would be well worth the effort. It took me a year to garner enough courage to do so; I am forever grateful that I did.

Amada's Place

After my initial visits to Amada's in February 1993, we started to correspond by mail. The first written communication I received from Amada was an Easter card that she sent March 15, 1993. She wrote, "I am *muy* simple and [an] old fashion[ed] lady, but you are always welcome to my humble home . . ." From that point forward, I began to see her regularly. It was a two-and-a-half-hour drive each way, modest by Texas standards.

Amada was always happy to have the company, and I often spent weekends at her home. It was amazing to see the number of people who visited her place. I learned how to help Amada make everyone feel comfortable, and I also kept up on news about the peyote harvest and its availability for NAC members. I gradually came to know a number of the regular visitors and began to feel part of a unique family-like community made up of Amada's friends and her family, including her son Claudio and his family, her sister, Andrea, and Andrea's daughter, Gloria. I remember driving Amada to see her sister and going out to lunch with these two charming "little old ladies." They looked so cute together that they drew attention and compliments from customers at Danny's, a local coffee-shop chain in Laredo. On our driving trips to Laredo and back, Amada would sit in the passenger seat, where she could barely see over the dashboard. Somehow she knew all the little cemeteries along the way, and she would thoughtfully cross herself and pray as we drove past each one.

There were also long periods of time when few visitors, if any, came to her house. These times offered me a window into Amada's life when it was quiet and peaceful. At these times, the sounds of the thorny brush lands were easier to hear: the melodic song of meadowlarks in the early morning, with their call of "shee-oo-e-lee shee-eelo-ee," the "whoo whoo" hooting of owls, and the howls and yips from coyotes at night. These could also be lonely times, so devoid of the voices of people and the energetic momentum of their activities as they came and went from the house. I think it was times like these when Amada appreciated my companionship the most. I usually slept in the spare bedroom when it was available. The arrangement brought me back to my memories of childhood and my grandparents, who helped raise me; I would frequently stay with them in their second bedroom. They were Jewish Romanian immigrants, and Amada reminded me of my grandmother, who was also very short in stature but had a Romanian accent when she spoke English instead of a Spanish one like Amada. And like my visits to my grandparents' house, Amada and I often passed the evenings together watching television. Unlike the spaghetti westerns, wrestling, and Lawrence Welk programs at my grandparents' house, Amada and I usually watched *Sábado Gigante* hosted by Don Francisco, her favorite *telenovelas* (Mexican soap operas), and *Noticiero Univisión* (nightly news from the Mexican station). Amada also felt like a mother to me, even more so after my real mother passed away in August 1993. When I shared my grief with Amada, she listened intently, retreated into her room, and brought out an exquisite Navajo beaded necklace and silver bracelets that had been gifted to her by Navajo visitors and gave them to me, letting me know that she cared about me like a mother. And she rejoiced in meeting Jim, my boyfriend, who eventually became my fiancé and then my husband. Amada enthusiastically accepted him as a son.

Whenever possible, I visited Amada over the holidays, such as Easter and Christmas. I made a special point of spending the Nochebuena (Christmas Eve) with her, and in December 1996 I drove us to nearby Laredo to join in the festivities of a beautiful Las Posadas celebration at the home of a longtime South Texas family, Rosie and Ricardo de Anda. Once Nora became Amada's caregiver and started taking her out more frequently, I often accompanied them on their errands in Laredo, even spending the day across the border in Nuevo Laredo for an early celebration of my birthday at the restaurant México Típico, a place Amada and her husband had frequented decades before. Amada joined in the festivities and had a piña colada with us before lunch. Another highlight from my visits with Amada was bringing my Huichol family to meet her. I had arranged for them to visit me and spend time at UTPA, giving presentations about their culture and demonstrating how they make their artwork. Fortunately, we were able to stay twice with Amada; during the second visit they had an opportunity to meet members of the NAC at her house for the February meetings.

Amada's Story

Over the years, as I grew to know Amada more intimately, I realized that I was no different in her eyes than anyone else in her life; she cared deeply about all of us. She had a profound influence on so many people's lives as a friend, mother, grandmother, healer, dealer, and, for some, a saint. It is rare to meet people of Amada's essence and character who walk this Earth, and I knew with her advancing years that Amada's story had to be told. Fortunately, several other people had written about her, however briefly, before I began writing this book. Geographer and friend George Morgan discusses Amada in his 1976 PhD dissertation in social geography, "Man,

Plant, and Religion: Peyote Trade on the Mustang Plains of Texas," as well as in a 1984 article that he cowrote with Omer Stewart in the *Southwestern Historical Quarterly*, entitled "Peyote Trade in South Texas."[3] Clarissa Kimber and Darrel McDonald, both geographers and professors at Texas universities, include a discussion about Amada in relation to the peyote trade in the chapter "Sacred and Profane Uses of the Cactus *Lophophora williamsii* from the South Texas Peyote Gardens," which they contributed for the 2004 book *Dangerous Harvest*. Brief mention of Amada is made in the article "Human Peyote Interaction in South Texas," written by Servando Hinojosa in 2000 for the journal *Culture and Agriculture*, and various newspaper articles have published snippets about Amada. Susan Maynard, Aida Franco, Bill Daniel, and Alan Pappe produced a visually beautiful short film titled *Amada of the Gardens* (2006 Maynard/Pratt & Brown production).[4]

The intent of this book is more encompassing. It provides an in-depth look into Amada and her life, from the cultural and ecological history that influenced her from the time she was born to the people and events in her life that contributed to her personal evolution. It describes interpersonal relationships she had with individuals and how her sage, penetrating loving-kindness found its way into the hearts and minds of multitudes of people from many walks of life.

The information presented in this book comes from a number of different sources. These include published information and film; my field notes and personal experiences, which span February 1993 to February 2011; references from the Special Collections at the Laredo Public Library; the Dr. George R. Morgan Memorial Archive at Chadron State College in Chadron, Nebraska; and Amada and the many individuals who graciously spoke with me, especially those who allowed me to interview them on tape. A list of the people I interviewed appears in the references section of this book. I was jubilant that the first interviews I carried out were with Amada in the 1990s. In the late 1990s and in 2000 I carried out half a dozen more with friends and family who came to her house. While I was on sabbatical leave from California State University, Chico, in 2004 I had the opportunity to interview many more people. I interviewed additional people in 2011. I intentionally sought out a number of these individuals in Alice, Austin, Houston, Laredo, Mirando City, Oilton, Rio Grande City, and San Antonio, Texas, and in Chadron, Nebraska. I happened to meet others at Amada's place who were more than willing to speak with me about this amazing woman. Some have called her an angel, Mother Teresa, a saint, a miraculous healer, peyote woman, and even peyote rose. The intention of this book is to tell Amada's story through her own voice and the voices of many of her family and friends, including me; after all, more voices make sweeter harmonies. I hope her life's story continues to be rekindled along with the sacred fires in hogans and tepees across the nation, and even in the family shrines and community temples of Huichol families. As humble as you are, and wherever you are, dear Amada, I hope you enjoy the storytelling within these pages, too.

Ooh, Los Ojuelos . . . everybody knew everybody. It was really nice. Across the street from my grandparents' home used to be the school. . . . Amada and her husband [still] lived there, too, the first couple of years when they were married. . . . I remember when we were living in Los Ojuelos that we would walk out of the little ranch and just walk the highway and walk back. And yes, I miss that. . . . I still think that it was very lovely. The sounds, the birds, the wind sometimes. Cold, the evenings were cool and no traffic, just talk, talk, talk and laugh and jump and skip. . . . And yes, it was something beautiful to grow up in.

—Gloria Sanchez Palacios, Amada's niece, interview, April 18, 2004

Well I suppose [I remember], even when I was a young child growing up, maybe three or four years old, when we lived in Los Ojuelos . . . we were pretty self-sufficient . . . we raised just about everything we needed for food. . . . my dad had about two or four vaqueros that worked with him and my mom used to cook for everybody.

—Claudio Cardenas Jr., Amada's son, interview, October 24, 2004

Chapter 1

Beginnings

The Land of the Peyote Gardens and Los Ojuelos

The Landscape

Amada S. Cardenas was born into this world in 1904 in Los Ojuelos, which is situated in Webb County in South Texas. South Texas, so distinct from the rest of the state, once joined other neighboring border regions to carve out their own short-lived country from January to November 1840. It was named the Republic of the Rio Grande, made up of proud Mexican separatists along with some Texans, frontier people seeking autonomy from the centralized Mexican government.[1] Within the reaches of this former empire, the vast Tamaulipan thorn scrub of the Mustang Plains in present-day Webb County is the land that Amada called home. This harsh landscape of thorny brush and small, tenacious trees was inhabited centuries ago by nomadic desert-dwelling bands of indigenous people. This section of the extensive Coastal Plain, crossed by the Bordas escarpment, is the northern reach of a unique ecosystem that includes the natural habitat of peyote (*Lophophora williamsii*), a plant whose range includes the Chihuahuan Desert, too, from West Texas south to San Luis Potosí, Mexico. These early peoples certainly became acquainted with peyote's amazing powers to heal both mind and body. Amada learned early in her life about the abundance of treasures hidden within the rugged natural beauty of this countryside and the unique cultural traditions that had evolved from such hardy, resilient settlers.

The first Spanish explorers to set foot in this region must have been awed by the Bordas Escarpment north of the Río Bravo (Rio Grande) and the sweeping views that it offered hundreds of feet above the extensive plains below. The first settlers to arrive here in the 1790s undoubtedly were impressed by the droves of wild horses and Texas Longhorn cattle that had escaped to this isolated land, prompting the explorers to name this territory Los Mesteños (the Mustang Plains) (Tijerina 1998:3).

Single individuals and impressive clusters of peyote inhabit the flatlands and rolling hills where Amada was born. Soils of gray caliche, red clay, and white limestone create a patchwork through dense scrub brush three to fifteen feet high of mesquite (*Prosopis juliflora*), *chaparro prieto* (blackbrush acacia, *Acacia amentacea*), and prickly pear cactus (*Opuntia* spp.) within the boundaries of Webb, Jim Hogg, Zapata, and Starr counties (Anderson 1969:301–303; Morgan 1976:12, 24–25; see also Longoria 1997:6–29).[2]

On this South Texas landscape, rainfall averages between seventeen and twenty-two inches per year. Dramatic rain showers bring startling flashes of light and deep resonating claps of thunder to the thorny landscape and cool the terrain from its humid, one-hundred-plus-degree temperatures in spring, summer, and fall. The weather can change "on a dime," and freezing "northers" bring wind, sometimes hail, in the winter, rapidly lowering the usually balmy seventy-five-degree weather to forty-four degrees and below.[3] For Amada, the variability of the weather had always been part of daily life and an important theme in her conversations with visitors to her home and in the letters she wrote to family and friends.

Amada knew when a storm was brewing before there was any indication in the sky—she observed the signs in nature. Laredo photojournalist Richard Geissler remembers, "Once . . . when I saw her on the porch and stopped to talk to her . . . the yellow jackets, the paper moths, they were circling the house and circling the house and she said, 'There is a big cold coming tomorrow.' And I said, 'Oh really? Why?' She said, 'See, when the wasps try to get in the house that's a sign that they are abandoning the nest and a big cold is coming.' And damned if the next day it came in blowing like a freight train" (interview, April 20, 2004).

In a letter she sent me in late May 1996, she devoted most of her thoughts to the weather.

> Mi buena amiga, los días han estado muy, muy calientes. Arriba de 104 degrees. Ay mi amor, que días tan calientes, nada de lluvia. Ya ves Stacy, qué seco están, ni lluvias, ni agua en las presas, hasta el Río se está secando, donde quiera no hay agua . . . (May 21, 1996)

> My good friend, the days have been very, very hot. Above 104 degrees. Oh, my love, what hot days, no rain. You can see, Stacy, how dry it is with no rain, no water in the reservoirs, even the river (Rio Grande) is drying up. There is no water anywhere.

This was no "small talk." For Amada, a keen understanding of the weather was essential. It was for everyone living in this environment, but especially for those involved in the peyote trade, for whom heat, rain, drought, and cold can affect the success of locating peyote in the brush and drying it for sale.

When the land is wet from rain, or a breeze picks up, a caravan of unforgettable scents dances through the air. Depending upon the time of year, one can catch the alluring fragrances of musky sage, the sweet honey-like aroma of *huisache* (*Acacia farnesiana*) and mesquite (*Prosopis*) blossoms, and the pungently sweet citrus scent of *anacahuita* (wild olive, *Cordia boissieri*). The land and sky are filled with the melodic songs of meadowlarks (*Sturnella neglecta*); yellow, orange-accented hooded orioles (*Icterus cucullatus*) with their "jeet-jeet" calls and rattling chatter; and the "pit-pitasee, pit-pit-pitasee, pitz" of vermillion fly catchers, whose crowns, throat, and underparts bring flashes of scarlet to the landscape. One can easily spot raptorial birds soaring above, such as Harris's hawks (*Parabuteo unicinctus*), tawny red-brown with patterned white and black feathers; *tijeretas* (scissor-tailed flycatchers, *Tyrannus forficatus*), with their astonishingly long tail feathers; and majestic crested caracaras (*Caracara cheriway*), the national bird of Mexico that knows no borders. For miles you can see these feathered raptors perched high upon telephone posts, keeping vigil from their lookout points for terrestrial prey, such as cottontail rabbits

(*Sylvilagus*), Mexican ground squirrels (*Spermophilus mexicanus*), voles (*Microtus ochrogaster*), and, of course, plentiful road kill if the coyotes do not get it first.

Some of the local youth clandestinely hunt these birds to sell to Native Americans traveling through on their quest to find their sacramental peyote. Amada, a great admirer of the birds' beauty and grace, and a conscientious upholder of wildlife laws to protect them, never allowed such activities on her property. Instead, she made her place a safe haven for creatures that wandered in from the brush. For years, Amada befriended a couple of *faisanes* (roadrunners, *Geococcyx californianus*) that decided Amada's yard was part of their territory. They would make their way boldly up to her house and unabashedly drink water from an old tin bowl that she put out for them. Families of feral cats found refuge on her property, living under the house. Amada had a soft spot for these cats that came in from the brush; they made their appearance when she left plates of food scraps on her back porch. In a high, singsong voice, she called out to them, "Here, kitty kitty, here, kitty kitty," doing what she could so that they would not starve to death. Only the wisest, most adaptable beings survive in these parts, humans included. Some of the most innovative were the original human inhabitants of the land.

Coahuiltecans

As early as eleven thousand years ago, this region was inhabited by Coahuiltecans, small bands of indigenous hunter-gatherer extended families in southern Texas and northeastern Mexico who spoke related languages and shared many cultural traits (Campbell 1983). They left behind projectile points and stone tools. The earliest description of Coahuiltecan people comes from the fabulous travel narrative of the Spanish explorer Álvar Núñez Cabeza de Vaca. He and three other shipwreck survivors wandered lost through what is now the American South for eight years, from 1528 to 1536. During that time, Cabeza de Vaca reveals in his writings the amazing turn of events in his life that led him from captive, to trader, to shaman and medicine man. He describes that some Coahuiltecans were tattooed, wore rabbit-skin and fiber loincloths, and donned capes of coyote and other animal skins. They also had domesticated a kind of dog that did not bark. Coahuiltecans were superb hunters with their bows and arrows, atlatl spears, and slings, and they could run down deer and antelope. They made effective traps and snares to catch animals and prepared camouflaged pits to catch javelinas (peccaries). Rabbits, wild turkeys, rodents, reptiles, insects, quails, doves, and other birds were eaten, as were cacti, maguey (*Agave* spp.) including lechuguilla (*A. lechuguilla*), and sotol (*Dasylirion texanum*). Mesquite beans were a staple, eaten fresh or dried and pounded into coarse flour. *Tunas* (sweet prickly pears) from the nopal or prickly pear cactus (*Opuntia* spp.) were relished (Newcomb 1961:37–44). Coahuiltecans also engaged in warfare, had ceremonies revolving around conflict, formed alliances, conducted rites of passage and healing ceremonies, and were said to establish contact with the supernatural. For a number of these ceremonies, they gathered and consumed peyote (Rueking 1953).

Various bands of these desert-dwelling Indians lived in what is present-day Webb County; they included groups known as Carrizo, Pacuache, Pastaloca, and Pitalac peoples, names applied by Spanish settlers.[4] By the early 1800s, these bands of Indians were severely impacted by the arrival of Comanches, Lipan Apaches, and other Indian groups displaced from their traditional territories and hunting grounds by Spanish colonists. Many survivors from the various bands of Indians known under the general cultural term Coahuiltecans ended up at missions in San Antonio (Campbell and Campbell 1981).

Los Ojuelos

In the mid-1700s, Spain was determined to protect the *frontera* (the northern border) of New Spain from raiding Apaches and Comanches and to strategically expand the lands north of the Rio Grande with fortified settlements. A buffer zone of *villas* (communities) was established along the banks of the Rio Grande (known on the Mexican side as the Río Bravo), and settlers were granted *porciones* (small tracts of land) to farm. Farther north, ranchos of larger parcels were granted for raising cattle, horses, and other livestock (Tijerina 1998:xxi). In 1755, don Tomás Sánchez de la Ibarrera y Garza and several other families established a settlement named

Laredo, a community that has grown exponentially to become the city of Laredo today (Thompson 1991:25–26).[5]

Amada's roots were established from this northern movement on the frontera to the place where there are springs, Los Ojuelos. It was mapped in 1830 by her great-great-grandfather, José Isidro Gutiérrez de Castro (Martínez-Laurel 2001:4). It was an emerald gem in this rugged landscape; crystal clear springs formed cool, refreshing ponds of water and made this shallow valley verdant and teaming with life. José Isidro Gutiérrez claimed a Spanish land grant of two leagues or 8,856 acres for his family (Tijerina 1998:8–9). He was never to see this land grow to be a working Tejano rancho. The precious springs had long before been discovered and claimed by American Indians that roamed the frontier. Arrowheads and other materials left behind by these Indians in times past grace the homes of some local residents today. Indians defending this precious watery place drove Gutiérrez back across the Rio Grande.

In 1857, nearly thirty years after Amada's great-great-grandfather mapped and claimed Los Ojuelos, and after the United States had taken over the Southwest under the Treaty of Guadalupe Hidalgo in 1848, Gutiérrez's grandsons—José Dionicio, Juan Nepomuceno, and José Maria Guerra—finally settled Los Ojuelos (Martínez-Laurel 2001:5). The Guerras welcomed family, guests, and migrant workers from the villas originally settled by the Spanish along the Rio Grande. From the 1850s to the 1870s, the last of the free-roaming Native Americans in the region either fled to Mexico, passed as mestizo, or were rounded up by the US government and sent to reservations in the newly created Indian Territory of Oklahoma. It was a bold, ruthless move that cleared the way for settlers to stake their claims to the vast territory that was now part of the United States.[6] By 1870 the settlement of Los Ojuelos had nearly four hundred people, and the cattle ranch, which stretched across twenty thousand acres, grew and prospered (Tijerina 1998:9). Los Ojuelos became a stop on the Pony Express route and a trading center along the road connecting Laredo to the west and Corpus Christi to the east, the port where the ranch would send oxcarts filled with wool and corn to market (Morgan 1976:63).[7] Los Ojuelos also served as a birthing center, complete with midwives who helped women from near and distant ranches bring new lives into the world.

Here, on October 26, 1904, Amada was born at Rancho los Ojuelos to Paula Guadiano and Ignacio Guerra, son of José Dionicio Guerra. From birth Amada was surrounded by a community where familial trust and cooperation were essential and where everyone relied on each other to survive. Establishing relationships as compadres—co-parents who, most often through church rituals, establish their roles as godparents to a child—they maintained strong bonds and linked several extended families together. *Compadrismo* was and continues to be a special relationship that creates lifelong ties between godparents, godchildren, and the children's parents. Community members of the rancho instilled in their children the virtues of hard work and respect for the family and elders. Children, related or adopted, were accepted into the household and treated the same as biological children in the family (Tijerina 1998:54–55). Amada's biological father led the life of a young vaquero who frequently spent days out on the range and did not have much of a presence in young Amada's life. Her mother later married Esiquio Sanchez, whom Amada recognized as the father who raised her. Her mother and Esiquio had seven more children, and five survived into adulthood. Amada took her role as eldest sister to heart and was a familial presence in their lives until she outlived them all, becoming the only centenarian among her siblings.

Male and female roles defined life in Rancho los Ojuelos. The men were vaqueros, a ranching tradition brought by the Spanish to the Americas and adapted by Anglo-Americans into the cowboy culture. The vaqueros wore wide-brimmed hats, leather chaps, and boots with metal spurs, and would spend their working days herding cows, horses, goats, and sheep (Tijerina 1998:48). Margarito Lopez, a former vaquero who worked in Los Ojuelos, knew Amada's whole family and remembers her when she was young. He reflects upon his vaquero life: "Tienes que juntar ganado, en ese tiempo se bañaba ganado. . . . Antes . . . tienes que buscarlas al monte, a caballo. Muchas veces tienes que acampar afuera, hiciera frío, hiciera calor" (You have to herd the cattle, in those days they were bathed. . . . Before . . . you have to look for them in the countryside on horseback. Many times you have to camp outside, whether it's cold or hot) (Margarito Lopez, interview, April 17, 2004).[8]

Margarito recalls that he was paid one *tostón* a day, which he calculates to be the equivalent of half a peso or fifty cents. Later he and his five brothers each earned a dollar a day. Times have certainly changed in the cattle ranching business in South Texas. Before, he would herd cattle on horseback, then with the horn of a truck; now it is done by airplane, and cattle are much more expensive.[9]

Back at the rancho, women tended fields planted with cotton, maize, sugarcane, beans, peanuts, watermelon, and other food crops. Closer to home women were avid gardeners. Deliciously fragrant Texas mountain laurel (*Sophora secundiflora*) and anacahuita, which bears clouds of snowy white flower clusters, were garden favorites. Vibrantly bright flowers were cultivated as well as sultry jasmine and medicinal plants, some more fragrant than others. Because of the springs, iridescent dragon- and damselflies would frequent the nearby gardens. Certain times of the year, monarch butterflies also filled the sky. Fluttery ribbons of bright orange and black dotted with white, they migrated south, riding the air currents to their wintering grounds in Mexico.

Women were also in charge of domestic duties and caring for the children. They put much of their energy into preparing food. Coffee, tortillas, beans, chorizo (savory sausage), menudo (soup made of beef stomach lining and spices), *barbacoa* (beef head baked in an earthen pit), tamales, and *cabrito* (young goat) were staples in the Tejano diet then as they are today.[10] Amada learned to prepare these dishes and continued to serve them up into her mid-nineties.

Amada felt comfortable and secure in this traditional ranch family culture. With a faint amused smile, she recounted to me and her caretaker Nora that she was a very mischievous child and that on one New Year's Eve she sneaked in to ring the rancho bells before midnight and ran off before she could get caught. Like most of the children of Rancho los Ojuelos, Amada attended school but, before completing her grade school education, she was recruited to help her mother with women's work in the household. Through home and formal education Amada became literate in Spanish. She made a point of learning English as her second language. The newspaper was her textbook, and until her vision clouded over with age and cataracts, she faithfully read the English and Spanish versions of the local newspaper, *The Laredo Morning Times*, and its various iterations. Amada regularly kept up on local and world news. In her later years, when I came to know her, Spanish was the language we used together. I noticed that she did not speak Tex-Mex; instead, she kept the two languages pure and separate in our conversations.

When praying, Amada preferred Spanish. Every day, throughout her waking hours, she reverently spoke or whispered her prayers, invoking El Padre (The Father), Jesucristo, La Virgen de San Juan (Our Lady of San Juan), and other saints. The faith that Amada lived was so deeply felt that it touched every cell in her body and was ever present in her thoughts and colored how she understood the world around her.

From earliest times, the Catholic religion in the borderlands was independent of Catholic priests who visited the ranching communities, such as Los Ojuelos, but never lived there. Devoted lay men and women developed a distinct form of Catholicism, one that recognizes the presence of the divine in the world in everyday life and within the framework of Mexican traditions and beliefs. In this so-called folk Catholicism, sacramental rites were of utmost importance. Taking Communion, praying the rosary, baptisms, first communions, *quinceañeras* (female coming of age rituals), and matrimony strengthened kinship ties in the extended family. The liturgical calendar provided families with opportunities to gather, worship, and celebrate together and was cause for entertainment among members of the rancho (Tijerina 1998:107–121).[11] The Feast of Nuestra Señora de Guadalupe; Nochebuena (Christmas Eve); *La Pastorela* (a Christmas play of Spanish origin of the prophecies proceeding the coming of Christ); Las Posadas (the reenactment of Mary and Joseph seeking accommodations so Mary could rest and give birth to Jesus); El Día de los Reyes (when the Three Kings or Wise Men bestow gifts on the Baby Jesus); El Miércoles de Ceniza (Ash Wednesday); Lent; Semana Santa (Holy Week), concluding with *Pascua* (Easter), were, and continue to be, some of the most celebrated days in the Catholic faith for Tejanos, Amada included. Equally important in Tejano culture is the celebration of El Día de las Madres (Mother's Day), which was always a special day for Amada.

"*Que dios te bendiga*" (May God bless you) was like a mantra for Amada. She also cherished the Virgen de Guadalupe, but the Virgen de San Juan was, as for many South Texans, Amada's special saint, and she dutifully burned candles in her home to this Virgen on a regular basis, evoking her grace, protection, and healing power. Later, when she married Claudio Cardenas, they made pilgrimages to the Virgen de San Juan de

Los Lagos in the Mexican state of Jalisco and to the Virgen de San Juan del Valle, where a replica of the Virgen de Los Lagos was commissioned and placed by Rev. Jose Maria Azpiazu, OMI, in the chapel to this Virgen in the Texas Rio Grande Valley town of San Juan.[12]

In Tejano Catholic folk tradition, faith was integrated with knowledge of bone setting and medicinal plants, especially when Western medicine was unobtainable. In Falfurrias, not far from Los Ojuelos, lived a legendary healer, don Pedrito Jaramillo, a man who heard God call to him after he suffered a terrible injury when he fell from his horse. He had no medicine to ease his pain except for mud, with which he coated his injury. According to the story, when the pain subsided, God told him that he was to spend the rest of his life healing the sick and injured. That is what he did, and his gift for healing was known far and wide (Brooks County Historical Survey Committee 1990). Amada told me her mother knew don Pedrito and had occasion to visit him, requesting his services as a curandero (folk healer) when there was no other recourse.[13]

When Amada was in her thirties, a *portador*, a gentleman sent by her hopeful suitor, Claudio Cardenas, came to the Sanchez home and asked Amada's parents' permission to ask her hand in marriage on Claudio's behalf. Claudio Cardenas had come with his family to Los Ojuelos in 1901 from the Mexican town of Hidalgo in the border state of Coahuila. Claudio's parents had heard Los Ojuelos was in need of hardy vaqueros, and this was an opportunity for the family, including Claudio and his six brothers, to try their luck at making a new life in Texas, a state that was a little more than fifty years old. It was the twenty-eighth state admitted to the union, with its final boundaries delineated in 1850 (Stemaler 2012).[14] Amada told me that in her youth she had many suitors in Los Ojuelos, but she always had her sights set on Claudio Cardenas, and she waited. Her patience was rewarded when he proposed to her. Amada reminisces with humor that they must have looked odd, because she was very short, and Claudio so tall. Regardless of these physical differences, theirs was an enduring, loving match that lasted until Claudio Sr. passed away in 1967. The newlyweds established residence right in the heart of the rancho between both their families. Claudio Jr. remembers:

We lived in the big house on the corner just as you go into Ojuelos. And my mother's parents lived straight back from there. My dad's parents lived right next door, Nicolas and Luisa. And then about four of his [my dad's] brothers lived right in that close area, too. So the Cardenas family back then was really close-knit because they were all pretty close together there. (Interview, October 24, 2004)

Within a few years of their marriage, Amada gave birth to her first child, a daughter whom they named María.

Years later, Amada told me the tragic story of the death of her first child.

> Cuando nació mi niña . . . esa noche . . . El doctor era un viejito que era aquí [Mirando City]. . . . no apuró para nada. . . . yo [estaba] muy mala, verdad . . . tenía bastante humo [por] la chimenea [en la casa]. . . . y pasó mucho tiempo . . . en el colchón había muchas cañas, muchas cañas allí y dondequiera porque no quería que se mojara. . . . tuvo que sacar [con el forceps] la niña. . . . estaba muy gorda, muy grande. . . . cuando nació mi niña tuve [que estar] muchos días en el hospital. . . . duró doce días [la niña] . . . ya cuando me dijo que se iba a morir, no más empezó [el sacerdote] a rezar la bendicíon. [Interview, November 27, 1993]

> When my daughter was born . . . that night . . . The doctor was a little old man who was here [in Mirando City]. . . . he didn't rush over. . . . I was very bad off, you see . . . there was a lot of smoke [from] the chimney [in the house]. . . . on the mattress there was a layer of reeds, there were many reeds all over, because I didn't want it [the mattress] to get wet. . . . he had to take the baby girl out [with forceps]. . . . she was very fat, very big. . . . when my daughter was born I was in the hospital for many days. . . . my daughter lived for twelve days . . . when I was told that she was going to die . . . and then the last rites were said [by the priest].

She attributed the difficult birth to her own wrongdoing, claiming it was because she ate so much ice cream and fatty foods, and the baby was too big. Years later, the loss Amada felt for her firstborn was replaced with joy when a young woman from the area, Nora Martinez, became her caregiver. For Amada, Nora became the daughter she had always desired.

Amada made sure that her next child was born in a hospital in Laredo with an attending doctor at her side. In April 1938, her son Claudio Cardenas Jr. was born. From early on, he was immersed in life on the rancho and in the life his parents began to immerse themselves in as peyote dealers to the Native Americans who followed the peyote religion. He became part of this unique cross-cultural network his parents shared with Indian peyotists and from which deep, reciprocal, heartfelt relationships were established and endured throughout his parents' lives.

Although the expression "Peyote Gardens" may have referred to past abundance of peyote, it could have meant, among Indians, the early settlement of Los Ojuelos, where they could obtain peyote.... Cultivated fields extended almost to the Peyote fields of El Bordo. Los Ojuelos was one of the early, perhaps the earliest, peyote trade centers where Indians coming to Texas could obtain their medicine (dry) and peyoteros probably guided Indians to El Bordo and the adjacent Mirando Valley, next to the cultivated fields ("Gardens") of Los Ojuelos (Morgan 1976:81–82).

—George Morgan, geographer, professor, and member of the NAC of Pine Ridge Reservation, South Dakota

It's where to come and get peyote. They call it the garden because it's where magic grows. But it don't look like no garden, all thorns, stickers, and everything. Maybe that's the way it's supposed to be. You know, a lot of times I'd go out there and take a smoke, and find this peyote, be just in the garden, feel like a good blessing. Make it down here for a certain reason, somebody's sick or something like that, take this medicine back home, have meetings for them.

—Robert Pedro, Southern Arapaho tribe[1]

My dad had some platforms they used to cure that medicine [peyote] on. And my grandfather, Esiquio, my mom's dad, also had some where he lived.... The first Indians that I remember came from Oklahoma, and then they started introducing it more to the southwest and the Navajos.

— Claudio Cardenas Jr., Amada's son, interview, October 24, 2004

Chapter 2

The Peyote Trade

The Peyote Religion: A View from South Texas

The peyote religion revolves around the sacramental use of a specific desert plant known as *peyotl* among the Aztecs, as *hikuri* to the Huichol and to the Tarahumara, as "medicine" among members of the NAC, and *Lophophora williamsii* to botanists. This sacred plant is revered by many for its psychotropic and medicinal qualities. Peyote contains over sixty alkaloids, of which mescaline is the major vision-producing agent (Anderson 1996:138). It has long been appreciated by those who consume it for the spiritual experiences it can provoke, for assuaging hunger and thirst, and for keeping one awake and energized. Scientific inquiries have demonstrated that peyote is also a medicinal plant containing antibiotic agents (McCleary et al. 1960). Experts have testified to its safety and benign qualities even among those who consume it extensively (Cabrese 1997, 2001; Halpern et al. 2005; Schultes 1938).

The borderlands of South Texas have always been the gateway for the peyote religion in the United States. Early hunter-gatherers exploring the Chihuahan Desert and Tamaulipan thornscrub ecosystems must have learned early on about the psychoactive and medicinal properties of peyote and that consuming this exceedingly bitter, unassuming, spineless cactus provided a door to the spiritual realm. Peyote appears in ancient sites from Coahuila, Mexico, to the Lower Pecos region of Texas, where necklaces of dried peyote, strung beadlike on fiber cord, have been found in shelters and cave burials that date from AD 800 (Adovasio and Fry 1976; Bruhn et al. 1978) to as far back as 5,000 BC (Furst 1989), with a few specimens recently dated to 6,000 BC (El-Seedi et al. 2005).[2] Some of the rock art in cave shelters along the Rio Grande north of Eagle Pass, Texas, may include intentional renderings of powerful peyote-related experiences and beliefs (Boyd and Dering 1996). Later on, peyote could very well have been a trade item which, like other precious goods such as salt and obsidian, was exchanged along trade networks established during pre-Columbian times (Weigand 1981, 1985).[3]

At the time of European contact, peyote was used by numerous indigenous cultures in what are now Mexico and the Southwest United States. Spanish clergymen and chroniclers referred to it as "the diabolical root" because peyote was used in religious and ceremonial traditions by indigenous peoples, and this interfered with missionaries' attempts to Christianize them. Acaxees, Aztecs, Carrizos, Caxcanes, Chichimecs, Coahuiltecans, Coras, Huichols, Opotas, Otomis, Pimas, Tamaulipecans, Tarahumaras, Tarascans, Tepecanos, Tlaxcaltecans, Tohono O'odham (Papagos), and Zacatecos were all said to have used peyote (Arlegui 1737; Hernandez 1790; Ortega 1887; Prieto 1873; Sahagun 1982; Santoscoy 1899; Stewart 1990). It should be noted that some Cora, Tepehuano, and Tarahumara still use peyote; however, the Huichol Indians are the only remaining indigenous people who make the annual pilgrimage to the peyote desert in the Mexican state of San Luis Potosí and, as a culture, continue to use peyote in their religious practices.

Spanish encroachment into the peyote lands disrupted peyote traditions and trading activities. In the wake of the chaos that ensued, the region along the present-day Texas–Mexico border was transformed into a refuge for fragmented indigenous groups. Some of the original inhabitants were already familiar with peyote and its curative and religious powers, while others, newly arrived, could have learned about peyote from them. The establishment of colonial presidios, missions, and settlements further impacted the border region on both sides of the Rio Grande. Interestingly, missionaries may have relied on converted Indians from the peyote-growing regions of what is currently northern Mexico and South Texas to assist in establishing new missions. Their movement away from the natural habitat of peyote could have been the means by which new Indian groups became aware of this sacramental plant (Stewart 1990:26).

Missions such as Dulce Nombre de Jesús de Peyotes established in Coahuila in the region of hills called *Lomería de Peyotes* (peyote ridge) and Presidio San Juan Bautista near Laredo were prime environments for the blending of indigenous peyote traditions and Christianity. In the early 1700s Padre Antonio Olivares, who had relocated from Dulce Nombre de Jesús de Peyotes to Presidio San Juan Bautista, observed at his new assignment, "I noted that only on the occasion of a *mitote*, or general dance, do they [the Indians in the Province of Texas] drink peyote and [the juice of] other herbs which cause a disturbance of the senses, producing visions and apparitions" (Slotkin 1955:220). Mission Indians from these locations were later relocated one hundred fifty miles north of peyote country to the missions of San Antonio (Stewart 1990:27): Mission San Antonio de Valero (the Alamo), Concepción, San José, San Juan, and Espada.

Evidently on at least one occasion, an officiating priest from the Texas mission of Refugio allowed Indians to make a pilgrimage to South Texas to collect peyote. Fray José Manuel Gaitán reports, "A short time ago my Karankawa Indians . . . told me there had been at Sierrita about fourteen of their men, only for the purpose of getting a supply of peyote for the year, and therefore taking their women and children. . . . I had approved their journey to the coast . . . to escape the smallpox we have at this mission" (Stewart 1990:47). Gaitán's superior explains this action in his letter to officials in Monterrey: "Indians from Refugio were permitted to go to Revilla-Laredo to collect 'la yerva nomrada pellote' which they customarily use, and had no malicious intentions" (Bexar Archives, Roll 56, Frame 659).[4]

Outside of the missions, Spanish chroniclers describe free-roaming Indians who occupied or raided areas within the peyote lands of Texas and the current Mexican states of Tamaulipas, Coahuila, Nuevo León, and Chihuahua. Southern Plains tribes descended upon Texas and traveled into Mexico, forming alliances with some tribes and fighting with others. From these written reports and other firsthand accounts, anthropologists James Mooney (1896, 1897, 1898), Omer Stewart (1990),

Morris Opler (1938), and Weston La Barre (1938) reconstructed the following scenario: the Mescalero Apaches occupied the peyote lands west of the Pecos River including the Big Bend area; Lipan Apaches, who were firmly established in the region by 1800, made their territory west of the Pecos River, including lands near Carrizo Springs and Eagle Pass. Comanches, who sometimes traded and raided together with Kiowas, spent months at a time in South Texas and south of the Rio Grande.

The Carrizo Indians, part of the general Coahuiltecan cultural group, were situated on territory from Laredo west along the Rio Grande, and they are credited by some as the purveyors of the peyote tradition among Indians in the United States. Add mission Indians and their use of peyote to the interactions and exchanges between these groups and the result is the diffusion of old peyote traditions and syncretic forms of Christian-influenced peyote religious practices (Schaefer 2013). In 1859 the US Government removed these free-roaming Indians in Texas to an area in southwestern Oklahoma that was part of the newly created Indian Territory (Stewart 1990:54–55). The peyote religion extended from these core Indian groups to other tribes in Oklahoma and across the United States and into Canada.

Lipan Apaches and possibly Kiowas appear to have been introduced to peyote by the Carrizo and may well have spread the seeds of the peyote religion that became today's NAC (Stewart 1990:45–53; Opler 1938:273; La Barre 1938:111, 122). It is quite plausible that other forms of the peyote religion also emerged due to different tribal histories, their interactions with other tribes and with the US authorities, as well as their contact with Mexican Indians, as has been proposed for the Mescalero Apaches (Mooney 1896, 1897, 1898; Schaefer 2013).[5] One of the first anthropologists to witness the religious use of peyote was James Mooney in 1891, when he worked among the Kiowas of Oklahoma (1896, 1897). He was employed by the Bureau of American Ethnology at the Smithsonian Institution and, after attending several more peyote ceremonies, he recognized the great importance this religion had for Native Americans. He recorded the oral tradition of the origin of peyote with his Kiowa-Comanche informant, Ga'apiatañ. Mooney later learned that this was the core story, with a few minor variations, of peyote's beginnings shared by Plains Indian peyotists, many of whom had recently lived a life of raiding and retribution in order to survive.

A summary of the story as told to James Mooney:

> Long ago two Mescalero brothers failed to return from a raiding trip far to the south. After a time, tribal leaders presumed them dead and announced a period of mourning. Their suffering sister roamed into the hills to wail and lament their passing until she collapsed into an exhausted sleep. While she lay on the ground, the "sun spirit" appeared in her dream whispering, "you will find [your] brothers—under your head something will bring them to you." After a few words of caution the spirit departed, and when the girl awoke, she found a seni (peyote) cactus growing near where her head had been. She cut off the top of the plant and returned to camp and asked medicine men to help her prepare a special tipi. They divided the peyote button and ate it and soon experienced visions of the brothers, alive but lost wandering the far mountains. A search party located the two men exactly as the peyote vision had predicted. Seni-Manyi or Peyote Woman lived to be very old. She made shields for her brothers which she blessed with special peyote powers; "You never get hurt and always beat [the enemy]." (Bogue 1977:467)[6]

Against the wishes of his superiors, Mooney encouraged peyotists to incorporate their religion under the laws of Oklahoma. In 1918 the NAC was established as a bona fide religion recognized by the federal government.

The peyote religion of the NAC spread like wildfire, with the Indian Territory of Oklahoma as the central point of its diffusion to tribes across the United States. It was estimated that in 1925 there were 13,345 peyotists (Newberne 1925:35). The peyote religion arrived at the Navajo reservation in 1920 but was not well received by Navajo tribal officials. In 1940 there was a public clash between peyotists and Navajo tribal officials resulting in outlawing the religion on the reservation (Stewart 1990:294). It was not until March 1967, when the Navajo Tribal Council formally accepted the US Constitution's Bill of Rights, that they also acknowledged that the peyote religion of the NAC fell under the First Amendment, which guarantees religious freedom (Stewart 1990:310). Today, Navajos make up at least one-fourth of the membership of the NAC, and as of 1987 they accounted for more than half of all the peyote sales from Texas (Stewart 1990:293). The number of Navajo church members and sales of peyote to them have undoubtedly continued to increase.[7]

The Emerging Peyote Trade

With the removal of most of the American Indians from Texas by the 1870s and the deployment of the Texas Rangers to keep Indians from reentering the state, procuring peyote became exceedingly difficult. Almost all of the Texas Indians were now confined to reservations in Oklahoma; however, the federal government rationalized that individual Indians posed no threat to the prosperity of Texas settlers, and they were permitted to travel to South Texas to acquire peyote and bring it back to the reservation (Stewart 1990:61).[8] Perhaps the best-documented case of the transport of peyote from Mexico through Texas to Oklahoma was that of Comanche chief and peyotist Quanah Parker, who forged diplomatic and business relations with US government officials and Texas cattle ranchers. He was so persuasive in his dealings with them that he was able to procure peyote from Mexico. Special Agent Johnson wrote to the Bureau of Indian Affairs, "It appears that Quanah Parker, under cover of an intimation that the Office had no objection to his getting a little peyote for his own use, sent a representative to Mexico and brought in 8,000 peyote. . . . In order to give the old Indians an opportunity to taper off, I have instructed my officer in Eagle Pass to permit Indians to bring in as baggage, not to exceed 500 peyotes. . . . In return for this concession, Congressman Ferris undertakes to dissuade Quanah Parker and his friends from the traffic" (Stewart 1990:76). In fact, the US government in the early 1900s tried to suppress the traffic of peyote to the Indians, but due to lack of funds, the government focused its efforts on eliminating the liquor traffic among Indians instead (Morgan 1976:67).

Peyote from South Texas does not survive well in colder climates north of its native habitat, not even in San Antonio (Del Weniger 1970). Dried peyote, however, lasts indefinitely, without spoiling or apparently losing much of its potency.[9] According to George Morgan (1976:43–45, 64–65), the practice of drying peyote was key to the diffusion of this plant beyond its natural habitat and was crucial to the spread of the peyote religion. The development of the railroad allowed for peyote to be transported in Texas. In 1881, the Texas–Mexican Railroad was completed, linking Corpus Christi to Laredo; shortly after, boxes and barrels of dried peyote were shipped on this railway. The merging of several railroad companies provided continuous rail service from Laredo to the southwestern part of Indian Territory at Denison, Oklahoma, and eventually to Vernon, Texas, about ten miles from the Kiowa-Comanche reservation (Stewart 1990:61).

Laredo was also a central supply point for peyote. Peyote traders acquired peyote from Tejanos living in Los Ojuelos, Torrecillos, and Aguilares; the latter two communities were stops on the Texas–Mexican railway (Morgan 1976:71–72, 74).[10] In the 1880s the pharmaceutical company Parke, Davis and Company purchased peyote from Laredo cactus collector and dealer Anna B. Nickels (Bender 1968:164). She sent them the peyote she had growing in her garden, numbering three thousand plants, and what she was able to find for sale. Ms. Nickels also informed Park, Davis and Company that one of the Mexican men who went with her to collect peyote had in the previous year (1887), "gathered 30,000 [peyote] . . . for a Mexican merchant of this place and he sliced and dried them here in Laredo and shipped them to some agency" (Stewart 1990:63). Dr. J. R. Briggs of Dallas, who was investigating the physiological effects of peyote use, reported in the *Medical Register* of 1887 that a Mexican man named E. A. Paffrath, a business associate of a general wholesaler in Vernon, Texas, supplied approximately 3,500 dried peyote buttons to Kiowa Indians for fifteen dollars a bushel (Stewart 1990:62).

Mexicans and Tejanos were, and continue to be, well acquainted with peyote's medicinal properties. It appears that they collected it themselves and, when none was available, they purchased peyote buttons from merchants in open-air markets and from businesses such as the cactus nursery of Ms. Nickels in Laredo. In her correspondence to Parke, Davis and Company she writes, "The Mexicans here in Laredo buy them [pellote buttons] off me at 5 cents each, 1 or 2 at a time to make a drink (they say for headache). They pound fresh ones and soak them in water, then strain and drink the water. They use the pulp left to bind any sort of sores" (Bender 1968:164).

Amada's niece recalls that Claudio Sr. "would mix the Mexican alcohol with the peyote, and I think it was the green peyote. He would mix it, and he would use it for his pain on his knees. He found comfort (from this remedy)" (Gloria Sanchez Palacios, interview, April 18, 2004).

Mrs. Teresa Johnson, mother of peyote dealer Salvador Johnson, describes how another of her sons uses peyote as a daily tonic for maintaining good health:

> Mi hijo hace su té. Es que es mucho mayor, es el más grande de mis hijos, tiene 64. He's going to be sixty-four years old. Y el hierve el peyote y lo pone en una hielera y en la mañana lo agarra. Y lo hecha tantito brandy, very tantito, y lo toma . . . sí, diario, y luego en la noche le toma un vasito y se siente bien. (Teresa Johnson, interview, April 10, 2004)

> My son makes his tea. It's because he is much older, he is the oldest of my children, he is 64. He is going to be sixty-four years old. And he boils the peyote and puts it in a cooler and in the morning he takes it out and adds a little bit of brandy, just a very little bit, and he drinks it . . . yes, daily, and then at night he drinks a small glass and he feels good.

Mrs. Johnson herself used the juice of fresh peyote for her cataracts. It was applied directly into her eyes and afterward she claimed that her eyes felt better. However the drops did not clear up her cataracts, according to her daughter Nora; her mother's cataracts were too advanced to clear them up. Even Texas Rangers in the past relied on peyote to endure fatigue and assuage hunger and thirst (Lumholtz 1902:358). Amada herself was in the habit of consuming a small amount of peyote each day. Perhaps that contributed to her longevity.

Los Ojuelos and the Peyote Trade

The first account of peyote trade in Los Ojuelos dates to 1909 and comes from W. E. Johnson, Chief Special Officer of Liquor Control, although there well may have been an even earlier peyote trade relationship between Tejanos and Indians. In this document Chief Officer Johnson lists eight peyote traders, four of whom lived at Los Ojuelos (Morgan 1976:63). One of these early peyote traders was Frank Cortinas, who started selling peyote in 1900 (Morgan 1976:72).[11] Amada's father, Esiquio Sanchez, was also a peyote trader in the early 1900s. Amada remembered when *carretas* (ox carts) transported peyote to the nearby town of Aguilares, where it would be loaded onto railroad cars and shipped to Laredo for further distribution (Morgan 1976:72). Due to distance and lack of transportation options, a few Indians arrived by train to fill empty trunks with peyote. As some Indians became more prosperous, they arrived in cars. Amada remembered when, in the 1910s, the first car she had ever seen arrived in Los Ojuelos, a Cadillac driven by an Indian couple from Oklahoma (Morgan 1976:74).[12]

> Había un señor muy rico. . . . yo creo [que] era Omaha. . . . y la primera vez que vino al rancho [Los Ojuelos] estábamos asustados porque era el primer Cadillac que habíamos visto, un Cadillac de Oklahoma. . . . Pues . . . no conocía a ningún indio, a ningún indio conocíamos, hasta que comenzamos a trabajar en el peyote. Sí, había indios antes en Oilton porque había el señor Frank Cortinas, fue el primero a comenzar a trabajar el peyote. Y otros venían a Aguilares también, de Oklahoma. Ellos [indios de Oklahoma] eran los primeros que nadie. Pero el señor con el Cadillac, se llamaba Pat Cheri[?]. . . . allí lo vimos. . . . nueve años [yo tenía]. En frente para adentro estaban las mesetas donde teníamos el peyote, y el señor, el viejito, era muy gordo, era uno de los ancianos, y el Cadillac era de los abuelos. [Interview, November 27, 1993]

> There was this very rich man. . . . I believe he was Omaha. . . . and the first time that he came to the ranch [Los Ojuelos] we were frightened because it was the first Cadillac that we had seen, a Cadillac from Oklahoma. . . . Well . . . I did not know a single Indian, not a one did we know until we began to work in the peyote trade. Yes, there had been Indians before in Oilton because that is where Mr. Frank Cortinas was, he was the first to begin working in the peyote trade. And others went to Aguilares, they were also from

Oklahoma. They [the Indians from Oklahoma] were the first ones. But the man with the Cadillac, he was called Pat Cheri[?]. . . . we saw him there. . . . [I was] nine years old. In front, inside were the tables where we had the peyote, and the man, the little old man, was very fat, he was one of the elders and the Cadillac belonged to the old people.

In the early 1900s, Indians sought out peyote traders and purchased fresh green peyote from them. They acquired larger quantities that were dried and more easily transportable from traders.[13] Peyote traders also helped Indians gain access to the peyote gardens. This meant getting permission from ranchers to harvest peyote on their properties, at which time they would also carry out peyote ceremonies in the heart of this sacred peyote land. Bob Fulbright explained, "As early as 1906 for certain, Indians were coming to Mirando Valley area (our ranch) to gather Peyote. . . . My grandfather told my father that the Indians told him in 1906 that they had been coming to the Mirando Valley area for years" (Morgan 1976:52).

The journey made by Native Americans to the peyote gardens was and continues to be considered a pilgrimage. Getting to this remote area, so distant from the homelands of most Indian tribes, is a hardship. This was especially true in the late 1800s and early 1900s, when access to the gardens was not guaranteed; if anything, the hope was to be able to spend time on the land and commune and pray to the peyote. According to a report on Shawnee peyote practices and beliefs, "You can get power by visiting the peyote patch in Texas, and telling it at evening that you want to help to cure people and get medicine. You sprinkle tobacco there" (Voeglin 1933–1934).[14]

On this pilgrimage to South Texas, some Indians stayed for an hour or less, since their primary goal was to acquire a supply of peyote to take home with them. Others remained for three or four days as they waited for the freshly harvested peyote to dry. The description of a Kiowa pilgrimage to the peyote gardens related that

> living beyond the habitat of peyote, all Plains tribes have to make pilgrimages for it or buy it. The journey is not ritualized, but there is a modest ceremony at the site: on finding the first plant, a Kiowa

pilgrim sits west of it, rolls a corn shuck cigarette and prays, "I have found you, now open up, show me where the rest of you are; I want to use you to pray for the health of my people." He sings and eats green plants while harvesting them; only the tops are taken, that the root may regenerate buds, a fine large one being saved as a "father peyote" for meetings later. [La Barre 1989:43]

In Los Ojuelos there were few places for the Indians to stay. Margarito Lopez recalls that there were still not that many Indians who came to Los Ojuelos, but those who did "ponían campo allá en el monte . . . se acampaban ellos (los indios) hasta que todo el peyote que necesitaban se secó. Pero uno no los ve, solamente cuando le ponía atención." (They [the Indians] camped in the countryside until all the peyote that they needed was dried. But one didn't see them, unless one paid attention to them.)

He goes on to say, "Nosotros no teníamos mucho cuidado porque la gente era más humilde . . . y sus padres hicieron a uno que no los moleste, o preguntar muchas preguntas o cosas así." (We were not very wary of them because the people were very humble, and parents made one not disturb them [Indians] or ask a lot of questions.)

Mr. Lopez adds, "Nosotros los veían pero los indios casi no hablaban inglés, nosotros tampoco . . . era muy raro que hablaran con nosotros, como ahora todos ellos tienen escuela." (We saw them but the Indians hardly spoke English, we did not either. It was very unusual that they spoke with us, but now they all have gone to school.) (Margarito Lopez, interview, April 17, 2004).

The Cardenases' Early Life as Peyote Traders

Peyote and the peyote trade were in Amada's blood. She was raised in the trade, helping her father, Esiquio Sanchez, who was one of the first peyote dealers in the region.

> Pues era muy joven. No me acuerdo qué edad tenía, pero siempre le ayudamos en trabajar el peyote. Otra gente lo traía, verdad, no me llevó al monte. Así es que otra gente lo conseguía, casi todos del

rancho [Los Ojuelos] hacían eso. Salían al monte a juntarlo, porque no había permisos todavía y nada de eso. Yo sabía cómo trabajarlo y lo secamos, también, seco. No teníamos rejillas tampoco . . . lo teníamos muy limpio en el piso . . . y yo empecé a aprender como trabajarlo, como cortarlo, y todo . . . [Interview, February 2, 1997]

Well, I was very young. I don't remember how old I was, but we always helped in preparing the peyote. Other people brought it from the hills, he [my dad] did not take me to the hills. Other people, almost all of them from the ranch [Los Ojuelos] went to get it. They went to the hills to gather it because there weren't permits yet, nothing like that. I knew how to prepare it and we dried it. We didn't have [drying] racks . . . we kept it clean on the floor . . . and I began to learn how to work, how to cut it and everything.

Amada recounted that when she was older and went out with her husband Claudio to harvest peyote, they would pray before cutting it. She told me that all harvesters prayed that way in those days; even those who did not pray in church did pray when they were in the peyote fields.

Nosotros teníamos como cuchillo, una palita, teníamos que ponerlo al ladito, al ladito, porque es muy fuerte la raíz del peyote, y [hacerlo] delgadito, delgadito, por el jugo del peyote. Así lo cortaban. . . . todavía tiene que cortar una pulgada de la raíz porque de la raíz sale otros peyotitos. Y luego cuando florea, la semillita con el aire vuele. . . . así es. [Interview, February 2, 1997]

We had like a knife, a little shovel, we had to put it in a little way from the peyote because the root of the peyote is very tough and [do this] gently, gently, because of the juice of the peyote. That's how they cut it. . . . even now one has to cut it an inch down on the root because from the root more little peyotes will grow. And then, when it flowers, the seeds are swept with the breeze. . . . that's how it is.

She continued, saying that they would eat peyote while they were working. They also consumed a beverage prepared by adding peyote to water in order to boost their energy. Although she never saw visions or colors or designs from ingesting peyote while gathering it, she did say it made her sleepy and also made her dream (personal communication, March 16, 1995). Amada said she ate peyote during both pregnancies because she was also harvesting peyote. She said nothing bad happened to her babies or during her pregnancies because of this, and that she didn't feel the effects of the peyote very much.[15]

Amada also related to me that she grew up with Indians frequently coming to the house. One older Cheyenne man remembers Amada when she was much younger, seeing her bring out large peyotes and place them on the table for those who wanted to buy them (personal communication, February 13, 1993). Shortly after the Cardenases were married, Claudio Sr. also took up the peyote trade, working often with Amada's father, who must have helped him learn the business.

> [Claudio] no sabía nada en trabajar el peyote, en '32 o '33 comenzamos a trabajarlo, pero él tenía que ir a pie a las lomas a traerlo. . . . empezamos a trabajarlo y muy pronto empezaron a venir los indios con nosotros. . . . ya comenzamos más o menos a juntar más y más. Y los señores [indios] ya sabían que podíamos venderlo, que teníamos para vender. . . . no hicimos [mucho] dinero con el peyote. [Interview, February 2, 1997]

> [Claudio] did not know how to work in the peyote trade, in '32 or '33 we began to work in the trade but he had to go on foot to the hills to gather it. . . . we began to work and very quickly the Indians began to come to us. . . . then we began more or less gathering more and more peyote. And the [Indian] men already knew that we could sell it, that we had peyote to sell. . . . we did not make [much] money from the peyote.

Amada and Claudio were among the few peyote traders who invited Indians to stay with them in their homes and treated them with familial hospitality, even giving up their beds so that Indian visitors could get a good night's sleep. Their son Claudio Jr. recalls the old house they occupied in Los Ojuelos, built, ironically, to ward off Indian attacks in days past. He also remembers clearly the generosity his parents showered upon their Indian visitors and the deep bonds of friendship that were forged in this way.

> We lived in a big white house. And it almost looked like an old fort . . . because if you went up on the roof it had little portholes and stuff. I was told . . . that the people who lived there used to go up on the roof in the late 1800s. Indians used to come raid up here, they used to come through here and they would have to fight them off. They would go up on the roof and shoot from there.
>
> That was the house that we lived in. But not only that, my dad had Indians that came, the first Indians that I remember that came were from Oklahoma. And then they started introducing it more to the Southwest and the Navajos, of course, they really started coming in. I remember this one, and I can't remember what his name was, he drew these beautiful Indian murals on the inside of our walls. And they were there for a long time. And also one time my grandfather Esiquio had killed a deer, and we used to tan the hides. We tanned this hide and the same man drew my dad's picture on a deer hide with an Indian bonnet. It was just beautiful. We had it for a long time, but of course it deteriorated.
>
> So I have a lot of memories from those days.
>
> First it used to be mostly men. . . . somebody would come with a pickup and they would have so many people that they would get medicine for, they would take it back. Then they would spread it around. And then later on, of course, their families started coming. The wife and husband, and then later on after that the kids would come. But it was kind of like a progression. They would all stay with us in the house.

Claudio also has memories of routine activities carried out by his family that revolved around the peyote trade.

> We used to have an old Model T that we went to the peyote gardens in. We never knew if we were going to make it back, and we used to load that truck, thirteen or fourteen sacks of peyote. And make it

back. But they started coming more and more, and the word spread. And they used to drive down, most of them.

Before the Indians came, what we did was the regular up there [in Los Ojuelos] . . . they used to come and they would either take it as we got it from the field or we used to dry it, the buttons, and they used to take it that way. But everything was done up there.

Yeah, in Los Ojuelos, my dad had some platforms they used to do that on, they used to cure that medicine on. And my grandfather Esiquio, also, where he lived he had some [platforms] where he did that. [Interview, October 24, 2004]

Amada and Claudio turned to the Indians to learn the sacred aspects of peyote and the most respectful way to harvest and just "be" with this highly revered plant. There were three important people early in their lives who were their guides into this realm. One was Anthony Davis, a Pawnee born into the peyote way of life. Both of his grandfathers were powerful roadmen in the early days of the formation of the NAC and he came into the world during an NAC meeting. As a youth he had worked as an actor for the Buffalo Bill Wild West Show and toured Europe, but he returned to the peyote religion and a more spiritual way of life (Jerry Patchen, personal communication, December 31, 2011). The other two were Allen P. Dale and his wife, Chris. Allen P. Dale was a prominent figure in the NAC; in 1946 he was elected president of the Native American Church of the United States, a powerful position he held for ten years. He came to the Cardenases' aid later on, when they were in need of legal representation during turbulent times in the peyote trade and the interpretation of Texas laws. Claudio Jr. comments,

> The way my dad talked to me about it and the way that he felt about it was that some of the first Indians that came down that he did business with talked to him about peyote religion and how they interacted with the medicine and so my dad mostly learned from them. And then he kind of adapted that to his own style, his own way of thinking about it. And he respected the religion. But, one of the first people that I remember beside that artist, but he used to go with my dad, was Anthony Davis.

> And I think he was one of the ones that taught my dad a lot about it, about peyote religion, because he used to stay with us for months at a time. And so he used to go with us out in the fields and he, too, would harvest. And he would come and help fix the medicine.
>
> And this one couple I remember came to the house, I guess it was to buy and be friends with my parents . . . the man's name was Allen P. Dale. He and his wife used to come over, down here about every two or three months and eventually we got along so well that we went up there and visited them in Oklahoma.
>
> I don't know if we have any pictures of them, but I remember them well when I was a kid. They were always around. [Interview, October 24, 2004]

Claudio Jr. recounts that his parents began to learn about and participate in peyote meetings carried out at their house in Los Ojuelos. Even as a boy, Claudio Jr. took part in the ceremonies.

> They would have meetings in the house. . . . Instead of a tepee they would have them in the house. . . . We had a huge fireplace, so they would just take coals from the fireplace and bring it in. . . . There weren't very many, maybe six or eight. . . . when I first started that I can remember, those prayer meetings were very formal. You went in at night and you started up and you stayed there all night. You didn't go out or anything, you sat there all night. And you drummed and you prayed and smoked and whatever. And in the morning you got up and you walked out. . . . these meetings are very informal now. You come and go when you want.
>
> In the meeting the designated leader was in charge and you respected that. You went in and you did what he guided you during the ceremony. . . . the water and everything was done afterwards at the time, that I can remember. The water and the food were done outside. . . . Even midnight water. And when they first started there was no roadman. Everybody [took part in running the meeting] . . . or whoever the person that was running the meeting, he picked out a person and he said you be the fire chief, or you take care of the

fireplace. That's what he did. But these persons were not picked out beforehand or anything. They were picked out after. And a lot of times even that wasn't done. There was just a fire in the middle and everybody sat around and they drummed and they did the peyote and the smoke and everything. So it was a lot different then, than it is now.

My dad had a feather fan. . . . And I kept it just the way he had it. And he used to drum and use the gourd and everything, the same. . . . he learned the Indian songs . . . he also had some songs in Spanish. He used to improvise. . . . And he grew up learning a lot of those songs from Allen P. Dale. And he learned a lot from some other people when they first started coming to Ojuelos. [Interview, October 24, 2004]

As time passed, Amada and Claudio became increasingly more involved in the NAC, participating in ceremonies and making lifelong friendships with church members. As the NAC prayer service evolved in South Texas, so did the role of men and women in their devotion to this peyote religion. Claudio Jr. expands upon this:

At first, it was all men. . . . My mother, I guess at that time my mother was more concerned about taking care of feeding the people and doing that sort of thing, and it was later on that she got asked to come in [the meeting]. But before that she just respected the fact that it was all men and that was it. . . . But then after a while when we got down here (to Mirando) then it changed. Then women could come in and do the ceremony. And then the water and everything started coming in. [Interview, October 24, 2004][16]

Amada recounted her memories of the first ceremonies at their place:

No sabíamos qué hacían en su ceremonia ni nada. Aquí comenzaron de poner lonas, y luego empezaron en el garaje. Siempre en el garaje tenían su *meeting*. Cerraron la puerta y en la noche tenían su *meeting*. . . . cuando comenzé [a participar en el *meeting*] lo tenían en el garaje. . . . [ya depúes] a veces tuve que meter el agua también . . . y la oracíon [sobre el agua]. Yo era más joven . . . pero sí, aprendí mucho. . . . tengo mucho respeto. [Interview, November 27, 1993]

We didn't know what they did in their ceremonies, nothing. Here they began to put up canvas [shelters] and then they started out in the garage. They always had their meeting in the garage. They closed the door and in the night they had their meeting. . . . when I began [to participate in the meeting] it was in the garage. . . . [later on] sometimes I would bring in the water . . . and pray [over the water]. I was very young . . . but I learned a lot. . . . I have a lot of respect.

The Cardenases' involvement in the peyote trade and in serving the NAC became a full-time occupation; they willingly immersed themselves in lives devoted to helping Native Americans who followed the Peyote Road.

Some of my brothers and I were working on a farm at Los Ojuelos (near Mirando City) when the first 'oil gusher' was discovered. We heard something like the sound of thunder, due north from where we were—we saw this "black stuff" up in the air, and we ran all the way, about a quarter of a mile to this rig. Since we were kids, we had a thrill seeing oil running through all those creeks nearby. We saw men dipping cups in the oil creeks and tasting the oil like they were drinking coffee.

—Luis Cardenas, Claudio Cardenas Sr.'s brother, in Black 1972:73

In Los Ojuelos, the family, I guess, must have gotten stressed out or whatever happened and they had to sell, and at that time my dad said, "Well, I'm not staying here anymore; I am not working in the oil fields anymore, I'm gonna do the peyote trade (full time)." . . . We moved down here to Mirando and then [the peyote trade] really took off.

—Claudio Cardenas Jr., Amada's son, interview, October 24, 2004

Chapter 3

Mirando City and the Peyote Business

The Cardenas family relocated to Mirando City in the 1940s, just shy of having lived in the same house in Los Ojuelos for ten years. They had no choice but to move after threats from the owners of Los Ojuelos, who feared that the Cardenases, as well as others living at the rancho, might invoke the legal provision known as Adverse Possession in the Texas Civil Practice and Remedies Code (Sec. 16021 et seq.), through which one may lay claim to ownership of property if he "cultivates, uses or enjoys the property" over a period of ten years.[1]

Amada, Claudio Sr., and Claudio Jr., along with Claudio Sr.'s brothers and their wives, and Amada's sister Pilar and her husband, bought adjacent lots south of the railroad tracks. The land Amada placed in trust comprises five lots that had been home to the extended family after they relocated.

Amada described the original house on the property that they had bought:

En la casa chiquita había una pareja de señores, ya grandes. Ella trabajaba poquito y el señor no tenía un brazo. Era en los '20s, era el "boom" de aceite.... nosotros pasamos por allí un día.... [queríamos comprarla]. "Pues Amadita, no puedo" [dijo el señor], pero más al rato movieron los Metodistas . . . veníamos a visitar allí [otra vez]. Dijo, "Ahora sí." Bueno, le dimos cien dólares por la casa. . . . los solares ya compramos estos. [Interview, November 27, 1993]

> In the small house there was an elderly couple. She worked a little bit and the man did not have one arm. It was in the '20s, it was during the oil boom. . . . We went over there one day. . . . [we wanted to buy it.] "Well Amadita, I can't," [the man said], but later on, when the Methodists [Anglos] moved away . . . we came to visit [again]. He said, "Now I can." Well, we paid one hundred dollars for the house. . . . we had already bought the lots.)

Amada described the property's land when they first moved there as "un bosque porque no limpiaba nada. Tenía muchos magueys. . . . más al rato la teníamos limpio. Nosotros comenzábamos a limpiarla. Habían muchas tacuaches entre las matas de maguey" (a forest because it wasn't cleared at all. It had many magueys. . . . later on we had it cleared. We began to clear it. There were many opossums between the clumps of maguey.) (interview, November 27, 1993).

The Cardenases' move was part of a mass exodus from the ranchos to the booming oil town of Mirando City, where people from different cultures and languages intersected in this South Texas town. Some aspired to make a home and a new life, while others were more interested in striking it rich. It was at this home that Amada and Claudio Sr. worked as a couple and became one of the major suppliers of peyote for members of the NAC. They also became a vital employer for community members in Mirando City, providing jobs as harvesters to meet the seemingly endless demand for this sacred medicine.

Oil Boom Town

The discovery of oil in Mirando Valley below the peyote fields north of Los Ojuelos in 1921 dramatically changed the lives of everyone in the surrounding countryside. Ranchers saw greater profits in leasing their land for oil and gas development than in cattle ranching, where unpredictable droughts took their toll on this traditional industry. Roads were carved through the open plains and scrub brush and huge trucks carried in the oil drilling equipment necessary to extract the black gold from as deep as 1,461 feet below the ground (Black 1972:10). By the turn of the twentieth century, ownership of Rancho los Ojuelos had changed hands within the extended Guerra family and the García brothers, Eusebio and José María, who had married into the family, became the barons of the original Spanish land grant that included the ranch and extensive range land.[2] The Garcías divided up their vast land holdings, selling land to create Mirando City and Oilton, and the latter merged with the older city of Torrecillas (Juan Guerra, personal communication, April 22, 2004).

Situated on an oil field surrounded by rigs in every direction, Mirando City was born (*mirando* is Spanish for "looking around"). The founder of this newly created town, Mr. O. W. Killam, was known as the "greatest wildcatter in South Texas" (Black 1972:11). He hailed from Missouri but spent significant time in Oklahoma, even when it had been Indian Territory; he came to the area as a speculator, seeking his fortune in discovering oil. Killam's efforts were rewarded north of Los Ojuelos, where he acquired acreage and secured permission by the railroad to build the town of Mirando City. Having recently arrived in Los Ojuelos from the town of Hidalgo in the state of Coahuila, Mexico, Claudio Cardenas, later to be Amada's husband, his brother Bruno, and their father, Nicolas, were hired to clear the land that would become the streets of Mirando (Black 1972:31). Killam laid out seven hundred lots and put them up for sale.

Mirando City was the quintessential budding new oil boomtown. A road was cut through the prickly pear and brush linking Mirando City to the established road connecting Laredo to Corpus Christi through Los Ojuelos. The first buildings to be constructed were associated with oil excavation. A pipeline was laid in town to supply natural gas from nearby fields. Electricity from a recently built power plant soon followed. The only drawback to the location was the lack of water. Developers looked to Los Ojuelos and its natural spring as a reliable water supply to sustain Mirando City. Wells were dug there, a pipeline was laid to Mirando City, and a storage tank and meters were installed. One of the partners in this water venture was W. W. (Bill) Sterling, a Texas Ranger who relocated to Los Ojuelos and was charged with keeping law and order in the region that was quickly populated by settlers looking to earn their livelihoods in the oil business (Black 1972:36; Sterling 1959).[3]

Businesses opened to supply and service oil-field equipment: a garage, a foundry and machine company, an oil-well supply company, a lumber company, and a gas station all came with the boom. Houses shot up, the Mirando City Bank was established, and the *Mirando City Record* began circulation. A pharmacy, a doctor's office, a grocery store, a dry goods and sundries store, a hotel, a boarding house, restaurants, and a bakery equipped with a soda fountain rose to meet the needs of the city dwellers. Mirando City attracted newcomers to the region—Anglos from the far reaches of Texas, the Midwest, and beyond. African Americans were brought in to work for Herbert F. Danmier, originally from Illinois, who established a truck business in Mirando City. There were Tejanos, many of whom relocated from the ranches in the outlying countryside, including former residents of Los Ojuelos who settled in the neighborhoods that delineated the city.

As with other neighboring ranchos, Los Ojuelos's population diminished, and it quickly achieved the status of a virtual ghost ranch. Gloria, Amada's niece who was born in Los Ojuelos in the 1940s, recalls,

> There were like one, two, three, four other Mexican American families that lived there. The other families there were the ranch hands and they were Anglos. . . .
>
> The only thing that was still there was the church. There was no school anymore. I do not recall a store. The only thing was the church on Sundays where the priest from Hebbronville came to do the service and sometimes they would come in on Saturdays to provide the preparation for the Holy Communion for kids. I do not remember school there; there was no school. There were no stores, no post office. You had to come down to Mirando for all of that, groceries and everything. [Interview, April 18, 2004]

The People of Mirando City

Churches and Mirando City High School were established, which contributed to a sense of family and community. Longtime Mirando City resident Raquel Mendieta remembers,

> When I came here, there was a Baptist Church, the Methodist Church, the Catholic Church. . . . I think there had been another one or two before then, but by the time I came, those were the only churches, and of course the school, and we had the Red and White Grocery Store and Cristan's Grocery Store and there was a little café . . . a couple of rooming houses. . . . in the mid '50s Lala, Lala Rodriguez, started a café, which is now, and still is, Lala's Café. And then, oh, there were a couple of beer joints. And there was an old well supply store. . . . Oh, and one time they had a Ford Motor Company, and I believe a Chevrolet and they had a theater. . . . There was quite a few more people then, than there are now. A lot of people lived, following the oil, well, the oil business. [Interview, April 17, 2004]

The arrival of the oil business brought a surge of Anglos to the area in the early part of the twentieth century. Like a chain reaction, their presence changed the cultural dynamics and political as well as socioeconomic power structure that had evolved over the centuries with the strong Tejano culture in the community. Before, Margarito Lopez reminisces,

> era barato todo. Levantabas la cosecha, también sembraban sandías, papas, tomate, adquieres leche y carne de la vaca, todas esas cosas. . . . ya comenzó a cambiar. . . . ya eran casi puros americanos, los dueños de los ranchos . . . tenías que comprar casi todo. . . . [en Mirando] había mucha gente. . . . de Los Ojuelos venías a Mirando . . . te sientes avergonzado porque no conocías a nadie. [Interview, April 17, 2014]

> everything was inexpensive. You harvested food, people also planted watermelon, potatoes, tomatoes. . . . you acquired milk and meat from the cows, all of these things. . . . it began to change, they were practically all Americans, the ranch owners . . . you had to buy

almost everything. . . . [in Mirando] there were a lot of people. . . . from Los Ojuelos you went to Mirando . . . you would feel embarrassed because you didn't know anyone.

With the shift from ranching to the oil business, some of the local Tejanos found work in the oil fields, working on the rigs, clearing brush and rocks, or driving trucks. Others worked as agricultural laborers, cultivating cash crops on land Anglos had bought. Many Tejano landowners may have been rich in land, but this did not translate into the monetary wealth necessary to exist in a commercial economy. Oil barons wanting to diversify their holdings also bought ranches from Tejanos. These new ranchers started to lease their property to hunters who came during designated seasons to shoot the native fauna—wild turkeys, quail, doves, peccary, and especially deer.[4] Land became a commodity as opposed to a place of cultural and familial heritage. This, in turn, uprooted Tejanos in the region who were no longer tied to ranchos; often they became laborers who worked for Anglos in order to make money, since that was the way to survive in the new capitalist economy.

Racial segregation was imposed in Mirando City in concert with the policies in the rest of Texas, which endured until the Civil Rights movement in the 1960s and the birth of the La Raza Unida party in Crystal City, not far away. Mirando City was divided into Anglo, Mexican (Tejano), and African American areas. Anglos and Tejanos attended the same school; however, the African Americans had their own school and church.

Mrs. Teresa Johnson, who moved to Mirando City as a young girl, recalls,

> Ah yes, there's a lot of people. We used to live, the Mexican people, we used to live across the tracks. . . . the black men . . . they used to live from the highway to that (east) side . . . and they used to have a big church . . . a school for the negro people. . . . the American people (gringos) lived over here (south of the railroad tracks).
>
> . . . And we had a big store where you could buy some shoes and clothes. The shoes never lasted, you buy a pair of shoes, they don't

last when you go to school here in that time . . . because of the oil . . . porque se llenaban (because they got covered with oil). [Interview, April 10, 2004]

Mrs. Johnson's son remembers, "There used to be oil in the road. . . . I remember when I was a young kid, too . . . I used to go to school and right near the railroad track we used to have a refinery . . . where they used to pick up the oil. And every time we used to go, there would be oil everywhere" (interview, April 10, 2004).

Churches and Schools

The religious faith and the church to which a family belonged delineated its cultural heritage in this segregated Texas community. Mrs. Catalina Inocencio, a devout Catholic and Amada's friend, explained, "Bueno, casi siempre los anglos tenían su iglesia bautista o metodista. Pero los mexicanos siempre tenían una católica chiquita, pero había. Pero también había americanos que eran católicos, pero eran pocos. Pero había." (Well, almost all of the Anglos had their own Baptist or Methodist church. But the Mexicans always had their own small Catholic church. There were also Americans who were Catholic; there were not many, but there were some.).

In the early part of the 1930s, at least ninety percent of Texas schools that taught Mexican students were racially segregated (Menchaca 1993:598).[5] Since Mirando City was a small community, Tejano children attended the same school as the Anglo children whose parents had come because of the oil boom. Catalina Inocencio, who was never able to complete school because her family moved back and forth between South Texas and Mexico, says that her husband was able to attend the same school as the Anglos. She refers to the teachers as *americanas*: "Pero sí . . . la escuela de los americanos . . . yo tengo fotos de cuando mi esposo estaba chico que sí alcanzó a ir a la escuela. . . . sí tengo fotos de todas las maestras, las americanas, todas." (But yes . . . the school of the Americans . . . I have photos of when my husband was small and he was able to go to the school. . . . I have photos of the teachers, the Americans, all of them.) (interview, April 21, 2004).

Mirando City—the Depression, World War II, and Afterward

During the 1930s Mirando City residents did not feel the impact of the Depression as much as many people living in other cities throughout the United States. Although there were divisions due to cultural differences, the economy was booming because of the oil. In fact, right before World War II, the price of oil went up, and demand increased. Some of the companies, such as the Long Brothers Drilling Company, used their profits to buy ranch properties (Black 1972:52). Mrs. Johnson recollects that in the 1930s and before World War II, there was no poverty, even among the Tejanos in Mirando City:

> Había mucho trabajo . . . había dinero. . . . fíjate, mi esposo, cuando nos casamos nosotros, él ganaba tres dólares por día, de troquero, y teníamos dinero en el banco. Porque la libra de frijol costaba un *dime*. Compramos quince centavos de carne y con eso comíamos y sobraba para la cena. Todo estaba muy barato. [Interview, April 10, 2004]

> There was a lot of work . . . there was money. . . . just imagine, my husband, when we got married, he earned three dollars a day as a truck driver, and we had money in the bank. That's because a pound of beans cost a dime. We bought fifteen cents of meat and with this we ate (at midday), and there was enough left over for dinner. Everything was very cheap.

Times were tough during World War II, however. Many of the men in Mirando City joined the military and their wives had to be resourceful to attend to the needs of their children and older relatives. Some women, such as Amada's sisters Pilar and Andrea, left Los Ojuelos and went to San Antonio to work in a factory to support the war efforts.[6] With food rationing, some families resorted to crossing the border to Nuevo Laredo, where food and goods were plentiful. Mrs. Johnson describes this time,

> Se puso duro durante la Segunda Guerra, que racionaron muchas cosas, como la manteca. Te daban estampillas para la manteca,

para el azúcar, todo eso. Y se acaban los ticketes, pues ya no compraba. . . . . sí había trabajo, pero racionaron todo, el gobierno. . . . Si me acababa la manteca o los ticketes para el azúcar, todo eso, pues yo tenía que ir hasta al otro lado a comprar manteca, a comprar azúcar, comprar tomate, todo eso. . . . en México no estaba racionada, te vendían bastante. [Interview, April 10, 2004]

It was hard during World War II; many things were rationed, like lard. You were given stamps for the lard, for the sugar, all of that. When the stamps run out, well, you didn't buy it. . . . yes, there was work, but the government rationed everything. . . . If I ran out of lard or ration coupons for sugar, all of these things, then I had to go across the border to Nuevo Laredo to buy lard, to buy sugar, to buy tomatoes, all that. . . . in Mexico they were not rationed, they sold plenty of things.

After World War II, a number of Tejanos who had served were eligible for the GI Bill and took advantage of this opportunity to go to college. As a result, some Tejanos elevated their socioeconomic standing and were able to own businesses that had previously been dominated by Anglos. This was true for one family in the Mirando City area, the Mendietas. Oscar Mendieta worked for Tom DeLay's family in their welding and machine shop.[7] Tom's father worked in the petroleum and natural gas industry, and they lived in Mirando City for two or three years when Tom DeLay was very young. Oscar and his brother, Armando Mendieta, bought the M & S Machine Supply Company from the DeLays and the company that pumped water from wells in Los Ojuelos (Raquel Mendieta, interview, April 17, 2004). Oscar Mendieta had the hands-on experience and, as Teresa Johnson explains, "Oscar's brother Armando was in the military and afterwards went to college. He returned to the area and knew how to do business negotiations. That is how they were able to acquire these businesses in Mirando" (Teresa Johnson, interview, April 10, 2004).

Mirando City Tejanos in the 1950s to the 1970s

Elvia Cristan's family owned a grocery store in Mirando City. Though she has been living in San Antonio, Texas, since the early '70s, she still remembers subtle segregation and underlying racism as a youth in the 1950s in Mirando and other parts of South Texas. By this time the African Americans who lived in Mirando City had all moved away, and Tejanos and Anglos made up the demographic mix there. Elvia explains,

> We used to go to school and for some reason we played [high school football] at some other town in San Ysidro and San Benito and all those small towns, we would go after school and they would not serve us because we were Mexican. So that was back then, and you could feel it. Even then, at my age when I was in high school, it was better, but still, you know. . . . Yes [it was] all over. Anywhere.
>
> It was in Mirando. It wasn't so bad, but it was the higher-ups, not our generation in school, we were all close, but there was just something behind that, you're not supposed to do that, you're not supposed to go with him. There's a difference. That was the thing. I was a cheerleader for four years and we had a lot of experience. . . . But we didn't care, we didn't know any better. To us everybody was the same, we didn't make any fuss about it, we just kept on. That's how it was. But you could see the difference.
>
> It was their western dances and the step, and we were separated in Mirando. . . . And when they had their big parties and dances, que puros americanos (all of them Americans, Anglos), we used to go see through the window from the outside, but they wouldn't let you in or anything. It was in the American Legion. . . . That's where we had all the dances and stuff. Theirs was theirs, and the rest was later. [Interview, April 23, 2004]

Amada's niece, Gloria Sanchez Palacios, remembers that even though she had Anglo friends, she felt different because of this underlying, often unspoken sentiment as a result of language and cultural differences highlighted at school in Mirando City, and in the atmosphere in surrounding communities. She relates,

I went to school in Mirando up to the fourth grade. And it's funny 'cause I was thinking last night, in '56 they had a Spanish-speaking kindergarten class, nobody knew English, we were all alike there. . . . how funny you think of it right now and so many things, and it did exist that way, too. Why did we have a Spanish-speaking kinder and then all-English kinder? We were such a little community, everybody knew everybody. But yet there was this. . . . division between the Anglos and the Mexican Americans. . . . I feel maybe I am wrong, I feel, now that I am thinking of it going back, but then most of our friends for me and Claud (Amada's son Claudio) when we were growing up were Anglo. . . . the very few close friends that I had . . . were Methodists. In Mirando, my mom's employer was Anglo; she was the postmaster there, Maria Long. [Interview, April 18, 2004]

The Tejano community of Mirando City maintained its language, as well as its religious and cultural traditions that originated in Mexico. One tradition that many from Mirando City remember is Las Pastorelas (Shepherd's Plays), which are theatrical events initiated by the Catholic Church in the thirteenth century and brought to the New World. Las Pastorelas are performed at Christmastime to celebrate the birth of Jesus. Some of the characters in the play, in addition to Jesus and Mary, are the shepherds, devils, and angels.[8]

Amada fondly remembers coming to Mirando City for Las Pastorelas before she got married, and even afterward. The family that hosted this celebration every year owned the *molino* (mill) in town, where they would grind corn into *masa* (dough), and people from the community would go there to buy it. Las Pastorelas took place in a fairly small wood house used especially for the occasion; another wood house next door served as the kitchen to cook all the food. *Faroles* (candle-lit paper-bag lanterns) illuminated homes and paths that special evening, and fireworks were also part of the festivities. Amada still remembered the songs that accompanied the event, and she sang a few refrains for me.

It was such a memorable tradition that many still reminisce about it. Mrs. Teresa Johnson recalls,

> At Lala's... Her mother used to have them en la tarde con todos los niños y dulces... tenía Pastorela, it was all nice... at the house... all night they make up two big things of tamales to give, there was a lot of people, American people that go over there... just to take pictures... where her mother tenía el altar. It was beautiful... and the Pastorela que tenía, el diablo, los angelitos que van arriba, los ángeles y los que cantan y luego adoran al niño Dios.... it was beautiful.... El 24 [de diciembre] she would feed the whole town.... oh yes, there were a lot of people. [Interview, April 10, 2004]

> At Lala's... Her mother used to have them in the late afternoon with all the children and candy. They would put on a Pastorela, it was all nice... at the house... all night they make up two big things of tamales to give, there was a lot of people, American people that go over there... just to take pictures... where her mother had the altar. It was beautiful... and the Pastorela they had, the Devil, the little angels that go up above, the angels and those who sing, and then they show their love for Baby Jesus.... it was beautiful.... December 24 she would feed the whole town.... oh yes, there were a lot of people.

Elvia Cristan's family helped host Las Pastorelas with Lala, her mother's aunt:

> The Pastorelas, well I was a little girl, and I remember at that time they didn't used to buy at the stores a lot of stuff or give us a lot of candy or stuff like that.... It must have been hard times for the parents, there were so many. But we looked forward to Christmas because of that big bag of food with an orange and an apple, and the *hojarascas* and all that, the cookies, that were given at the Pastorela. So we would stay up all night and be there, it was a rosary, the most important thing, but we didn't go for that; we wanted the cookies, the candy from the padrinos, that was the stuff we wanted. And then the other people would stay up to midnight and my grandfather's sisters would make the tamales and make the altar for the *niño Dios* (Baby Jesus), and

have a Pastorela. And there was a gentleman who would do the whole thing on the Pastorela, they would sing it out, they really worked it out, they would have the *diablo* (Devil), they would have all these costumes, it was really something, it was really nice.

And they would *arrullar al niño Dios* (sing lullabies to the Baby Jesus), cradle him and wrap him with the scarves and sing and all that, and then they would pass out the candies and the *colaciones* (candy made of sugar-covered aniseed). It was really fun, that's what we looked forward to, that was Christmas to us because there were no Christmas trees, we looked forward to the Pastorelas and *levantar al niño Dios* (raising up Baby Jesus). . . . everybody was involved, everybody, everybody looked forward to it. And if you could afford a Christmas tree it would be one from the woods—a mesquite tree. They would fix it up.[9] [Interview, April 23, 2004]

Amada and Claudio: Integral Community Members

Amada and her husband, Claudio, were active members in this community of Mirando City, and they contributed all they could to the school and to the Catholic church. Amada, having grown up in the Tejano, Spanish-speaking rancho of Los Ojuelos, and Claudio, who came to South Texas from Mexico in search of a better life, dedicated their energies to giving back and enriching the educational and civic welfare of the community, especially the children. They helped families raise money to build an auditorium that benefited the school and the community. Mrs. Raquel Mendieta explains, "A lot of other people donated money, too, but they were so generous, everybody said. And so, we got the community auditorium built and then later they turned it into a cafeteria and of course an auditorium, too, but they built a kitchen and that is where the kids eat their meals" (interview, April 17, 2004).

Both Amada and Claudio wanted the best for their son and their niece, Gloria, whom they helped raise when she was young. Neither Amada nor Claudio had learned much formal English and were attentive to providing the tools they thought would enable their children to do well in the Anglo, Tejano, and Mexican worlds. They insisted that the children learn

English first, then Spanish. Claudio Jr. recalls, "I learned Spanish when I was about four years old because I used to sit with my dad and he used to read me the newspaper. And then he'd say, 'Now you read it. You read what I read.' And I started reading it and I started figuring out the words, and then I could spell them, just like that I learned. So by the time I was in second grade or whatever, I knew how to speak English and Spanish" (interview, October 24, 2004). Amada also encouraged her son to learn, and she was a dedicated reader of the newspaper. Claudio Jr. recounts,

> Yeah, she was interested in the news as well as what was happening in these local communities. And another thing, too, about my mother, she was always involved, not only in my school activities, but she was in the Parent-Teacher Association, and she was into all those things like that, she was very supportive.
>
> I always had good memories of school. It went by like a blur. I played sports and speech club and one-act plays. . . . I really got into that stuff. And spelling bees, all that stuff. And of course being a small town I went to school with the same people, grade to grade until I graduated, so it was kind of nice. You got to know the people, you were right there together until you graduated. It was special. [Interview, October 24, 2004]

Due in large part to the influence of his parents, Claudio Jr. did not remember feeling any prejudice or discrimination. "You know, I think about that sometimes, and as far as I remember, there wasn't any. I got along with anybody. And I used to have a lot of white friends and everything, of course I went to school with them, too. But no, not that I remember, there was nothing, no friction that I can remember. It was pretty mellow" (interview, October 24, 2004).

Amada and Claudio Sr. were loyal fans of the high school football team, for which their son Claudio Jr. was a star player. In the 1950s, as much as today, high school football in Texas, even in South Texas, has been elevated to an extraordinary level of community pride and honor. Gloria, Amada's niece, remembers about her aunt and uncle, "They were very involved in the school. Very much so. And Claud was always playing football. So they were there for every game, they followed him everywhere he went to play. . . . I remember when Claud graduated in '56, I was coming into school . . . and Amada had a cheerleader uniform made for me . . . of the school colors. And I would wear it to the football games" (interview, April 18, 2004).

The elder Cardenases were extremely proud the day their son graduated; he was the first member of the family to complete high school. Their comadre, Guadalupe Lira, remembers that day in 1956: "When their son graduated we came over, we used to give little presents to the graduate and I remember it so well. . . . I can see it right now, a table full of shirts that he had received . . . and we brought him one. And they were all colors and all shirts, he had a lot of them. . . . And she was so happy for her son, he had finished high school" (interview, April 21, 2004).

Amada and Claudio Sr. were also dedicated to the Catholic church in Mirando City, named for St. Agnes. Raquel Mendieta provides an overview of this saint:

> She was a young girl. . . . her father had promised her in marriage . . . and she refused to marry this older man. . . . She had dedicated herself to the Lord and so she had made up her mind and she was not going to marry anybody, and so she was killed for that reason. So she was canonized as a saint. She's our saint. And, we did a real nice Easter Vigil Mass Saturday night, that's when they . . . turn the lights off and we'd go outside and then they'd build the fire and that's where they'd light the Easter candles from. And then all of us would light our candles from the Easter candles. We'd go into the church and there's no lights except the candlelight and it looks beautiful. [Interview, April 17, 2004]

Amada and Claudio attended mass regularly, and Amada, along with other women in the community, was a member of the Altar Society. Raquel Mendieta, a fellow member, says, "And, for the church, we were members of the Altar Society and, of course, we had fundraisers for the church. So, we worked together a lot. We used . . . to make tamales to sell at the school carnival and we would work practically all day making the tamales and Mrs. Cardenas was there and her sisters. . . . But . . . we were involved in anything that came around; we were there" (interview, April 17, 2004).

Amada's friend and another member of the Altar Society, Maria Esquivel, fondly remembers Amada and how much she contributed, even donating jewelry that NAC members had given her as gifts: "She was a very special, special lady . . . We had a big society . . . and she was always helping . . . whatever we were doing for fundraising, she would always volunteer and give us whatever we needed. Sometimes she would give us one or more of (her) Indian necklaces . . . so the church could make money. Such a special lady" (interview, April 21, 2004).

The Cardenases' Home Life

On the home front, Amada and Claudio Sr. created a loving, caring environment that stressed the virtues of responsibility and respect for others. They raised Claudio Jr. and his cousin Gloria with these values. Gloria's mother, Andrea, was the youngest of Amada's siblings. Amada and Claudio Sr. helped support her sister and niece and treated Gloria as if she were their own daughter. Gloria and her mother would spend the workweek at Amada's and Claudio's house in Mirando City and the weekends with Amada's parents in Los Ojuelos until they all moved to Laredo when Gloria completed the fourth grade.

Both Gloria and Claudio Jr. remember the reserved, strict manner by which Amada instilled in them the values she and Claudio Sr. shared.

> So, and there were little tiny things that today do make a difference in our lives. Like, you prepare your clothes for school the day before. You polish your shoes every day. You take a shower every day, I don't care if you have a headache, you're sick, you're lazy or what. And she was very strict about it. She was always very strict about prayer. Prayer before we went to bed, prayer before we had our food, and there was no cussing in front of them. Never can I even begin to start to imagine a bad word out of her mouth or out of my uncle's. Never.
>
> It was not that you felt fear because of the disciplinarian that she was, but she made you feel respect; it was respect within the discipline. And you learned it.

And it was like, she always stressed grace before we eat, grace before we went to bed; we said our prayers. They were very devoted. Religion played an important part (in their lives). [Gloria Sanchez Palacios, interview, April 18, 2004]

You know, my mom, she was very laid back and she always, it was like she was kind of in the background, you know, and she wasn't a very assertive person, but she had her moments. She did all the discipline, and my dad was the one that was the soft one. My mother used to send me to my room without food when I did something wrong, and my dad would sneak some food out the side door and come back in my room and give me some food, that's how softhearted he was.

Yeah, she was really strict, but at the same time she did it with a lot of love. And, like I say, she was kind of in the background. But if you got out of line she was right there. You know, sometimes she used to chase me around the house with a broom . . . but on the other side of that, she taught me how to dance.

. . . We used to go to dances and my dad wasn't too much into that kind of thing, but my dad, he was my dad, and he kind of sat around, like a lot of men do. But my mother, she liked to go to dances and when she went, her and I would dance all the time. Like I said, we would go step for step and she would put some music on and she would say, here, this is the way you do it. So she taught me how to dance pretty early . . . mainly Mexican *corridos* and ballads. [Claudio Cardenas Jr., interview, October 24, 2004]

In the 1940s and 1950s, Nuevo Laredo, the "New Laredo" across the border from the US Laredo, offered a number of affordable entertainment venues, and the Cardenas family frequently drove to Laredo and then crossed over the border by foot to Nuevo Laredo. Claudio Jr. reminisces,

There used to be a restaurant down there, you know where the big market is? Right across the street from there. It's not there anymore. . . . it was called the Alma Latina. And we used to be regulars there. All the time, every time we went there, they knew my dad by first name and my mother. . . . my dad really loved it. My mother, she liked to go there and have dinner and a little bit of wine. . . . We used to go to the bullfights all the time. When I was small, I hated to see those bulls get killed so I would hide behind my mother until the bull got killed. So after a while my dad got the message and he decided that he wasn't going to go anymore because it was pretty hard on me. But the three of us, we used to do just about everything together. We used to go to the bullfight in Nuevo Laredo, We used to go to the ball game in Nuevo Laredo . . . baseball, the Tecolotes.[10] We used to go to wrestling matches. We did a lot of things. That's one memory that really sticks out. [Interview, October 24, 2004]

Being devout Catholics, the Cardenas parents would also take Claudio Jr. on religious pilgrimages in Mexico. They would visit a shrine northeast of Guadalajara to receive blessings from the Virgen de San Juan de Los Lagos. Known as the patroness of journeys, she is also venerated by followers who make *promesas* (vows) to her. Claudio Jr. remembers the family's pilgrimages to the Virgin. "My dad loved the Virgen de San Juan de los Lagos. . . . He used to pray to her all the time and he would petition for different things. And when he got what he asked for, we would go there, and he would get on his knees and walk, go into the church—way from the courtyard all the way to the altar. This was when I was maybe about ten."

In 1949 a replica of the Mexican Virgen de San Juan was brought to San Juan, Texas, in the Rio Grande Valley (Arreola 2002:180–182). The Cardenas family would also make pilgrimages to this shrine to the Virgen de San Juan del Valle and collect holy water to take home. Claudio Jr. recounts, "San Juan, it is the Virgen de San Juan de los Lagos, and she is in the Valley, but the original one is in [Mexico]. That's why she loves that place" (interview, October 24, 2004).

Life as *Peyoteros*

From the time that the Cardenas family made Mirando City home, all members worked full time in the peyote trade. All of the townspeople knew when they saw Native Americans coming through town that they were headed to the Cardenases' place to buy peyote, and they accepted this. Claudio Jr. explained that there was no conflict between his parents being good practicing Catholics and also being involved in the NAC: "There was never any conflict. . . . from the beginning on, they balanced everything out and there was never a problem. . . . they were very accepting of it . . . once they [the community] understood the reason why they [the Indians] came, we were to harvest it [peyote] for them to take it back" (interview, October 24, 2004). Gloria stresses, "I think everybody understood their purpose and what the peyote itself stood for. I do not recall any conflict whatsoever. . . . I cannot recall anybody there in Mirando ever questioning or doubting what they were doing" (interview, April 18, 2004).

Amada stressed the importance of respecting the Indians who came to Mirando and their peyote ceremonies:

> Muchas veces la gente cree que es una cosa curiosa [las creencias de la NAC], y yo les digo que no, es una cosa seria, porque son oraciones. Cantan y rezan, le dan lugar a otra persona que rece, que describa su vida, yo creo es como una confesión . . . muchos de ellos son católicos. Yo me he fijado que muchas veces ellos rezan y bendicen el agua, la comida, la fruta, la carne, lo que meten a la tipi y ponen donde está la lumbre. [Interview, November 27, 1993]

> Many times the people believe that it is a curious thing [the beliefs and practices of the NAC] and I tell them no, it is a serious thing because they are prayers. They sing and pray, they make room for another person to pray, to talk about his life, I think it is like a confession. . . . many of them are Catholics. I have noticed that many times they pray and bless the water, the food, the fruit, the meat, everything that they take into the teepee and put by the fire.

The sound of the water drum used in NAC ceremonies on the Cardenases' property on the southern outskirts of the city sometimes resonated through the town at night. Mirando City resident Raquel Mendieta remarks,

> I was glad or happy to see that they could stay there. . . . I could hear them, sometimes. We had some new people move into town, on the next corner here, and when they came . . . three or four days later, the man said, "Was that you playing that music so long during the night?" I think, "What music?" I didn't hear them that night. He said, "Well, I heard something and it sounded like drums." I said, "Oh! That was the Indians having their ceremonies." Because they stay up all night, they start at seven o'clock in the evening . . . and they stay until the sun comes up the next morning. And, every once in a while you can hear the drums, and he said, "Was that what it was?" I'm sure that's what it was. I didn't hear them that night, but I've heard them before. [Interview, April 17, 2004]

Mrs. Terry Johnson comments, "I lived over here [near Amada's] so I used to hear [the drums]. I like it because I like music, you see" (interview, April 10, 2004). Some of the local townspeople would occasionally talk with the Native Americans who came through, but their children were more likely to mingle with the younger Indians who came with their families to the Cardenases' house.

Mrs. Mendieta says,

> I thought that was very interesting, because, like I say, we used to say hello to them and talk. Well, I remember one time this Indian woman, I think she told me she was from Minnesota, but what attracted me to her was she was wearing the soft leather boots up to her knees and they were beaded; they were beautiful. And so we got to talking, and she told me she was from Minnesota. It has been so many years ago, and you know, talk to them and say hello to them . . .
>
> And, my daughter made friends with a little girl . . . an Indian girl . . . and for several years after they would come and they would see each other; my daughter still remembers that little girl. [Interview, April 17, 2004]

"When the Indian families came to Amada's," Mrs. Johnson fondly remembers, "they would bring their children, including their teenagers.

Where Amadita lives over there, they [the Indians] used to bring a lot of teenagers . . . and Nora [her daughter] and her friends used to go and talk to the young people . . . and they liked the Indians, the teenagers" (interview, April 10, 2004).

Amada always made sure that the local Mirando City youth were respectful of the Indians who came to her house. Salvador Johnson, Mrs. Terry Johnson's son, clearly remembers this when he was young:

> The thing that sticks with me was that she always protected the native people that come down here. . . . she was very strict about it. . . . It was not because she was selfish or none of this; it was something that, I believe, she had a lot of respect, and she just didn't like people bothering them when they were praying. You know, we didn't know, and people don't understand why a lot of people are there. But this is the way it is.
>
> We would we go up there sometimes when we were kids and talk to them and just be around there and she would run everybody off. . . . if you didn't go there for a purpose that she'd call you up there, you had to come knock on her door and ask for permission. You just couldn't go in there, no, no, no. I understand now being involved with the church, I understand where she comes from. Because four or five, ten trucks there and fifteen, twenty, thirty people there who were praying and trying to accomplish the mission they had taken to come all the way out there to the holy land. And for us to go out there and interrupt them, which we didn't know what we were doing, and she was the only one who knew. And we didn't, we didn't know any better. But now I know, and it wasn't because she was mean; we just didn't understand why these people would come all the way over here. Like I said, you have to really understand or be involved . . . with the Native American Church to understand. [Interview, April 21, 2004]

A few of the Mirando City kids became more involved than others with the Native American youth and with the ceremonies that took place on the Cardenases' property. Neighbor and comadre to Mr. and Mrs. Cardenas, Guadalupe Lira recounts,

> Yeah, they would come all the time there (to the Cardenases' property) and build a tepee. Yeah. And they would pray. . . . they would invite you to go to the meeting. But I never did go. . . . but I remember that and there were a lot of Indians, a lot of them would come . . . some, I believe, in February. . . . I didn't think nothing of it. It was part of, I guess, the tradition in this town for them to be here . . .
>
> Javier . . . my son, he likes, he loves the Indians, and he would sing. It's a song in Spanish, because he loves Indians. . . . he must have been about sixteen . . . and as soon as they would get there, he was over there with them, talking to them.[11] He's very outgoing. . . . he would write to this girl; he made friends with them. And he likes whatever they wear. . . . and they gave him some rings. . . . he takes a little bit [of peyote] in the meeting; he eats peyote. He is a very strong man. . . . I know it is good. That's why they [Indians] come over here to look for it, because it is their *medicina* [medicine] and they are used to it. [Interview, April 21, 2004]

Various Tejano townspeople who worked in the oil fields or on ranches supplemented their earnings by harvesting and selling peyote on the side to Native Americans who came to Mirando City.[12] Others in search of work harvested peyote and sold it to traders such as the Cardenases. Still others would go out with Claudio Cardenas Sr.—sometimes Amada would accompany them—to the gardens to work side by side harvesting peyote to take back to clean and dry. Amada remembered some of the places where she and Claudio secured permission to harvest peyote.

> El primer lugar que conseguimos [permiso] fue en Curvitas con la familia Muñoz. . . . Era muy buena gente . . . y había tanto peyote. No más sentábamos y estábamos cortando, cortando, cortando [peyote]. Había muchísimo, y sí, muy grande. Ya después no nos dejaron entrar . . . porque habían muchos petroleros y nos pasamos por El Garceño. También había mucho peyote en ese lugar. Fuimos varios años cortando peyote. . . . conseguimos [permiso] por escrito. . . . No, nunca entramos a un portrero donde no teníamos permiso. . . . en el lugar que le dice La Casita . . . nos dio el papel escrito que nos dejara entrar . . . también allí lo cortamos.

Cuando nos faltaba peyote íbamos al [área de] Rio Grande [City]. Teníamos amigos que nos ayudaban, que cortaban el peyote ellos y nosotros no más íbamos a recoger[lo].

Jacinto Villareal y ella [su esposa] tenían mucha familia. Allí nos campamos con ellos y vamos juntando el peyote.

Fuimos también [con] David y la señora. Y luego nos campábamos en el rancho el viernes, y el sabado y domingo trabajamos. Era solo el potrero. [Interview, February 2, 1997]

The first place we got [permission] was in Curvitas with the Muñoz family. . . . They were very good people . . . and there was so much peyote. As soon as we sat down, we were cutting, cutting, cutting [peyote]. There was so much, and yes, it was very large. Later on we were not allowed to enter [the property] . . . because there were many oilmen and we moved on to El Garceño. There was also a lot of peyote in this place. We went there many years cutting peyote. . . . we got written [permission]. . . . No, we never entered land where we did not have permission. . . . in the place that they call La Casita . . . we got a written note that allowed us to enter . . . and there we also cut [peyote].

When we didn't have enough peyote we would go to [the area of] Rio Grande [City]. We had friends who helped us, cutting the peyote themselves, and we just went there to collect it.

Jacinto Villareal and his wife had a large family. There we camped with them and we would gather peyote.

We went also [with] David and his wife. And then we would camp at the ranch on Friday, and Saturday and Sunday we worked. We were the only ones there.

For a time Claudio Sr. and Amada employed a significant number of people in Mirando City to help them in the peyote trade. Gloria remembers that "some of Claud's friends would go with him to get the medicine, [on] the ranches where they were granted permission." Today, Salvador Johnson is one of the few remaining peyote dealers; he got his start at age eleven working for the Cardenas family. He remembers,

I met Ms. Cardenas in, I'd say, about 1956, I think; actually that was about when I started. I was about eleven years old when I started harvesting peyot [sic], . . . it's something that, I guess, came natural to everybody because almost all the kids around here, we used to work for them, involved in one way or another . . . [they] always needed somebody to go out there and harvest peyote. . . . And we did that for Amada Cardenas and Claudio for years and years and years. After we grew up and we left, but we always, we used to go out with them to harvest peyote. . . . We would go where they would go early in the morning and they would give us a baloney sandwich, potato chips, and a coke. And we stayed there until the evening and that was it.

We had two places where we went. There is a place they used to call the Texaco. And the name of the Texaco was La Mota Ranch. Why they called it La Mota, I have no idea . . . but that was one of the places. In that time everything was open, we called it "open range," we would go to all the different ranches. Another place that we used to go was Robert East's ranch. It's part of the King ranch; that ranch consists of 187,000 acres.

Those were the two ranches where we used to go to harvest peyot [sic]. The owners of the ranches, I don't know who the owners were, but at that time everything was open range so we would go there. [Interview, April 21, 2004]

The Cardenases' comadre, Mrs. Guadalupe Lira, describes how, years ago, she and her husband would accompany the Cardenases out into the brushland to harvest medicine, and that sometimes she and her husband would go on their own to harvest peyote to sell to the Cardenases. She also reflects upon how challenging the work was with their first child in tow:

I used to be over the hill [from] where she lives, on the other side. There used to be a little house, and I and my husband was living there, and so we were neighbors. . . . What I remember best [was that] her husband used to go get the peyote, and they had a little truck. . . . so we would go out and get the peyote and then, they had boards like tables, they would put the peyote there and dry it. . . .

We used to watch that. We used to go, my husband and I, often to get peyote. Because you could do that then, now you have to have papers or something, but we used to go and get some peyote [and] sell it sometimes to them. . . .

There were friends that had ranches . . . and my husband would ask permission and they said we could go in. But now you have to pay and you have to have papers and no, no, no, just forget it. But we used to go; my husband would make *peyotavos* [cutting tools with handles] from old hoes. . . . I had a lot of them here. . . . I gave one to each of my sons and daughters, in remembrance of their father and what we used to do. Later on in years we had my first baby, and I would lay him in a basket where you put your clothes . . . an oval one . . ., and he would lie there with his bottle. He would get ants all over him. Oh, poor baby. . . . we didn't have anybody to look after him. Now there's a lot of people who can take care of babies in my family, but then I didn't have anyone. . . . It was hard work because you are out there in the sun. [Interview, April 21, 2004]

Mrs. Catalina Inocencio explains,

Cuando nos casamos él, después de su trabajo con el Sr. Killam, juntaba peyote. Se lo traía al señor Claudio y la señora Amadita, muy amable y lo recibieron de él. Veníamos del rancho Cuéllar, allí trabajó mi esposo por mucho tiempo. Y ella muy amable nos ofrecía lo que tenía. Luego después ella iba con su esposo a Cuéllar. Los dos iban a recoger el peyote que mi esposo juntaba en los costales y lo traían. Ellos eran tan amables. [Interview, April 21, 2004]

When we were married, my husband, after working for Mr. Killam, gathered peyote. He brought it to Mr. Claudio and Mrs. Amadita; they were very kind and they received it from him. We would come from Rancho Cuellar; that is where my husband worked much of the time. And she [Amada] was so hospitable and offered us whatever she had. Later on she would go with her husband to Cuellar to pick up the peyote that my husband had gathered in burlap bags and take them. They were so kind.

Mrs. Inocencio and her husband did not have much contact with the Indians who came to the Cardenases' house to buy peyote and knew virtually nothing about their religious use of this revered cactus. But she said, "Amadita no más nos decía que ellos son gente creyente y buena" (Amadita simply told us that they were believers and good people).

From the moment they went to harvest the peyote to the time they returned home and prepared it for sale, the Cardenases always carried out their work in a respectful manner and were faithful caretakers of the peyote for the Native Americans.

Their niece, Gloria, remembers this vividly when she was a girl:

> I do have to stress that their line of work was done, in my point of view, very professionally because they really took it to heart. It was not something that they were out there to make money from. No, they understood what it stood for, and that's the way they valued it. It was hard work, they would leave very early in the morning, come back six, seven at night, and even then, even after a hard day I can remember, Claud, my uncle, he would boil water, wash the medicine first, spread it out, all out on those little wood tables he had out there.
>
> And they always took real good care of it. And she [Amada] always stressed that this is for religious purposes, so you have to respect it like so. And I can remember, it was like a day in the afternoon when all the other chores were taken care of, everybody would sit with their little bucket, start cutting them, the little roots so that they could put them, all the peyote in a line, very neatly, for them to dry so that they could have the dry peyote. They would grind it to make the powder, they would keep the fresh. But everything was done, yes, like special treatment, I could say. They really took real good care of what they were doing. [Interview, April 18, 2004]

The Native Americans who came to their home in Mirando City knew this well. More and more of them sought out Claudio Sr. and Amada for their sacred peyote. And in the coming years the Cardenases' lives became more deeply intertwined with the NAC and many of its members. A large number of them became close friends and family.

Map of Northwest Mexico, South Texas, and the Natural Range of Peyote Cactus

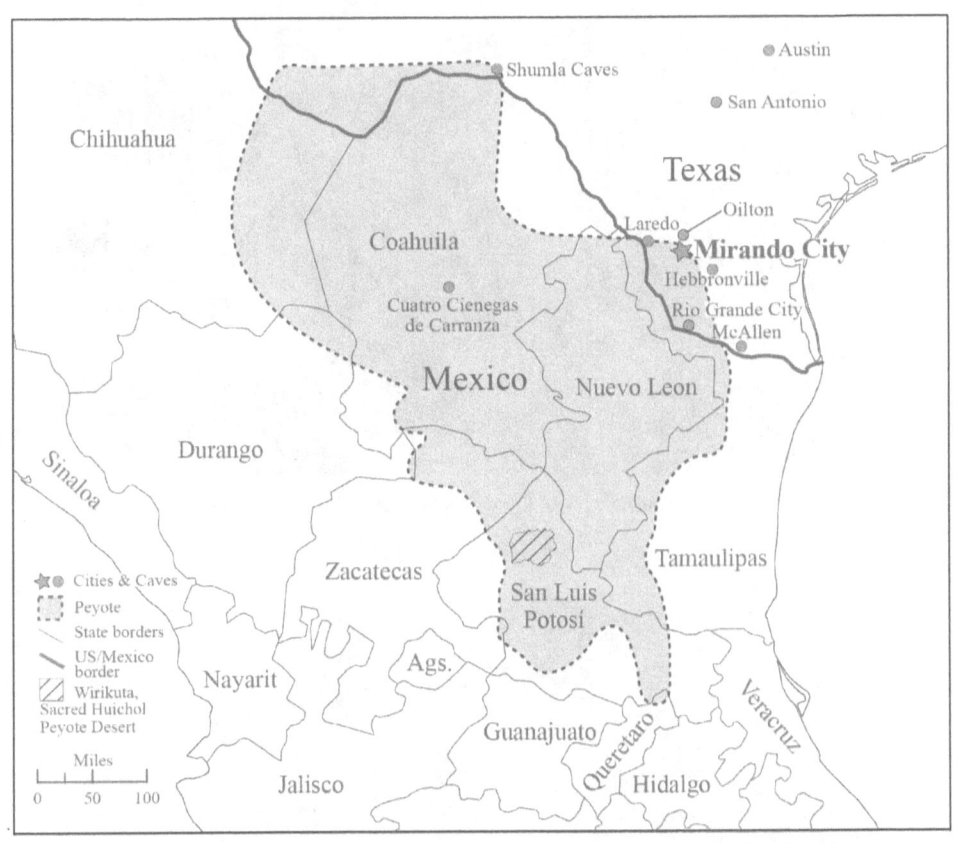

Map by J. Bauml, Nov. 24, 2014, adapted from ESRI World Basemap, 2006. Peyote distribution from M. Terry, 2008. Wirikuta area from Conservación Humana.

Amada (right) and family in Rancho los Ojuelos, late 1910s. Courtesy of Claudio Cardenas Jr.

Expedition to harvest peyote in the gardens of South Texas. The burlap bags are filled with freshly cut peyote. Claudio Cardenas Sr. (standing) with Claudio's brother David Cardenas (kneeling), David's wife, Morena, and David's son, Rene (seated in truck). Photo taken by Amada Cardenas with her box camera, circa 1946. Courtesy of Claudio Cardenas Jr.

Claudio Cardenas Sr. cleaning fresh cut peyote to dry. Photo taken by Amada Cardenas with her box camera, 1950. Courtesy of Claudio Cardenas Jr.

Amada and Claudio Cardenas Sr. in December 1966. Courtesy of Claudio Cardenas Jr.

Amada as widow and peyotera with dried peyote, November 1972. Courtesy of Linda Patchen.

Amada as La Reina de San Valentín (Valentine Queen), Civic Center, Laredo, Texas, 1987. Courtesy of Claudio Cardenas Jr.

Officers of the newly reinstated Native American Church of the United States at Amada's place, February 1988. Left to right: Jerry Etcitty, Frank Takes Gun, Jerry Patchen, Amada Cardenas, Rutherford Loneman. Courtesy of Linda Patchen.

Amada standing with food for a prayer meeting on the tepee grounds of her property, February 1988. Courtesy of Linda Patchen.

Amada with Nora Martinez coming out of a prayer meeting service in a tepee on the Cardenas property to honor Amada on her ninety-seventh birthday, October 2001. Courtesy of Linda Patchen.

Amada and Mrs. Mary Jacquez. Courtesy of Linda Patchen.

Amada and Nora. Courtesy of Michelle Mackey.

Amada with her birthday cake at age ninety-two, October 1996. Courtesy of Linda Patchen.

Amada with family and grandson, Alan Cardenas, blowing out candles on the cake for her ninety-third birthday, October 1997. Courtesy of Linda Patchen.

Amada with family and great-granddaughter, Nicole Harris, blowing out candles on the cake for her one-hundredth birthday, October 2004. Courtesy of Jim Bauml.

Amada's birthday cake and photo on her one-hundredth birthday celebration at the Civic Center in Mirando City, Texas, October 2004. Courtesy of Jim Bauml.

Amada and family members in front of the tepee where a prayer meeting to celebrate her ninety-third birthday had taken place, October 1997. Photo courtesy of Linda Patchen.

Judge Kazen with his wife, Drusilla Perkins Kazen, and granddaughter Lisl Kazen Friday as they arrive at Amada's place to visit her during her ninety-sixth birthday celebration, October, 2000. Kazen wears the red-and-blue blanket and carries the eagle feather presented to him by the NAC after the 1968 ruling on *The State of Texas v. David Clark*. Courtesy of Linda Patchen.

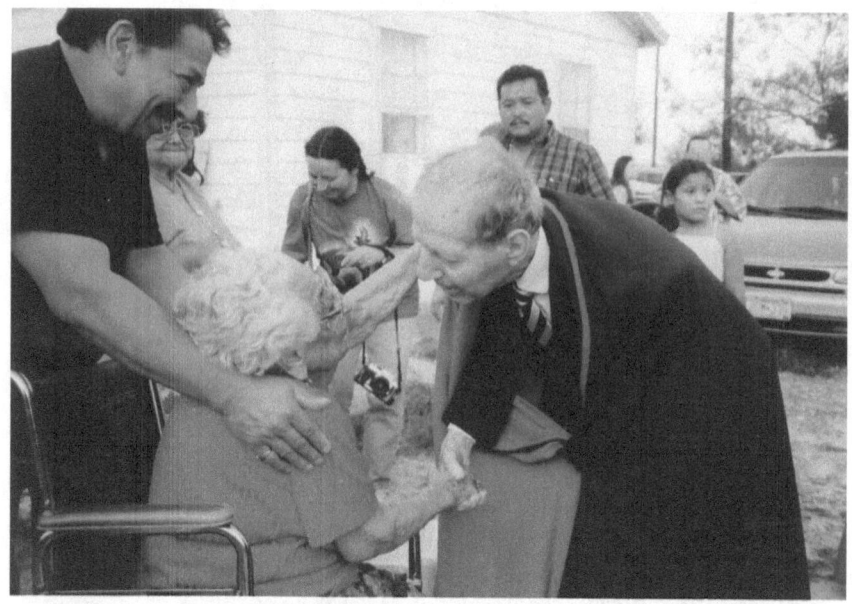

Judge Kazen greeting Claudio Jr. and Amada on her ninety-sixth birthday, October 2000. In background: Nora's tía Ana, the author, and tía Ana's son-in-law, Sylvester. Courtesy of Linda Patchen.

Amada and Claudio Cardenas Jr., October 1995. Courtesy of Stacy B. Schaefer.

And there were lots of gifts that they [Claudio Sr. and Amada] received. And the really funny part about it I couldn't understand back then was the bond between the people and my uncle and aunt. I could see that glow when they got here, when they arrived, they embraced, and there was a glow, and there was laughter and talk, and she always kept a book where they would sign in, and they would go through the book and see who had come in, left, or whatever.

But the connection that always left me like that bond . . . that was really the bond, when they were getting ready to leave. There were tears with the good-bye. There were gifts that were given to them, to my aunt and uncle. And there was always that expectation that we will see you again soon.

—Gloria Sanchez Palacios, Amada's niece, interview, April 18, 2004

And I remember there was a lot of peyote in the [Cardenases'] backyard; they were really big. . . . My mother really took it to heart that this was a sacred place, a really holy place, on these premises, and she was very touched by the fact that there were people that lived way out here that respected the peyote just as we do. . . . Everyone knew that Mr. and Mrs. Cardenas are the people who took care of the medicine out there and they would pray for them. . . . So that was when I was a little girl, that was always in my mind. That stayed with me throughout all these years.

—Geri Arviso, Navajo, interview, February 16, 2004

And for a while the Indians used to come down here, the only way they could get peyote was to come down here, but eventually my dad and mom got a permit from the Texas Department of Agriculture so they could ship it.

—Claudio Cardenas Jr., Amada's son, interview, October 24, 2004

Chapter 4

Tepees on the Landscape

The Cardenases and the Native American Church

Native Americans at Amada's and Claudio's in Mirando City

Once Claudio and Amada Cardenas had moved to Mirando City in the 1940s, the number of Native Americans that came to their house increased dramatically. The Cardenases offered their home and grounds, equipped with drying tables and garden patches of peyote plants encircled with rock barriers, as a safe and welcoming place for Native Americans to come to purchase peyote, to visit, and to pray. The land was still "open prairie," and few fences excluded people from the hillsides and scrub brush where peyote grew. The fortunate ones were able to get permission to go into the countryside where they could pray and harvest peyote for their own consumption. Regardless of whether or not they had access to gather peyote themselves, more peyote buttons were always needed, and dried peyote was portable. Additionally, the welcoming environment and friendship that Claudio and Amada extended to the Native American pilgrims created lasting bonds with their families. From the 1940s through the mid-1960s, the Cardenases became well-known and respected peyote traders, and their home became an increasingly popular place for American Indians to visit in South Texas.[1]

Their son, Claudio Jr., remembers,

> They'd come, a lot of the time . . . most of them would come in the summertime when their kids were out of school. But then, after a while, they started coming any time of the year. So we always had steady people coming in and out. And originally they would stay (with us) in the (little stone) house here, but it got to be so much that we used to accommodate them in the garage (the tin shed), but back then it was a nicer place; we had it fixed up a lot nicer. And of course some of them would bring their tents. They would put tents up and that sort of thing. It wouldn't be strange to see as many as ten or twelve people here on a given day. It was busy. . . .
>
> Some of them would stay, some of the men would come and they would stay for like two or three weeks and help my dad around to cut the peyote and work it and dry it and all that. We always had people at our house, always, every night . . . Indians. [Interview, October 24, 2004]

Amada's niece Gloria remembers that when she was a young girl living at their house in Mirando City, she, too, assisted with hosting their Native American guests:

> And I met tons of people that came. I used to pray at the table with them. . . . They [would request], "We want the little girl to pray for us." So back then that was what I could pray, that was what I would pray, "The Lord is my shepherd." There were times when we would all [pray], because they would take their food for them when the people came, Amadita and my uncle. And it was at that older little house where I grew up, and they [Amada and Claudio] would say, "Okay, we are going to fix breakfast for them, the people that came in last night at two o'clock in the morning."
>
> So they would go and call them; they would come to the main house; they'd sit down. They would pray or they would say—people had already gotten to know me, they knew I was living there and staying with them, so sometimes [they would say], "We'll have the little girl pray for us." And I would. And sometimes they would do

their praying in their own language. And there was food for everybody—whether it was breakfast, lunch, supper, whatever.... No matter how many people came in, there was always enough. If somebody left and somebody else came in, okay, there was another table ready for whomever came in. [Interview, April 18, 2004]

Bertha Grove Davis, a Ute, tells how she came to know the Cardenas family:

My name is Bertha Grove Davis, Red Earth Woman, and I am a Ute of the national tribe.... I was about eighteen or nineteen when I first met Mrs. Cardenas.... Way back in the late '40s... my son, Alden, he was just a little baby then, when I first came... At that time there were no fences, everything was open country. The peyote, you could drive out there and camp out there.... then they started fencing things up and they started clearing the place.
 ... Mrs. Cardenas and Claudio, her husband, they were a young couple. They lived here.... They didn't have teepees or nothing down here way back then. They had meetings in their house then. Later on we brought out teepee poles. We brought our teepees, brought our old one down and put it up.... There's an old shed over there where they dried peyote—her and Claudio. They sold it. We bought some medicine from them, besides what we cut out there....
 My grandfather was a Sun Dance chief and I grew up in a Sun Dance way. And he was a medicine shaman, helped people, healed people. He was that kind of person. That's the way I grew up; that's how come I know how to move around. There is a certain way that you got to understand the medicine. You got to be careful. I learned that early cause I grew up in it. But when I got married, I married into the Native American Church. It's all I knew [the Sun Dance tradition], but over the years I learned that all things work together. But you got to learn to understand it, all things, no matter how you might see it, no matter how you might worship, or how you do your rituals, it's all the same....
 When you are young, you just come along and you just listen. You learn by being aware and you just listen. When we first came

down to the Cardenases' house I didn't do much talking, just listening to the talking, the joking around with her and her husband. We had good visits with them. My father-in-law at that time, Joe Naranjo . . . he was from Santa Clara Pueblo . . . he knew Claudio and Amada. [Interview, February 21, 2004][2]

It was not uncommon for Amada and Claudio to form special friendships with the children that came with visiting families. Some were made to feel so welcome that they considered the Cardenases to be part of their family. Geri Arviso, a Navajo from Arizona, tells her story of coming to know Amada and Claudio when she was a young girl:

We would come every year in March during spring break. Sometimes the spring break would occur like in April, at Easter time, and so we would come down to visit every year. My mom made a point every year to be here. . . . I know Amada from when I was like maybe eight or nine years old. When we first came, her husband Claudio was the kindest man that I remember. He treated us like his kids, me and my brother. . . . My mom and my dad would bring us here to go out into the fields to pick medicine. . . . My mother would start taking medicine from home . . . drive all the way with medicine, singing songs all the way here, and offer a prayer, and then go out into the fields the next day. . . . we would be out there all day in the heat, you know it's hot. . . . we got used to it. . . . you don't even feel those cactuses that get on your legs, they'd be all over you, your back, everywhere . . . and then you feel it. . . . and I remember for me, being a child, able to go underneath the leaves and crawl underneath. . . .

At night Mr. Cardenas would go outside and peel the medicine. He'd go out each night to peel it, and I think that he was trying some out. He would do that every night. The people would come here, he would talk and visit, then my mom and Mrs. Cardenas would be inside the house talking about things. But for me being a child, you just ran around exploring things. . . . When I met Mr. Cardenas he treated me really good, he gave me medicine and he told me to eat and he told them [my parents] that [my] name was not going to be Geraldine, but Geraldina, so that is how I got my name, from him saying that. . . . He made me look at the peyote that was all right there and he told me that "This will always know you forever, into the future, when you grow up, when you become my age, when you have white hair." and Mr. Cardenas, he and [Mrs. Cardenas] wanted me to stay; [they] wanted me to be a part of them at that time. So they were considered my godparents from that point on. [Interview, February 16, 2004]

Not-for-Profit Peyote Trade

Although the Cardenases dedicated their lives to the peyote trade full-time, they did not choose this line of work in order to make a profit; rather, having been inducted into the Peyote Way, they saw their work as an important service to Native Americans who were devout members of the NAC.

Claudio Jr. expresses it this way:

I think he (my dad) really enjoyed being around Indian people and medicine. He participated; he was like one of the guys. . . . I think that made a big difference, too. It made him closer than usual, not just selling—but he participated in the ceremonies, and that was natural. So he got really close with people. So did my mother. . . . yes, she would go. And my dad would take medicine, and my mother and I would take tea at that time. Well, we all did. We enjoyed those ceremonies. We would stay in there all night. [Interview, October 24, 2004]

In a conversation with Melvin George, a roadman of the Yuchi tribe who is a member and former president of the NAC of Oklahoma, Claudio explained that his parents did not view their work as a business; they were different from some of the other peyote dealers.

Everybody wanted the money up front. . . . I think my dad . . . when he was in Ojuelos, and by the time he moved down here [Mirando City], he was more interested in accommodating the Native American people than whatever else he was doing. I think so. . . . He spoke pretty good English. He learned a little bit of English, of course, from the time that the Indian people started coming; he had to. [Interview, October 28, 2000]

Mr. George reminisces,

When we first came here in '58, we already had green peyote. My father told my mother, "Let's go visit my friend Claudio." So we came over here. Anyway, my mother and my father, they were visiting with your parents . . . and then my father told my mother, "They have some dried peyote. . . . let's get some dried peyote." So my father told [Claudio], "We'll take one thousand dried ones." And he asked him how much. Five dollars . . . One thousand, they were all big. And then after he gave him the five dollars they [Claudio and Amada] ran in and brought out another big paper sack. It was another five hundred they had in there—all of that for five dollars. . . . now the peyotes are small. . . . those peyotes were bigger than silver dollars. . . .

And there were times, too, when it seemed someone needed the medicine, and they would give it to them. . . . There was no money involved. They just gave it to them. You don't hardly see that today. . . . My uncle Allen Dale and his wife, Chris Dale, they came from White Oaks, Oklahoma.[3] And they were having a real hard time financially. And your mom took them in, and they lived with your mom [and dad] for a long time, until they got straightened out. Your mom is a kind-hearted person.

Claudio interjects,

Sure. . . . And there would be a lot of times that people would come down here and their car would break down or something would happen; they did not have any way to pay for their medicine. He [Claudio Sr.] would just let them have it. . . . but these same people would come down the next time and say, "This is what I owe you from the last time." Very honest. It worked both ways. . . . it was always the case that eventually they would get whatever—that it would come back [to them]. They never worried about that. If they could accommodate someone, they would. [Interview, October 28, 2000]

The exchange of peyote was completed in a respectful as well as celebratory manner. The Cardenases' niece Gloria remembers,

> I . . . recall the sound of the drums, I can recall that and the little rattle. I can recall all of that. . . . I do remember those sounds very much set in my mind because they would play the drum and rattle, while my uncle would count whatever amount of medicine they were going to take, they would sit, squat, would squat on the floor inside of the home, which would be, we could call it, the small living room, and they would play on the drums and they would sing, the Indians. So, yes, I can remember all of that. [Interview, April 18, 2004]

Peyote Prohibition in the Navajo Nation

When the time came for the visiting Native American families to return home, it was often an emotional, bittersweet farewell that included an exchange of hugs and good wishes and blessings that the Cardenases would bestow upon these friends for their travels home, which were sometimes thousands of miles away. During the 1940s through the 1960s, there was little consistency from one state to the next and from one reservation to another regarding the laws and provisions for the religious use of peyote by members of the NAC.

Geri Arviso vividly remembers when the use of peyote, even for religious purposes within the NAC, was forbidden on the Navajo reservation:

> My mom [and dad], they felt like giving help to other people. So she [my mom] always had medicine for other groups of people. . . . [Returning from South Texas] we would have gunny sacks full and there was a time we used to take home fourteen bags. . . . all I remember is that there were fourteen bags and there'd be bags and bags in the whole truck. They'd go halfway, the bags would go halfway and my dad had to sit on top of that with boards,

two-by-fours. . . . he'd cover it with mattresses or something, you couldn't see, you can't tell, and there would be a front part right there where it looks like there's food.

I never knew why these things were going on, but I think back now and every little law that has come about. I think back to those days . . . when I was little. I don't remember any other way of life, you know, it was normal to me, for me to be hiding in the mattress. Covering me so deep, my uncles would be carrying me up the mountains to [hide] . . . and my mom said when I was a baby, you know, I was still breastfeeding, we got thrown in jail and all the people in jail, all the ladies that were in jail would look at my booties and say, "Oh, what cute peyote." . . . even then, before, when my mother was pregnant with me she got thrown into jail. [Interview, February 16, 2004]

In 1967 Navajo peyotists were finally guaranteed the right to practice their religion when the Navajo Tribal Council formally accepted the Bill of Rights of the US Constitution, which includes the First Amendment guaranteeing freedom of religious practices. The Navajo Tribal Council passed an amended ordinance to the First Amendment, stating, "Provided that it shall not be unlawful for any member of the Native American Church to transport peyote into Navajo country, or buy, sell, possess, or use Peyote in any form in connection with the religious practices, sacraments or services of the Native American Church" (Stewart 1990:310).

Anti-Peyote Laws and Legal Entanglement

From the earliest times of their establishment in North America, the Catholic Church and other Christian churches aggressively formulated policies and practices to eradicate the use of peyote among indigenous peoples. In 1899 the Department of the Interior embraced this edict, and under administrative orders, the first statute intended to criminalize peyote use was approved by the Oklahoma legislature (Botsford and Echo-Hawk 1996:126).[4] Indian Territory, in present-day Oklahoma, was established as a place to settle "uncooperative" tribes from disparate areas of the country away from the movement of white frontiersmen and women who were fulfilling the ambitions of the United States to populate and develop the West. With the move to formally ratify Oklahoma into the union as a new state, Indian and Oklahoma territories were merged. Concern on the part of American Indian peyotists over anti-peyote legislation slated for the newly incorporated state of Oklahoma brought peyote leaders together with the Medical Committee of the Constitutional Convention in 1907. Quanah Parker, a prominent figure in the peyote religion, persuasively argued from the standpoint of the First Amendment's freedom of religion clause that American Indians had the right to use peyote in their religious practices, and from a medical perspective, that peyote had health benefits as a cure for alcoholism. In response, the 1899 statute criminalizing peyote use was repealed (Maroukis 2010:32–33). However, this did not stop the Bureau of Indian Affairs from continued efforts to harass peyotists and to prohibit peyote use.

Legal strife over the use of peyote by members of the NAC spilled into Texas through its anti-drug legislation. Despite the mounting body of evidence of the benefits of peyote use to Native Americans, especially within a supportive, religious context, there were opponents set on outlawing it.[5] Following a 1916 ruling by a federal judge in Deadwood, South Dakota, that the prohibition of liquor did not pertain to peyote, and in spite of the 1918 federal recognition of the NAC in Oklahoma as a bona fide religion, a dozen anti-peyote bills were introduced in Congress between 1916 and 1963. None of these bills, however, became law (Morgan and Stewart 1984:290). Opponents then turned to the states for legislation to prohibit peyote. The first states to make the use of peyote a criminal offense were Utah, Nevada, and Colorado in 1917, followed in the years between 1923 and 1933 by Arizona, Kansas, Montana, North Dakota, South Dakota, Iowa, New Mexico, Wyoming, and Idaho (La Barre 1989:224; Stewart 1990:227; Botsford and Echo Hawk 1996:128).

In 1937 Texas enacted its first anti-peyote law, which did not actually pertain to its use in Texas, since few Native Americans lived there; most tribes had been relocated to Oklahoma. Agents in the Texas Narcotics Bureau and Texas Department of Agriculture "allowed peyote to be harvested, sold and transported, and eaten in Texas for religious purposes" (Stewart 1990:240; Slotkin 1956:56). Instead the law was specifically intended to prevent the transportation of peyote. Commercial peyote suppliers circumvented this law by shipping peyote only into states where it was legal. Oklahoma, the cradle of the NAC, allowed peyote use. Packages containing this sacrament were sent to Oklahoma, and from there some of the peyote supply was then distributed to peyotists elsewhere, because incorporation into the NAC in Oklahoma also extended to other states (Stewart 1990:226, 229). In the same year that the Texas legislature passed its anti-peyote law, a federal senate bill submitted by Senator Dennis Chávez of New Mexico "aimed to prohibit the interstate transportation of anhalonium, commonly known as 'peyote'" (Stewart 1990:237–238). The bill was defeated after testimony by experts, many of whom were anthropologists led by the Commissioner of Indian Affairs, John Collier.[6]

Alarmed by the legal threat to peyote use at the discretion of state governments and concerned about how this might impact members of NAC chapters outside of Oklahoma, a national branch of the NAC was incorporated in 1944. Known as the Native American Church of the United States (NAC–US), and later as the Native American Church of North America, its elected president in 1946 was Allen P. Dale, and the elected vice president was Frank Takes Gun, an activist from the Crow Tribe (Stewart 1990:239–240, 242–243).[7]

Claudio and Amada Cardenas understood the importance of providing a supply of peyote to their Indian customers and friends, and they shipped orders of dried peyote out of the state. Anthropologist Ruth Underhill, who studied peyote use among Cheyennes and Southern Arapahos in the 1950s and accompanied them in search of peyote in South Texas, writes, "Numbers of Mexicans work in [their] spare time gathering the heads which they sell for $6.50 a thousand to Claudio Cardenas in Mirando City. He dries them and ships them all over the country at $10.00 a thousand on the understanding that they are for sacramental use" (Underhill 1950:3). Amada and Claudio had high moral standards and a compelling sense of social justice. Their support for the religious freedom of the NAC and the members' right to use peyote furthered their efforts to provide fresh and dried peyote to Native Americans who sought their help. This did not sit well with some Texas authorities. Amada described the series of events that led up to Claudio's arrest.

Veníamos con quince mil peyotes, yo y mi esposo, no más los dos. Veníamos con quince mil peyotes en la troca y cuando veníamos llegando a la loma, mira lo que estaba allí, era un policía. Bueno, ya estaba oscureciendo. Era Cucu, Cucu Pérez. Él nos miró, descargamos el peyote. Y el otro día en la mañana, llegó allí [a la casa en Mirando City] el FBI. [Interview, February 2, 1997]

We were returning with fifteen thousand peyote, me and my husband, it was just us two. We were traveling with fifteen thousand peyote in the truck when we arrived at the hill [on the road to Mirando City] and look what was there, it was a policeman. Well, it was already getting dark. It was Cucu, Cucu Perez. He looked at us and we unloaded the peyote. The next morning, the FBI arrived [at the house in Mirando City].

Their son, Claudio Jr., remembers the fateful day in 1953: "I think what happened is that the Department of Agriculture started getting really nasty about peyote because they decided it was hallucinogenic. And they wanted to put a complete stop to it. They didn't want it sold, and they didn't want it shipped. And so my dad tried to test it and see how far they would go. And so he shipped some out and a few days later the FBI were here, put him in [hand]cuffs and took him to Laredo." Claudio states that this event did not take place when there were Indians at the Cardenases' house to buy peyote. "No, not at all. He shipped it and, at that time, I guess they decided that it was illegal." He elaborates,

Well, that particular day, it started out like a normal day and then around noontime, I think it was, a couple of cars drove in the yard, and parked, and some men in suits got out and my dad went to greet them and they asked his name. And they said, "You are under arrest." So they turned him around and they put [hand]cuffs on him and they took him to Laredo.

She [Amada] was surprised, but she just stayed pretty calm. She just said that . . . they were trying to pass some laws that would restrict the Indians from obtaining the peyote and that they were trying to make a case through him [Claudio Sr.] and that was about all she said. Not to worry, that everything was going to be okay.

Claudio asserts that his mother was supportive of his dad's actions. "Oh yeah, absolutely. He wanted her to go [to jail]. . . . Yeah, he wanted them to take her, too. And she was calm, she didn't get . . . excited or anything like that. She took it all in stride because my dad stayed calm. My dad didn't say a word or anything. So, off they went. That's the most I can remember" (interview, October 24, 2004).

Gloria was also present at this event: "They had struggled and gone through a lot to get where they were at. And they were doing the best they could. . . . Yes. I can remember, I cannot give you dates because I was fairly young, but I can remember feeling the stress that was going through back then, when they were driven to court because of the peyote. I can remember the stress, the pain, sometimes even concern and crying" (interview, April 18, 2004).

Amada continued the story,

> Y le arrestó [a Claudio] y le dijeron que le iban a llevar para la cárcel. Y se lo llevaron. "Yo voy a ir con él." Y sí, fui con ellos. . . . yo le dije que no le dejo solo . . . Nos tuvieron en Laredo, no conocíamos a la policía . . . no conocíamos a nadie. . . . entonces nos llevaron con un juez. . . . fue el Juez Viegas. Él se asustó. "Porque no es causa ninguna, mijo, es peyotero," [decía]. Estaba Alan Dale aquí con nosotros, Kazen era el prosecutor. Alan Dale nos dio una buena recomendación. Y como Claudio no hablaba mucho inglés, el Sr. Kazen [nos dijo], "No hables tú, yo voy a hablar por ti"—el prosecutor. Él dijo, "Aquí no hay causa ninguna." [Interview, February 2, 1997]

And he [Claudio] was arrested and they said that they were going to take him to jail. They took him. "I'm going with him." And yes, I went with them, I told him that I would not leave him alone. . . . They had us in Laredo, we did not know the police . . . we didn't know anyone. . . . then they took us to a judge. . . . it was Judge Viegas. He was surprised, [he said], "There is no justification, none, he is a peyotero." Alan Dale was there with us, Kazen was the prosecutor. Alan Dale gave us a good recommendation. And since Claudio didn't speak much English, Mr. Kazen [told us], "Don't speak, I will speak for you"—the prosecutor. He said, "There is no case at all."

The Cardenases' friend, Allen P. Dale, then President of NAC–US, retained the legal services of a highly respected Laredo attorney, Manuel J. Raymond, to represent Claudio Cardenas. The charge was presented on March 15, 1954, to the grand jury of the 49th circuit court in Laredo, which agreed, upon the recommendation of District Attorney E. James Kazen, not to prosecute Claudio Cardenas Sr. (Morgan and Stewart 1984:290). "I can remember the glow when it was all over," recalls their niece Gloria (interview, April 18, 2004). "That is exactly how I would picture him," says Navajo Geri Arviso, "going ahead and going to jail, to make other people realize. But then you would think there is a reason why that judge thought that way, you know, maybe it is the peyote way of life, the way he [Claudio] took care of those peyote, they helped him" (interview, February 16, 2004).

After the hearing, Claudio's lawyer, Mr. Raymond, was so compelled to see justice served that in the following month, in a special session of the Texas legislature, he had the Texas Narcotic Drug Act amended by striking the words "Peyote" and "Mescal Beans" (a former ceremonial plant) (Morgan and Stewart 1984:291).

Becoming Active in Native American Church Ceremonies

The Cardenases, their friends, and officers of the NAC–US and the NAC of Oklahoma were elated by this decision and its implications for securing peyote for dealers and peyotists. Following suit of this monumental ruling, the charter for the NAC–US was amended on July 12, 1957: the name was changed to the Native American Church of North America (NAC-NA) and the Cardenases' home was designated as the official NAC-NA headquarters in the state of Texas. Amada and Claudio Sr. became members of the board of trustees at this time.[8] They and two other trustees, Frank Takes Gun and Jimmie K. King, were present to sign the document amending the Articles of Incorporation. The Cardenases and the other trustees were entrusted with the duties that "shall be in the nature of Delegates-at-large for the Native American Church of North America in the State of Texas." Concerned with firmly securing the right to provide peyote to church members within and outside of Texas, the Articles of Incorporation also included, under Article VII, "That Frank D. Bushy of Rio Grande City, Texas, and Claudio Cardenas of Mirando City, Texas, shall be and are the authorized supply agents of sacramental Peyote to the members of the Native American Church of North America, and further be it known, that these dealers shall have the right to sell, transport, and ship this sacramental Peyote in and out of the State of Texas to members of the Church."[9]

These events further strengthened the bonds between the Cardenases and the NAC and its members as well as deepened their commitment to the NAC and participation in church meetings. Enriching their own knowledge of the peyote plant, they became familiar with Native American convictions in the powers of peyote as a sacrament and medicine for mind and body. Claudio Jr. reminisces with Melvin George about his father's integration into the NAC: "Well, I remember my dad was pretty well versed in everything, because he was really close to these people and they would come down and he would learn the songs, and the gourd [rattle], and he learned to drum, he learned to tie a drum. . . . he learned most of his songs from Oklahoma." Melvin said, "Well, he would take tunes and put them to his own words . . . in Spanish. . . . my father sang some songs he learned from Claudio [Sr.]."

Claudio Jr. added, "But also, I don't know if your dad had any, but my dad used to make drumsticks. There was some kind of wood that my dad used to get—I don't know the name of it, but it was a special wood, a real hard wood. And he would work that and he would make some really special drumsticks, really nice sticks, I remember" (interview, October 28, 2000).

The February Meetings

In the 1960s some Native Americans began to arrive in February to hold an annual peyote meeting on the Cardenases' property.[10] By this time, Claudio Jr. had graduated from high school in Mirando City and attended college at Texas A&I Kingsville (now Texas A&M University–Kingsville) for a few years, leaving to enlist in the Air Force. He recalls that the February meetings began because the Indians

> always came on the twenty-second of February; there were a lot of . . . [things going on] down there . . . oh, the parade that's in town, yeah, George Washington's birthday parade.[11] They had really big events in Laredo. . . . yeah, they came for that. . . . they loved stuff in Mexico, bullfights and everything like that. . . . my dad's birthday was in March. . . . the twenty-second of February was very close to my dad's birthday. I think it was the first or second week in March. [Interview, October 24, 2004]

Archie Hoffman, a member of the Cheyenne and Arapaho tribes in Oklahoma, explains how he came to understand this February meeting:

> My father's name is Fred Hoffman and his dad's, my grandfather's, name was Albert Hoffman. . . . My grandfather journeyed down here and he met these folks that live here, Claudio and Amada Cardenas, years back. My grandfather was telling me he conducted a peyote meeting, a prayer meeting. . . . I guess that Claudio got ill, very ill. And soon my Cheyenne people, Comanche people, they showed up over here at this house. And Claudio wanted help with this peyote. He asked my Cheyenne people to conduct a prayer meeting for him, and so they done that. And through this peyote, Claudio regained his health. And so they carried that ceremony for four years. And I don't know how long ago that's been.[12]

Jerry Patchen, a Houston attorney who, with his wife, Linda, met Amada in the 1970s and became involved in the NAC, recalls what had been told to him about the origin of the February meeting:

> Well it all started, there was the incident I know you heard about where Ernest Mycoby [Comanche], Raymond Stonecalf [Cheyenne], Sam B. Dear [Cheyenne], Bert Youngman [Southern Arapaho], Amada, and Claudio were there. All of them were there. That

meeting was over forty years ago. They were in the old house, Claudio was sick, and they had a meeting for Claudio . . . this would have been in the 1960s. . . . But Claudio got well, he got healed in that prayer service that they had. These men had traveled down from Oklahoma and they were buying peyote and they wanted to have a meeting. And they had it in the little old grey house that is torn down now, it literally fell down, the first house that Amada and Claudio lived in. . . . Claudio . . . wanted to have this meeting every year. And they took a smoke. They took a smoke, and they agreed to have this meeting every year, and that when those among them went on, that the remaining [Indians] would continue this prayer service and pray for their families, pray for everyone's family." [Interview, April 29, 2004]

Passing On to Another World

Claudio Sr. died suddenly on October 24, 1967. Amada recounted how it happened:

> Detrás de la casa puso el troquito. . . . Yo estaba lavando unos vasos en frente de la puerta de la cocina. Él iba a enjuagar peyote que iba a trabajar. Pues no alcanzó porque yo creo iba a abrir la llave del baño, porque había un bañito que estaba allí, shower. Pues el no alcanzó. Cayó, fulminante el ataque [del corazón], tiró al suelo y le arranqué a levantarlo. No abrió los ojos, nunca abrió la boca tampoco. . . . murió en mis brazos porque yo le levanté . . . como quiera se falleció.
>
>   Nunca se quejó que "me duele" o "tengo dolor aquí." . . . nada me dijo. . . . nada más estaba diciéndome [un poco antes] que me iba a traer a Laredo . . . que íbamos a ir a Laredo a sacar un retrato del treinta y cinco aniversario, porque en diciembre es cuando nos casamos. Íbamos a cumplir treinta y cinco años de casados. [Interview, November 27, 1993]

He parked the truck behind the house. . . . I was washing some glasses in front of the kitchen door. He was going to soak peyote that he was going to prepare. Well, he didn't get there because I think he was going to turn on the faucet in the little shower we have over there but he didn't get there. He fell, he had a full-on heart attack, he fell to the ground and I pulled him to lift him up. He didn't open his eyes, he never opened his mouth either. . . . he died in my arms because I lifted him up . . . but regardless he died.

He never complained "I'm in pain" or "I hurt here." . . . he didn't tell me anything. . . . he had just been telling me [shortly before] that he was going to take me to Laredo . . . that we were going to Laredo to have our thirty-fifth anniversary picture taken because in December is when we were married. We were going to have our thirty-fifth wedding anniversary.

Claudio Jr. relates that in memory of his dad, "the February meeting became an annual tradition after my dad passed on in '67; they just made it sort of official that every twenty-second of February they would meet and honor my dad for his birthday" (interview, October 24, 2004).

Claudio Sr.'s abrupt departure left a deep void in the hearts and minds of many. His niece Gloria reflects upon how much he meant to her and the legacy he left:

My uncle had a very big heart. And he didn't care who you were or what background you came from. If you needed help, he was there to help you. And if he just had to, if he didn't even have to, he would make the best of it for whomever. . . . [they] were little things . . . but they always made you feel not only that you were not forgotten but that you were special. And yes he was a very honest, hardworking man who truly loved what he did. He was just a great person. There is no other word to describe him. [Interview, April 18, 2004]

The Cardenases' Navajo friend, Geraldina Arviso, remembers now, as an adult, the otherworldly realization she had as a child that Claudio would no longer be there at his house to greet them:

We drove up, my mom and dad just drove up and they went inside. And I heard Mr. Cardenas singing songs, and he would always sing songs, you know. When he was cleaning the medicine he would be singing songs. And so I woke up because I had heard he passed away, and so I woke up thinking he was around. So I jumped out of the back of the truck and went inside and he wasn't around. So my mother and father told me I was dreaming and I said, "No, I could still hear him, and I could still hear him around." So they had known him and they had to pray for me and everything that I was [not haunted] by his spirit. . . . my mom and dad finally had to explain to me . . . what it meant to be gone . . . from the physical [realm]. But I was thinking, they're lying, you know, he's still around, maybe singing behind the old garage or something. . . . I would think that. [Interview, February 16, 2004]

Claudio's untimely death left Amada alone, a widow, surrounded by the peyote gardens to which she had dedicated her life with him. I would like to suggest that the last few words on this page be followed by a moment to remember and honor Mr. Claudio Cardenas Sr. and his remarkable life as a father, son, uncle, compadre, peyote dealer, and friend who genuinely cared about people and deeply understood how to respect and care for the peyote.

They made such a nice couple. They would go everywhere together. If you could see Amada without Mr. Cardenas, it is not Amada . . . everywhere. [The two were] something [to] see, where there's love, you know, caring about that person. And she came to get [her] hair fixed, he would be here to pick her up. And, he'd get out and help her get in the truck. So, they were a really good couple. Her heart broke when he died.
—Maria Esquivel, Amada's friend, interview, April 21, 2004

A lot of people figured out after a while there was money to be made [in the peyote trade], and they started getting out of hand, and then my mother wanted no part of that. That's not the way she operated.
—Claudio Cardenas Jr., Amada's son, interview, October 24, 2004

Chapter 5

The Mustang Plains

Amada's Place in the '60s and '70s

Life as a Widow and a Peyotera

Grief stricken over the sudden death of her husband, Amada found solace in her family. Her son, Claudio Jr., married and with two small children, was then living in Minnesota. He visited her as often as possible, but with his work and young family to support he had already made Minneapolis his home. Amada's sister and brother-in-law did their best to help her adjust to life without Claudio Sr. Shortly before his death, Claudio and Amada had been preparing to move out of their tiny stone house into a new construction they had purchased and transported to their property: a two-bedroom, one-bath wood house that still sits on the property today. Amada's sister Pilar and her husband, Severo, had acquired two lots adjacent to the lot Amada and Claudio's old stone house occupied. Pilar and Severo chose not to live on the property, and they had agreed to allow Amada and Claudio to use these two lots to construct a new home (Claudio Cardenas Jr., personal communication, October 24, 2004).

Amada explained to me about her house one day when we were running errands in nearby Hebbronville. On the way back to her home, she pointed out the business on the side of the highway where she and Claudio had bought the prefabricated wooden house in 1967. She exclaimed that it cost them $2,500, plus $300 to move it onto their property, connect the electricity and plumbing, and add a porch. They diligently paid $100 monthly toward the mortgage until the house was theirs. Amada said the money they earned from collecting and selling peyote is what bought the house.[1] The house arrived in September, but, as Amada lamented to me, Claudio never got to enjoy it because he died in October, two days before her birthday and before they had moved in. Pilar and Severo stayed with Amada on the property after Claudio passed away (Amada Cardenas, personal communication, December 14, 1996).

Claudio Jr. reflects upon this time: His father "had just almost finished the house. . . . he had reworked it, worked the outside. . . . at that time Pilar and Severo were living here with her, after my dad passed away . . . then Pilar also passed away here at Grandma's house . . . a few years after that. It was kind of a double [tragedy]" (interview, October 24, 2004).

Amada remembered this event as she told me that her sister Pilar was worried that all the paperwork for the legal transfer of ownership of the two lots where Amada's new house stood wouldn't be complete before she, Pilar, passed away. Amada and Pilar went into Laredo to transfer the title to Amada. That night Pilar died at Amada's house of a heart attack, the same malady that had taken Claudio Sr.'s life (Amada Cardenas, personal communication, March 29, 1997).

Amada's son, Claudio, described his mother's resilience through these tragedies:

> My mother had this philosophy that she mourned for a year and then she said, "That's it, I'm done, I'm moving on." And that was it. And I didn't know if my mother was going to make it because she was so dependent on my dad. He drove her everywhere. And of course he took very good care of her. So I thought, well, I don't know what is going to happen. And of course, ever since that happened . . . I've been wanting to take her to Minnesota. . . . But she is a very strong person. And like I said, she mourned for a year, let it go, and then went on with her life.

Claudio Jr. viewed his father as the public figure in the peyote trade business, while his mother was in the background. "She was just off somewhere. . . . I guess at that time my mother was more concerned about taking care of feeding the people and doing that sort of thing" (interview, October 24, 2004). Once Claudio Sr. had passed on, her role—one might say her persona—was transformed. Now she was the one who was first on the scene to greet and interact with visitors. Amada maintained the peyote business. She hired some of the men and boys in the community to go out into the brush country and harvest peyote and bring it to her.

One of Amada's friends, Florinda Sheeran, met her during this time. Mrs. Sheeran, her husband, and her children had moved to Los Ojuelos, where her husband worked as a vaquero:

Venimos [a Los Ojuelos] en '64 y ya venían los indios a la casa de Amada, venían. Oí decir que venían *once a year*. Se estacionaban allí [en frente de la casa de Amada]. Y ella, pues, vendía peyote. Siempre veníamos y cuando sabíamos que había indios, pues veníamos tambíen, cuando oímos el *tomtomtomtomtom* [del tambor]. Mis hijos, pues, juntaban el peyote. Como eran jóvenes, *they didn't mind, you know*. Andaban en todo eso, *you know, looking for peyote*, en ese rancho de los Ojuelos. Y se lo vendían aquí a Amadita. Venían a Amadita's, y ella se los compraba. Se venían y fue cuando comenzamos a que conocimos a Amadita. . . . entonces conocimos a Amadita, *maybe '77, '78*, yo conocí a Amadita . . . ya ella estaba aquí sola cuando yo la conocí. [Interview, April 21, 2004]

We came to Los Ojuelos in '64. The Indians were already coming to Amada's house. I heard that they came once a year. They parked there in front of Amada's house and she, well, she sold peyote. We always came when we knew there were Indians, well, we also came when we heard the *tomtomtomtomtom* [of the drum]. My children, well, they gathered peyote. They were young, they didn't mind, you know. They worked in all of this, you know, looking for peyote on this ranch, Los Ojuelos. And they sold it here to Amadita. They came to Amadita's and she would buy it from them. They came and that's when we began to know Amadita. . . . so we met Amadita maybe in '77, '78. I met Amadita and she was already living alone when I met her.

Amada remained true to the spirit in which she and Claudio Sr. had always approached their line of work as peyote distributors. Amada was fair in her dealings, kept her doors open to all, and provided loving hospitality to Native Americans and others who came to her home.

Mrs. Beatrice Weasel Bear, Oglala Sioux from the Pine Ridge Reservation, remembers how she came to meet Amada at this time and then maintained a great friendship with her from that day forward:

> Well, some years back my uncle Joe T. Sierra, he was living.[2] He used to make his travels down there to Texas. He was the very first Indian person that ever traveled down there to get peyote for our people here down in Pine Ridge, South Dakota. . . .
>
> He is the one who introduced me to the medicine. And I went to the meetings with him. I sat with my uncle and he talked to me. I learned a lot of things from him, he's the one who used to transport medicine to the Pine Ridge reservation. He traveled to Texas and . . . he did the harvesting, him and Claudio did a lot of harvesting . . . and Mrs. Cardenas, they done a lot of harvesting together, and they prayed together. And he used to bring back lots of medicine for the Oglalas, and the Rosebud reservation, and Lake Andes, where the Teton Sioux live.
>
> He used to bring the medicine back to them at Christmastime . . . and then he would go back in February for the medicine to be used for Easter and all that. So that's how he made acquaintance with them and called them his brother and sister. He continued on like that and, in 1970, I finally . . . was able to go over there to Texas, and that's when I met Mrs. Cardenas, Amada.
>
> When I first went to her home, it was raining and we got there late and I went to her door and knocked . . . and somebody told me to come in and it was her. She was laying right in the doorway there with a little carpet to lay on . . . nothing to cover her with. But she gave all her rooms to all the relatives and people that came there and got the

medicine, peyote, and it really made me think about my mother. Because my mother was like that, too. And she laid there, and she still wanted to make room for me. But I told her no, we are okay, we are in the car, I just wanted to let you know that we are here, and I introduced myself to her. And then she wanted to offer me something to eat and I said, "No we are going to go out to bed, I'll visit you tomorrow," and I left. I went back to the car and the next day I visited with her and we wrote our names down in the book.

Every year we go, we write our names down in the books . . . and I always followed her around. . . . it's really wonderful, you know, you think . . . she's all by herself, and she always tells me, "Don't do anything, don't do this. Let me go clean up. You don't have to do it, you gotta rest. You haven't rested." I'm like that at home, I'm never sitting still . . . so when I was there I wanted to do something, I wanted to clean up or help, but she won't let me do it. . . . and that's how I came to know Mrs. Cardenas.[3] [Interview, July 16, 2005]

Mrs. Weasel Bear's daughter Loreta Afraid of Bear Cook visited Amada on another journey to South Texas in the 1970s. She describes how Amada took her and her companions out to harvest peyote:

And fortunately I spotted the first medicine so we stopped; they laid prayers down, and we crawled around all day. It took me all day, from eight in the morning until probably around four, when it was so unbearably hot that you couldn't be out there anymore. And she [Amada] was very, very cautious, telling us how to cut. "Don't pull the whole thing up. Do it this way, take your time. Just slice the tops off. Leave the root." So she came out to the fields actually to show us how to do that and how to be about it, to be gentle.[4] [Interview, July 16, 2005]

Amada and the 1969 Peyote Legislation Test Case

Amada never wavered in her firm belief in the Native Americans' right to religious freedom and, now *sola* (alone), she courageously engaged the legal system on behalf of members of the NAC. In 1967 the Texas legislature, following the lead of California and New York, passed the Texas Dangerous Drug Act of 1967, which made possession of peyote illegal in Texas, even for Native Americans. This law sparked intense debate and concern from church members. If possession of peyote was illegal in Texas, how would they be able to come to the gardens, pray, and ritually gather peyote, or buy it from peyote distributors in South Texas to bring back to their homes and churches? How could the peyote dealers even harvest peyote if its possession was a felony?

A number of peyotists representing various chapters of the NAC–NA began to petition the State of Texas for an exemption for the church that would enable them to possess, transport, and use peyote for religious purposes (Stewart 1990:246). Others used a different strategy. They decided that by making a test case that challenged this law, it would have a greater impact on the legal systems in the State of Texas and beyond, and as a consequence educate lawmakers about the NAC and awaken legislators to the rights of Native Americans and their religious use of peyote. Frank Takes Gun, a Crow Indian activist who served many years as the president and vice president of the NAC–NA, took action.

Houston attorney Jerry Patchen, who was friends with Amada and involved in the NAC, knew Frank Takes Gun. He explains what happened,

> Ah yes, . . . in '68, but the test case was in '69. The Texas State Legislature [had] made peyote illegal. And of course, the Native American Church was alarmed and in a state of serious concern, and Takes Gun took the initiative, and there was a big debate about what to do and how to handle it. Well, Takes Gun took the initiative. There wasn't any stopping him, Takes Gun.
>
> So he went down to South Texas, he was the Johnny Appleseed of the Native American Church, but I won't go into his history, but some of the things he did were marvelous.[5] . . . he was a good friend of Amada's . . . and he was President of the Native American Church of North America. And when that occurred, he fought the Woody case over in California, he fought the Mary Attakai case in Arizona, he handled the legislation, he shepherded the legislation in New Mexico and Colorado and Montana that got peyote legalized through the legislature. The man was amazing.

Frank Takes Gun was not a lawyer. No, no, no. That was the amazing thing about him. He was a master strategist. And he had worked with the ACLU on Attakai, and on the Woody case, and he knew how to marshal the resources, so he got the ACLU to support him, a young lawyer at the time, Sam Houston Clinton, who later became a judge on the Court of Criminal Appeals in Texas, to agree to represent the Native American Church, and so he was putting together a test case that would challenge the constitutionality of Texas law.

And so he goes down to South Texas, and he has this young Navajo Indian, David Clark, with him. And they are going to have this test case. And so he goes to all the peyote dealers, he knows all the peyote dealers; he goes to all of them, the dealers, the men, the male dealers. He said they were afraid; they were all afraid, and they wouldn't give him any peyote for his test case. And so he went to Amada and she said, "Sure, yeah," without hesitation. Brave, Amada is brave. . . . Amada provided the peyote and David Clark drove right out of her driveway, and they had alerted the DPS because they wanted him to get arrested, and so, sure enough, right out of her driveway, David Clark driving Frank Takes Gun's Ford . . . he was arrested. And Sam Houston Clinton [the defense attorney] did a remarkable job, and Judge Kazen, who was known as a very strict judge, a tough judge, he [ruled] on behalf of the Indians. And that became a remarkable experience for Judge Kazen; he came back and went to a [peyote] meeting there [on Amada's property].[6] [Interview, April 29, 2004]

Judge E. James Kazen, the presiding judge in the 49th District Court, was familiar with the legal plight of peyote dealers and the religious use of peyote by Native Americans. His niece, Cathy Kazen, Amada's longtime friend, explained that her uncle was well prepared for this case. He was the prosecuting District Attorney in 1954 when Claudio was arrested for shipping dried peyote out of state, for which he recommended to the Grand Jury that the charges be dropped. Cathy Kazen's grandfather, Manuel J. Raymond, was the defense attorney for the Cardenases in the 49th District Court at that time (Cathy Kazen, personal communication,

February 11, 2011). For this charge the Honorable Mr. Kazen, weighing legal and religious rights, ruled that the Texas law was unconstitutional on the grounds that it violated the religious freedom of members of the NAC. In his ruling, Judge Kazen wrote, "In view of the . . . evidence and findings, the Court finds and concludes that Article 726-d of the Penal Code of the State of Texas is unconstitutional as it applies to this defendant [David S. Clark] herein, who possessed and used peyote in good faith in the sincere and honest practice of Peyotism, a bona fide religion; and therefore, the defendant is found not guilty" (*State of Texas v. David S. Clark*, No. 12,879, Official Ruling of the 49th Judicial District Webb County, Texas, [1968]).[7] Judge Kazen dismissed the case against Clark. This was a historic decision that was implemented by the Texas Legislature with the Texas Narcotic Law of 1969, in which the Texas Dangerous Drug Act of 1967 was amended to state that the law does not apply to members of the NAC when the peyote is for use in a bona fide religious ceremony. The exemption in the law, it was determined, applied to any person with at least 25 percent Indian blood (Stewart 1990:246–247; Morgan and Stewart 1984:291).

Barbara Kazen, Judge Kazen's daughter, still vividly remembers the progression of events revolving around the resolution of this issue:

> Yes, they made him an honorary member of the Native American Church. . . . Allen Dale was, I guess, daddy's primary contact, even though Clark had been the defendant, Allen Dale was the person at that time who was the most influential. . . . My understanding is that they picked David Clark because he was young; Mr. Dale was quite elderly at the time, he and his wife. And they were the ones who had the most contact with Mother and Daddy. And . . . Frank Takes Gun . . . and I think they handpicked Clark because he was young and aggressive, I think they thought he could withstand the trauma . . . although Sam Houston Clinton was prepared, the defense lawyer, he was prepared to post bond immediately and I don't think Clark actually spent any time in jail. But I think they wanted to spare the elders from that, and Clark was chosen, was my understanding.
>
> And so then they had the trial, and it was in my daddy's

courtroom because he was the criminal district judge of this county, that's the 49th Judicial District Court, and so they put on the evidence . . . and one of the expert witnesses . . . David Aberlee, Professor of Anthropology . . . he used to be a professor in British Colombia. And he wrote this wonderful letter to Daddy that he admired the way the case was handled and that he was impressed with the dignity of the proceedings and the way the issues were brought out and the way that Daddy had expressed himself in his opinion.

And so it was sometime after his decision, his decision actually was in 1968, and brother Allen Dale wanted to honor Daddy in a very particular way, and they asked him, they advised him first of all, that pursuant to his decision, they were going to be coming to Mirando City to gather the peyote, and I think they wanted the protection of Daddy, of the authorities knowing that they were going to be here to avoid any incident. And then on top of that, they wanted to honor him. And Daddy asked if I wanted to come and of course I did. I was teaching at the University of Texas Law School at the time, and they invited my mom.

. . . It really touched my life. I felt that the sincerity, the spontaneous, instant devotion and their effect was so beautiful, everyone praying in their own language. There were leaders from the tribes from all over the United States. They were all different tribes. They were all praying in their own tongue and so fervently and devotedly. They explained enough of what was going on that we realized that our prayers were going through the fire up through the hole to the Great Spirit, and they would bring in water ceremonially and they were very kind to help us, assist us with all that was going on. And they really made us feel a part of it. . . . in the middle of the ceremony they made him an honorary member of the church and presented him with the robe and the pin that he was wearing last night. And then at the end of the all-night ceremony they presented him with the [fire] stick and they had given him the white eagle feather and they named him "White Feather."

Judge Kazen's daughter then brings Amada into the discussion about her father:

The way that Amada and my daddy have always been linked in the Native American Church is that they have always felt that Amada and her family traditionally have provided a beautiful place for them and their sacrament, but that they would not have been allowed to use the sacrament if it hadn't been for Daddy's opinion. So they have linked them completely together and then members of my family . . . like Kathy Kazen, stay close to Amada over the years. [Barbara Kazen, interview, October 29, 2000]

The amendment to the Texas Narcotic Law also formalized the work of the peyote distributors. The provisions in the amendment included the creation of a bureaucratic structure in which the dealers had to apply to the federal government and to the State of Texas for a license to sell peyote. They also needed to record the details of each transaction. The dealers were authorized to sell peyote only to certain members of the NAC: custodians, roadmen, or other officials who were of at least 25 percent Indian blood and whose names were listed on a membership roster along with the officers of their church chapter that was sent to the Texas State Board of Pharmacy (Stewart 1990:247; Morgan and Stewart 1984:291).[8] Then, in the 1970s, the regulation of the peyote trade was placed under the supervision of the Texas Department of Public Safety (DPS), Criminal Law Enforcement Division, Narcotics Service (Morgan and Stewart 1984:291).

Amada conscientiously complied with these requirements and became one of the first federally licensed peyote distributors in the United States. According to DPS guidelines, when distributors apply for or renew their licenses, they must indicate where they will obtain their peyote and who owns the property where they will be collecting, as well as the names of harvesters. Peyote distributor permits are only issued in South Texas, since that is where the greatest abundance of peyote exists. Distributors must also review a purchaser's travel permit to review the person's full name, percentage of his or her Indian blood, and that it is printed on official stationery of the NAC (DPS Drug Rules 13–14, Sec. 13.50). Amada even went a step further by continuing a tradition of keeping a daily guest book in which all visitors to her house were encouraged to sign their names; they also now provided detailed information to indicate their tribe or church membership, where they lived, the amount of peyote purchased—whether from her or another dealer, and to make comments. Amada's guest book signing ritual was a welcomed tradition through the decades by which visitors could review the entries and see whom they recognized who had also made the long pilgrimage to the peyote gardens and to Amada's house.

Hippies in the Gardens

The arrival of hippies in the peyote gardens of South Texas in the late '60s and through the '70s fueled the ire of the DPS, local residents in the Mirando Valley, and members of the NAC. Hippies were drawn to peyote by the psychedelic drug movement and the writings of individuals such as Aldous Huxley and Carlos Castañeda. Huxley, in his book *The Doors of Perception*, vividly describes his experiences under the influence of mescaline, peyote's most active alkaloid. Carlos Castañeda, in various books, writes about the "magical" world Yaqui shamans accessed with their peyote use. His stories read more like allegoric tales than factual ethnography (Stewart 1986). Geographer George Morgan writes that a representative of the State Board of Pharmacy in Austin told him, "People from the 'drug culture' necessarily trespassed; some lived for days to weeks undetected in the vast Texas brush-lands, gathering peyote for their portable outdoor laboratories ('kitchens') in order to produce 'pure mesc' for the drug-using group" (1976:103).

Mirando City resident Raquel Mendieta describes meeting hippies out in the countryside:

> There were some young people that would come sometimes, and they were the ones that make the trouble. Going into pastures looking for peyote and they were not supposed to be there. But what did they used to call them? Hippies? . . .
> . . . No, they were not Indians. . . . I remember one day my husband had to fix a broken waterline and I and the kids . . . we went with him and he was working on the line and I saw this car go by on the highway and pretty soon they came back and before we knew it, one of the young men was standing right beside us.

I said, "What are you doing here?" He scared me. . . . And he said, "Oh, we are looking for tarantulas." I said, "Well, let me tell you, this is the wrong time of the year and the wrong time of the day to be looking for tarantulas. Now you get out of here right now." He looked at me kind of. "What are you doing here?" I said, "Can't you see my husband's working?" And I said, "And you better hurry up and get out of here." So they did, they left. [Interview, April 17, 2004]

Richard Geissler, a photojournalist for the *Laredo Times* in the 1970s, traveled to Mirando City to cover a few stories about Amada Cardenas, the NAC, and the peyote trade. He recalls seeing hippies in the countryside and remembers how out of place they looked:

Oh, god, yes, which is part of the reason the law, the DPS [Department of Public Safety] [took action, because of] these space cadets. I mean string all over the hair, backpack, walking . . . and you go out there, you know, [and you see] somebody walking down the side of the road, it is not like toolin' down Ventura Boulevard. . . . and everybody would go, "Ah . . . hippies looking for peyote." And so, we were telling them, you know we were '60s children, too, we would go, "Yo dude, everybody knows what you are doing." "What do you mean?" "Well, you came here looking for peyote." "Ah! Do you know where it is?" "Man, you are going to get busted if you get any. They are going to bust you." They would have hand-drawn maps, Laredo, go out this way, or they would have maps with little red lines around it, you know, and six miles after the railroad tracks in Mirando City, or 6.2 miles stop, and then go south, go to the south, you won't find nothing to the north of that road, which is true. And they would hand out these little handmade maps.

And then it became a conflict because there was as many hippies as there were Indians. . . . Yah. And, there was a constant clash. The Indians' song was, "Hey, you don't even know, you are just out here, dirty hippie. You are just trying to get high." The hippies going, "Hey dude, yes, just like you." "Naw, naw, it is different for us." [Interview, April 20, 2004]

While Amada welcomed anyone who came to her house, she would politely talk in a mater-of-fact way to the few hippies who ventured up to her doorstep, informing them that it was illegal for them to use peyote, harvest it, or take it with them. Perhaps it was the reputation of the Texas rangers; maybe it was the heat, the thorny terrain, the rattlesnakes, or the stares from locals they received. Whatever the factors were, most hippies passing through from out of state did not stay long in the peyote gardens, or in Texas, for that matter.[9] However, local residents and law enforcement kept alert whenever young hippy-looking Anglos showed up in peyote country.

George Morgan, Geographer and Peyotist

In the '60s and '70s, in addition to the hippies, an assorted retinue of non–Native Americans found their way to Amada's home. George Morgan, geography professor at Chadron State College in northwestern Nebraska and member of the NAC of the Pine Ridge Reservation in South Dakota, came to know Amada while doing his PhD research. The title of his dissertation was "Man, Plant, and Religion: Peyote Trade on the Mustang Plains of Texas." Morgan carried out his research under the direction of the most prominent scholar of the NAC religion, anthropologist Omer Stewart from the University of Colorado.

Before undertaking this research, Morgan had already been integrated into the NAC traditions; he walked a unique road between cultural worlds. His former student, geography professor Darrel McDonald from Steven F. Austin State University in Nacogdoches, Texas, remembers his mentor:

> I knew Dr. Morgan, as he would say, he would go through the cultural veil, on the weekends . . . he would leave Chadron, Nebraska, and go to the Pine Ridge Reservation [South Dakota], where he would become an important member of that particular peyote group. He was a secretary for the Native American Church for the Pine Ridge folks. . . . he would leave the white world. . . . he understood so well that cultural barrier and that cultural veil that he walked though each weekend that took him from the Western

culture into a culture that very clearly transcended Western culture. And yet every Monday he would be back in his classrooms, prepared, insightful, philosophical, and competent. . . . He was a scholar and a gentleman in his passions among friends and there must have been countless hundreds of people that he visited with to gain insight into that church.[10]

George Morgan's research took him to the peyote gardens, where he meet with peyote dealers, ranchers, and law enforcement agents in order to determine the nature of the peyote trade and to develop strategies to secure the future of the peyote supply and healthy peyote populations. Morgan met Amada in the 1970s and recognized that among all the "Hispano" peyote dealers, there was a special kindness, warmth, and openness that Amada shared with all her visitors. He wrote about Amada and her home in his field notes and dissertation, and he was inspired to draw and paint watercolor scenes of Amada's property.

Darrel McDonald elaborates on the relationship between Morgan and Amada:

> I found them the truest and deepest and dearest of friends. There was a genuine respect on both sides for who they are and what they did and who they helped. Amada was always proud to know that there was a professor that visited her, and he was extremely pleased to know that she was such an important role for people's lives to be enriched through the medicine. So in an individual way, they were just treasures to each other and it was genuine. [Interview, April 27, 2004]

During the years 1973 to 1977, George Morgan journeyed down to South Texas, sometimes with his second wife, Mary Walker, an Oglala Sioux from Pine Ridge, or with his son George Morgan Jr. Amada's house was his home base, and she helped him meet local people in the peyote trade. On some occasions she also acted as translator, as was the case when he interviewed Mr. Rodriguez about the trade in the early 1900s (December 26, 1974). His field notes included his observations of Amada's place and of her work as a peyote dealer. Some entries speak of her worries about too much rain and spoilage of peyote that had been cut and was drying (January 2, 1975), or of the number of peyote buttons she sold and the Native Americans that came to her house as customers and friends.

The entry in his journal for December 27, 1974, states,

> People who come to Mrs. Cardenas's feel at home, many adoptions made [informal kinship bonds established]—exchange of pictures, presents—each car that pulls away with peyote Mrs. Cardenas blesses.
>
> Dec 29, 1974, Crows leave, Navajos leave—pictures—Mrs. Cardenas, "They sure like to take pictures and also to drink pop."
>
> Crows left no money for staying—Navajo left $20.00. It has been a *very* busy week, many people, different tribes, hospitality shown to all—Mrs. Cardenas—sign of the cross "In the name of the Father, Son, and Holy Ghost, carry these people with the sacred medicine home safely."

Morgan even notes that on a few occasions, he helped Amada process peyote, and when Amada did not have enough peyote, she would contact other dealers and send Native Americans to them so that they could fill their entire peyote order.

George Morgan described the coming together of cultures at Amada's place, so poignantly represented by the stone-lined garden beds of peyote around her property, which also contained old grindstones used in both ancient and contemporary Mexican cooking.

He noted in his journal that some were disrespectful of Amada and her home and her garden beds, writing in the entry dated January 6, 1975, "Someone stole peyote from Amada's garden!" At times there was factionalism between some church members from different tribes who came to Amada's. Morgan writes, "Tensions between Comanche and Navajo—Mrs. —— 'We have a church, but now with all of these other tribes, I don't know what you call it!' Said in presence of Navajo. Tension between tribes for limited resource."

The membership of Navajos in the NAC increased exponentially from 12,000 or 14,000 in 1951 to 70,000 in 1975, after the Navajo Tribal

Council no longer prosecuted church members and permitted religious use of peyote in Navajo country (Aberle 1966:124; Morgan 1976:112). A number of Navajos from the Four Corners area were enrolled in the NAC-NA; however, some Navajos (southern Arizona peyotists) had a political falling out with the church and struck out on their own as the Native American Church of Navajoland (Stewart 1990:311–312). The growing number of Navajo peyotists also meant more members were taking to the highways to venture to South Texas to pray in the gardens and buy peyote. From the total peyote sales recorded in 1972–1973, the Navajos of Arizona purchased over a third of the supply (38 percent); in 1973–1974 they purchased over half (53 percent) of the annual sales of peyote (Morgan 1976:112–114). The demand for peyote and its occasional scarcity was felt by everyone. The desire to have a place to stay and carry on a prayer meeting in the gardens also strained relations between different tribes. Amada's guest books showed a dramatic increase in visitors beginning in 1968; most were Navajo (Morgan 1976:112).

George Morgan observed these tensions playing out at Amada's house as he continued to visit her after he completed his dissertation. He writes in his field notes for June 19, 1977,

> It seems that since the major user of the Peyote plant today is the Navajo, that they want to control the space in which it grows—the only space which they feel a control with confidence is the small acreage of Amada Cardenas at the south edge of Mirando City—the Navajo consider this small space Navajo country. . . . Indians from other tribes view the frequency of so many Navajo into Texas as a kind of territorial intrusion. . . . [there are] whispers and uneasy thoughts that since the Navajo have come to Texas in large numbers, there has been an unfavorable balance between supply and demand.

During this time, Amada, like the other peyote dealers around her, experienced a shift in the peyote business that took customers farther south to the Lower Rio Grande Valley around Rio Grande City and Roma. Claudio Jr. remembers, "There used to be medicine around here, too, but everything got harvested, and everything started to move south. But when we started we would go maybe twenty-five miles and find medicine. And then we started to find less and less and had to look further away" (interview, October 28, 2000). The amendment in the Texas narcotics laws that now regulated the sale and transport of peyote within the state of Texas, coupled with greater Native American demand for peyote, enticed more local Tejanos to become dealers. These newcomers saw the peyote trade as a business and a means for profit.

Morgan found that in the Mirando Valley, many ranchers, incensed by trespassing hippies, no longer allowed peyote dealers or Native Americans to harvest peyote on their properties. Fences went up around ranches, gates cut off access to the peyote gardens with multiple chain locks that festooned the ranch gates. Later, incentive monies from Texas state programs in agriculture encouraged ranchers to use heavy equipment to root plow to eliminate the brush (and peyote), and to plant buffelgrass (*Pennisetum ciliare*) as forage for their cattle (see Longoria 1997:33–39, 57–64). Native vegetation, including peyote, was seriously endangered by such radical actions to "tame" this harsh environment into land in which the cattle industry could prosper. Local Tejanos felt the impact of the privatization of the ranchlands, with the development of the petroleum and natural gas industries; vast acres had changed owners, a number of whom were Anglos. When Texas attained statehood, the federal government recognized title to these lands that had formerly been awarded by the Spanish and then the Mexican governments. The Tejanos did not primarily see the land as an economic asset; rather, more importantly, these ranches were part of the history and cultural heritage of generations of Tejano families. The peyote dealers in the Mirando Valley had to form new relationships with the ranch owners to gain access to the peyote on their lands. Not all ranchers were keen on such an arrangement and many did not allow the peyote dealers and their workers onto their land. Others charged the dealers for access to their land, and formal lease agreements were contracted. The ranchlands that had not been destroyed by root plows were havens for all remaining native wildlife. Some ranchers also leased their land to hunters during the hunting seasons, further limiting the year-round accessibility for the peyoteros to harvest peyote.

Peyote dealers to the south had access to ranches. Unlike the area to the north in the Mirando Valley, smaller tracts of ranchlands remained in the hands of Tejanos. Often dealers were related to the ranch owners, or they had family members who worked for ranchers and were able to obtain permission to harvest peyote. Morgan also feared that the increasing demand for peyote, and the commercial interests driving some peyote dealers, would ultimately lead to overharvesting, and that the methods used by some to collect peyote impacted its ability to survive and resprout and were thus not sustainable. He most likely would have wanted to see a solution for the looming peril he foresaw through conservation, appropriate harvesting methods, and propagation strategies. His life's destiny did not allow him to further his work on peyote. In 1985, when he was teaching an evening class, he felt ill, left the classroom, and "died of an apparent heart attack shortly after he was stricken" (Chadron State College Office of Information, November 8, 1985). George Morgan was fifty-three years old.

George Morgan's death devastated Amada. Darrel McDonald, Morgan's former student, describes taking her to the funeral:

> On the advice from some folks in Nebraska, that I could be a conduit for Amada to get to the funeral . . . I drove to Mirando City that night. Slept overnight in my car. The next morning, about six thirty, Amada and I got into my S10 Chevrolet pickup and drove to northwest Nebraska nonstop. . . . we had long conversations on the trip up; it was about twenty-two hours each way. . . . when we got into the Panhandle we ran into a winter storm, and we drove on packed snow and ice for the rest of the journey. . . . A good period of time she spent with a shawl over her head praying for us as we drove down the road. . . . We got in town, in Chadron, Nebraska, attended the funeral . . . and [afterward] made it safely to her doorstep. . . . she blessed me [with her holy water], and I drove on. [Interview, April 27, 2004][11]

Leaving the Peyote Business

By the late 1970s, Amada decided she no longer wanted to work in the peyote business, and she let her permit expire in 1980 (Jody Patterson, Texas DPS, personal communication, 2011). Claudio Jr. remarks that when his parents worked the trade full-time for many years, there were probably only two or three peyote dealers, including Claudio Sr. and Amada. In the late '60s through the '70s, however, Amada faced significant competition. Claudio Jr. relates,

> What happened was a lot of people here got really greedy and the peyoteros didn't include her; they had control at the ranches and they finally figured out there was money to be made. So it started dwindling and dwindling and my mother, of course, she was licensed from the Department of Agriculture [and later on DPS] every year to sell. And after a while she decided that it wasn't worth it because there were too many people getting into it and acting ugly. My mom didn't have that kind of mind, she just wanted people to have the medicine and that is the way she went about it.

Amada explained why she no longer worked in the peyote trade:

> Es mucho trabajo para una sola. Ahora tienes que tener un lease. ¿Dónde voy a buscar un lease yo? ¿Con quién? No, no. Y ¿quién va a traer [peyote] acá y luego trabajar por aquí? Es una cosa en que tienes que tener mucho cuidado con el [peyote]. Lo trabajas [preparas para secar], tienes que ponerlo en la mesa, y voltearlo, y tener mucho para cubrirlo con lono o algo. Y [si] viene una tormenta en la noche, ¿cómo voy a salir si no puedo andar bien? No, no. Vale solo con mi esposo. No quería seguir trabajando [como peyotera]. [Interview, November 27, 1993]

> It's a lot of work for a single person. Now you have to have a lease. Where am I going to find a lease [on a piece of land]? With whom? No, no. And who is going to bring the peyote here and then work here? It [peyote] is something that you have to take a lot of care with. You work it [prepare it to dry], you have to put it on the table and turn it, and you have to have a lot of canvas or something to cover it. And if a storm comes in the night, how am I going to go out if I can't walk very well? No, no. It's only worth it with my husband. I didn't want to keep on [as a peyotera].

Without income from peyote sales and with limited resources, Claudio Jr. further elaborates that Amada subsisted on her "social security benefits, and I helped her out. And my dad left her without any debts and the house and property was all free and clear. She didn't have a lot of problems." The Indians "still kept coming and then, of course, they helped her out, too. To this day they have always helped her out. It's been a good marriage, you know" (interview, October 24, 2004).

A number of Native Americans who knew her through the years, as well as newcomers to her home, appreciated Amada and all the help she selflessly provided. Those who could would send or give her personal donations. Never asking for a penny, Amada was grateful for the financial contributions from Native Americans and non-Indians who considered her to be a friend or an adopted relative.

Having retired from the peyote trade, she continued to open her home to all who came through; she also helped Native Americans acquire peyote. Loreta Afraid of Bear Cook, Oglala Lakota from Pine Ridge who was good friends with George Morgan and who also traveled down to Amada's place in the '70s, recalls, "She would tell us to let them [the peyote dealers] know that we were over at her place, at Amada's. And she said, 'They'll treat you good.' Sure enough, they did. They didn't overcharge us, they were open."

Loreta also remembers that many people came to Amada's place, and that along with the wonderful openness and generosity Amada shared with everyone, there could be friction among some of the visitors. "So it was through her efforts we met people that were nice people, and we met some people on her place that were not so nice, too. They were being mean to each other. But somehow she even managed to go over there and get them together. The powers of harmony, I think, were her best thing" (interview, July 16, 2005).

Maker of Peyote Chiefs

One tradition that Amada continued from her days in the peyote trade was the art of making peyote chiefs for special people who requested them and to whom she wished to gift a powerful talisman or a central ritual object for the altar at NAC prayer meetings. The peyote chief is a large button, selected for its size, form, and numerous segments. There is a special art to making a chief. Amada spent days, often weeks, forming each peyote so that it would dry correctly, with its magnificent fuzzy areoles like a crown of white hair in the center. During peyote meetings, it is placed in the center atop the crescent moon altar made of sand; sometimes it rests on a piece of fabric or a miniature weaving. The chief embodies the power of Father Peyote, the power of the sun, and is considered to be the messenger between humans and God or the Creator. The chief is said to guide communication among members in the ceremony through songs, drumming, ritual actions, prayers, and expressions of their thoughts and emotions to the Divine. When not in ritual, peyote chiefs are reverently placed in beaded and fringed buckskin cases that are safely guarded in the roadman's cedar box or hung around his neck. Peyote chiefs are said to protect the person in possession of them and also to have healing powers (La Barre 1989:25 n. 11, 72–73; d'Azevedo 2006:6; personal communication and observation).[12]

Since not just anyone can make chiefs, many roadmen sought out Amada to make chiefs for them because she truly understood the peyote. She was born in the gardens, she knew this sacred plant intimately, and she was also well versed in the peyote religion and participated in the NAC ways. She prayed for its future owner over each chief while she formed it to perfection. She prayed that blessings be bestowed upon the recipient and his family: good health, safety, and a good life.

Amada shared some thoughts about her special talent for making chiefs:

> Yo lo aprendí de los indios. Mi papá [y] Claudio me enseñaron. [Empecé a hacerlos] yo sola. . . . como Claudio fue en '67, yo comenzaba sola.
>
> [Sobre] todo [chief] debo de hacer una oración. . . . mis oraciones que tengo de la antigüedad, sí. Me manda a rezar para [tal persona] que está enferma . . . algo especial, una oración especial y hago un smoke [del tobacco cuando rezo y soplo el humo encima del chief].
>
> [Si no piden una oración especial] no más yo rezo mis oraciones . . . para mi salud y para ellos también [los que pidieron el

> chief], para todo el mundo, para todos los vivos, para mi hijo y su familia, todos los que vienen en el camino por acá, que Dios les dé su mano, les cuide en el camino . . . para su familia, todas mis amistades, para todo el mundo. [Interview, February 2, 1997]
>
> I learned it from the Indians. My father [and] Claudio taught me. [I began to make them] by myself. . . . since Claudio passed away in '67, I began to make them alone.
>   [Over] every [chief] I need to pray. . . . my prayers are ancient, yes. Someone asks that I pray for [a certain person] who is sick . . . something special, a special prayer, and I take a smoke [of tobacco when I pray and blow the smoke over the chief.]
>   [If one does not ask for a special prayer] I just recite my prayers . . . for my health and for them [who requested the chief], for all the world, for everyone who is alive, for my son and his family, everyone that is traveling on the way to get here, that God may lend them a hand, that he watch over them on the road . . . for their families, all of my friends, for all the world.

At age nineteen, Claudio Jr. joined the Air Force. Amada, concerned about her son's safety, made a peyote chief for her son to keep with him. His tour of duty extended into the Vietnam War, during which time he was stationed primarily in Laos and Cambodia. True to the intentions it embodied, it must have protected Claudio so he might live to tell the story of the chief and what became of it. He describes those times:

> I was attached to the 101st Airborne. We did ground-to-air communications . . . well, we would also do recon, when we did that air-to-ground because we used to call in air strikes. . . . I just worked on the ground.
>   Yeah, she sewed it [the chief] in a piece of silk. . . . I carried that for a long time . . . with my dog tags, and one time we were out on a mission and we got into a firefight and we got ambushed, and it got kind of nasty. Just to make a long story short, someone had to play dead because the Viet Cong were coming around with their bayonets and stuff, and they were coming around and they were taking your

watch, and they took dog tags, and they ripped that [the peyote chief] off. . . . Yeah, and I never saw it again. So somebody might have it over there. And I don't talk too much about that stuff.

. . . She sent it to me . . . to an APO. . . . I never told my mother where I was at or what I was doing, I didn't want to worry her. All she knows is that I was in the Air Force and that is about that. [Interview, October 24, 2004]¹³

The great majority of the chiefs she made were for Native American roadmen; however, she also made a chief for a few other individuals important in her life. She made one especially for George Morgan. Beatrice Weasel Bear describes the miraculous reappearance of this chief after a fire:

And she once gave our chief peyote to Dr. George Morgan Sr. She made it for him. It was a beautiful chief peyote. And she gave it to him, and after he passed away, his wife gave it to one of our ministers of the Native American Church, and that medicine was used in many prayer meetings. But at one time that minister's home burned down, and everything burned up, even his instruments, and he was feeling bad because even that chief peyote was in there. But later on, a couple of years or more, one of them found that chief peyote intact, nothing wrong with it, no burnings, nothing. So that was the blessing of Mrs. Cardenas, my sister. She's really a wonderful lady. [Interview, July 16, 2005]

Amada as Healer

Amada's spirituality grew even stronger in the eyes of her friends, adopted kin, and visitors once the peyote trade no longer occupied so much of her focus. One day Amada modestly shared this with me:

A veces estoy haciendo oraciones especiales—para un muchacho joven que su madre se pena mucho porque no le puede reducir. Yo creo que se junta con alguien que usa droga. Y ella batallando mucho con él y me mandó que le hiciera una oración especial, y me dijo que ya se está mejorando, que va a comenzar a ir a la escuela. Yo les hago oraciones.

Ya ves que vino un señor que tenía un stroke, pero él no tenía nada malo, no más sentía mal, él. Me dijo, ¿Se le podría curar? Pues le tuve curando y sentía muy contento y muy aliviado—la fe. Yo hago como voluntario, la fe, porque primero la fe. No hay que perder la fe. Como le digo, "Don't lose your faith." Hombre, se fue contentísimo. [Interview, November 27, 1993]

Sometimes I am making special prayers—for a young man whose mother is suffering because she cannot control him. I think he got together with someone who uses drugs. She was struggling a lot with him and she asked me to say a special prayer for him, and she told me that he is getting better, that he is going to start to go to school. I say prayers for them.

You see, a man came that had a stroke, but it was not serious, he just felt bad. He asked me, could I heal him? Well, I was curing him and he felt very content and soothed—faith. I do it voluntarily, the faith, because faith comes first. One should not lose faith. As I say, "Don't lose your faith." Well, he left very contented.

Various people witnessed the amazing healing powers they believed Amada could access through the peyote. Loreta Afraid of Bear Cook describes one such event:

In the early '70s, late '60s, we made a trip down there . . . and at that time I was married . . . to a Shoshone man, and he was really ill, he was really quite young but he already had a prostate illness and it eventually killed him. But he had a festered boil, it looked like a boil to me, about the size of a fist, and he was crying and in so much pain and when we had gotten down there, we had traveled maybe two days down, and by the time we got there he was very ill. And she came out and she blessed him, and even though he didn't want to show her where the boil was, she reached in the back of his leg and touched it, and knew where it was. She blessed him and prayed for him. . . . And she gave him a peyote, she told him, eat this and you will get well from it, you'll get home and you'll be okay. And so we wanted to believe that.

And so early the next morning, as the sun was coming up, she took that medicine and she showed it to the sun, and let the sun's rays hit it, and we had to lift him out of the bed, so the men had him and she was saying in her language prayers with this peyote and she gave it to him. And she told him to start eating it now. So he forgot his pains for those moments and for me it was like she had performed a miracle because that thing that came out of his wound, it exploded, it's just like it perforated the skin, just right as she is saying these prayers, and this awful-smelling stuff came out, and it was just running down his leg so we had to quick do a bath. We couldn't take him to a local hospital because we were native peoples and naturally we did not have insurance. So there was no way.

So she told us to believe in that medicine and to believe in that prayer, the power of prayer. And we did. And we got him home like that. He survived it, but spent twenty-seven months in the hospital with that illness. And then was told not to do other things, which he did engage in, and it killed him. But for that moment, she caused him to live, she caused him to, he had so much pain he wanted to die, that's the way he felt.

I've seen that miracle that she worked with that medicine, it was just like we trusted her because it was Indian things, like as far as we know, native things, indigenous ways, and was a practice of our ways. [Interview, July 16, 2005][14]

From livelihood as a peyote dealer to the lifework of a healer with deep religious faith, Amada was heralded in her elder years as a spiritual icon, and her reputation grew legendary throughout Indian Country and beyond.

Hasta los sacerdotes, los franciscanos, la aprecian, ellos la quieren mucho, la buscan para estar en su compañía. . . . ella tenía tanto amor para los demás . . . y nos educaba con su ejemplo.

Even the priests, the Franciscans, appreciate her, they love her a lot, they seek her out to be in her company. . . . she had so much love for everyone . . . and she educated us by her example.

—Catalina Inocencio, Amada's friend, interview, April 21, 2004

So there were things he had told me about Amada. "You should come down and spend time with her. And Grandma, she'll tell you amazing stories." And he said, "She really believes." And I said, "I don't doubt it." . . . And she saw me and she said, "You're Rutherford's daughter." And she kissed me on the cheek, just like I was her own. And that healed me, and I said, "Nobody does that to me anymore, I don't have that many older people in my life."

—Margaret Behan, Cheyenne Arapaho, interview, February 27, 1997

Amada opened the door. She was so glad to see us, she invited us in. . . . that wonderful, openhearted greeting that we received on her doorstep was amazing. I'll never forget that magic moment. And she was, I mean, we were just in awe that we were received so openly. . . . And she insisted that we come in. She did not know us, did not know a thing about us, but she was so delighted that we were there. And her greeting, and that's the keyword is greeting, the way she greeted us. That's just one of the most marvelous experiences in my life to this day, just a peak experience.

—Jerry Patchen, Amada's friend and lawyer, interview, April 29, 2004

Chapter 6

Amada's Home

A Worldly Place

Community Member and Friend of the *Peyoteros*

In the community of Mirando City and throughout the surrounding countryside, Amada was known as an unwavering, upstanding, law-abiding citizen and a kind and caring member of the community. She faithfully attended church and participated in community activities. Her comadre Guadalupe Lira remembers, "She would come to church. . . . We would go to the priest, and confess our sins, and they would give use our holy wafers . . . but she would be a very religious person. She would come to church, Amadita. And everybody around here knows her. . . . we used to sing and Amadita used to come to church" (interview, April 21, 2004).

Amada's friend Maria Esquivel also reminisces about Amada's involvement as a member of the community: "Well, she never failed to go to church on Sunday. And you know everything there is for the church, she would go, bingos, *comidas* (luncheons), fiestas. Maybe some do not think that is being a real Catholic . . . but she is a very moral, religious person" (interview, April 21, 2004).

Amada also remained active in the peyote trade, befriending all the dealers in the region. Her primary concern was whether the American

Indians who came to visit her from their faraway homes would be able to acquire peyote. Dealers also benefited from her phone inquiries to them and by her sending Indians to their homes to purchase medicine. Mauro Morales became one of the new peyote dealers in the business at the end of the 1980s. He had worked harvesting peyote for one of the prominent dealers in Rio Grande City, Roque Reyna. That was over twenty years previously, followed by an equal number of years working as a seasonal dock worker in Delaware and Indiana, advancing from the position of laborer to foreman. But his family and roots were in South Texas, and he decided to work in the peyote trade. Mr. Morales says, "I had heard about her before, years before, from guys that work around here, the peyote pickers, or you know, people, see I got some relatives in Hebbronville. . . . they said that there were meetings over there in Mirando. That's what we heard, but . . . I never went until I became a dealer. But, we heard of her a long time ago." Amada helped Morales in his new endeavor by referring Indians to him.

> I appreciated her because she did that and I respect her in a lot of ways. I don't know how to explain it, but in Spanish . . . Porque ella era una señora que platicaba muy bien de la gente, de los indios, de uno, y ella decía "Ayúdalos" o "Ay, te voy a mandar unos amigos" (Because she was a lady who spoke well of people, of the Indians, of anyone, and she would say, "Help them," or "I am sending some friends down to you"), like friends.
>
> I said, "Sure, just tell them to call me when they get in town." And they would, and I went and picked them up and brought them over and from there on, they became, how do you call it . . . amigos y ya despúes ellos traían alguien más (friends, and later they would bring another person along). It grew up a little bit more. The only thing that I can tell you about her is that she is a very nice lady.

When he first met Amada, he recalls,

> Well, one thing, she reminded me lots of my mother. . . . She was a little short lady, and she was very nice. She would make you feel at home. That's her thing; you can always feel at home. . . . At first, I used to visit her like every month, because she would call once or

twice a week saying she was going to send some natives. I had to return the call, so I went and visited her often. [Interview, April 16, 2004]

Amada always appreciated that Mr. Morales came to see her; most times he would bring her a gift such as a bag of grapefruits or melons from the lower Rio Grande Valley. On one memorable occasion, he brought her a large pot filled with a cluster of beautiful mature peyote that had grown from the same deep root; every peyote button contained a multitude of sections to it, bestowing the status of chief peyote for each. Amada was delighted and prominently displayed the peyote on the front porch near the entrance to her home.

Other dealers also came to visit her. Salvador Johnson helped her with some improvements to her property. Miguel Rodriguez, also from Rio Grande City, brought her flowers, cards, and sweets on special occasions such as her birthday, Valentine's Day, or Mother's Day. They, and other dealers from the Rio Grande City area, including Roma and the Mirando City region, would come to see her when the February meetings took place at her home. Amada religiously kept a piece of paper with all the dealers' names and telephone numbers taped on the wall of her living room next to the telephone, ready when she needed to call them on behalf of Indian friends.

Visits to Indian Country

Amada did not always stay at her home in South Texas; she was also quite a traveler to Indian Country, depending upon the time of year and the occasion. Her altruistic nature resonated deeply with many Native Americans who had come to know her; she had ties with some families for generations, since the time when she and Claudio were a young married couple. The legacy of Amada and Claudio's generosity, their hospitality, and their commitment to caring for the peyote and participating in NAC meetings were never forgotten. Starting years before, Indian families wanting to express their appreciation and reciprocate their good deeds invited the Cardenas family to their homes. This tradition continued after

Claudio Sr.'s passing. Their son, Claudio Jr., remembers,

> We went up there and visited the Dales, Allen P. Dale and his wife, in Oklahoma. . . . Sure, we used to go to Window Rock, Arizona, and Shiprock, New Mexico, and after I left she would make those same trips. And also she would go to South Dakota to the reservations. . . . Yeah, Pine Ridge. She made several trips, Oklahoma—Ponca City, Oklahoma, and those areas there. She traveled quite a bit. . . . the people, they would come and get her and then they would drive her and she would spend several days, or a week or whatever, and they would bring her back. The only time she went not by herself—her sister was with her—was when she came to visit us [in Minnesota]. They would get on the bus—you know, two little old ladies. [Interview, October 24, 2004]

Mrs. Weasel Bear remembers when Amada came up to the Pine Ridge reservation for a visit as an honored guest for a Mother's Day meeting:

> Mrs. Cardenas, my sister, she's really a wonderful lady. She came over here to South Dakota after Dr. George Morgan passed on. And my daughter and her husband, my son-in-law, Tom and Loreta Cook, we sponsored a Mother's Day meeting for her. And Jerry [Patchen] brought her over and we had a tepee meeting and we had Mother's Day cakes for her and I, and we celebrated Mother's Day. We really had a nice prayer service for us. And from that time on, she became my sister. [Interview, July 16, 2005]

Amada's Meeting during the February Weekend

Back at her home in Mirando City, the largest annual event continued to be the February meeting, which had become a tradition in memory of her husband, Claudio Sr. According to Claudio Jr., sometime after the Saturday prayer meeting for his father was in place, a second meeting was established on Friday of that same weekend to honor his mother (interview, October 24, 2004).

Jerry Patchen explains,

> My understanding of how that meeting came to be . . . Amada wanted to have a meeting. So they started a [second] . . . night meeting. . . . Nick Micoby, the last year that he was down there, he was in poor health and he said he wasn't coming back. And so he took a smoke with Rutherford Loneman and with a Ute Indian . . . and he . . . passed that Saturday night meeting to Rutherford . . . and that the Ute was to take the Friday night meeting. And Rutherford went back up to Oklahoma and because Rutherford was not the kind of guy that would do anything without permission, Rutherford met with the Cheyenne Arapaho chapter with the Oklahoma state organization and said, "Look, this is what Nick Micoby is asking me to do—take care of that Saturday night meeting." And they told Rutherford, "Okay, we will help you the first year. We are having trouble up here, we've lost a lot of elders. . . . we will give you your food and your wood for the first meeting. After that you are on your own." And Tennison Goodblanket came down with Rutherford and hit drum [played the sacred water drum] for Rutherford. [Interview, April 29, 2004]

Alden Naranjo, the Ute roadman who has run the Friday-night meeting many times, relates how Amada's prayer meeting takes place:

> Well, I came down here to make a prayer for her. I come down here to conduct the services for her on Friday night. I come down here to make sure people are respecting her . . . provide the supper. I don't want her to have any expenses to provide the food; we provide the medicine; we provide whatever we can. We set up camp here. We do it here in our tent but by cooking our food because we don't want her to be . . . we don't want to bother her in her home. Even though she has said, "Yes you can use that, you can do that," we feel that if we do it over here, we don't use her, we don't use a lot of her facilities. That's what we want to get away from, them doing that, to defray the expenses she might have, and we told her, "Don't worry about anything, we'll take care of all this stuff, we'll be the ones to take care of it. Just be here." We run that meeting Friday night,

make a prayer for her, and we bring her in the morning and fan her off [with cedar smoke] and make a collection also to help her with people, maybe, who have been using her home, whatever to help her defray that expense that she has. But, all year long we make a prayer for her. Every time we go to a Native American Church ceremony, we make a prayer for her that she might be in good health and be here when we come here.[1] [Interview, February 22, 2004]

The Friday and Saturday meetings came to be known as "the February weekend," and over the decades various well-known roadmen have run the meetings for the Cardenas couple on their property. Jerry Patchen recalls some of them: "Virgil Franklin led it one year; Danny Sandoval led it way back there. There was another Navajo with the name of Tommy Nez that came down and led it. Rutherford's teacher, Gregory Blackburn, led it—Northern Arapaho, but he lived in the South. His family was from up north, the Wind River Reservation" (interview, April 29, 2004).

Rutherford Loneman and the Patchens

Everyone was a treasured individual to Amada. Nonetheless, Rutherford Loneman had an especially warm relationship with her. For years he came down to the Cardenases' house and stayed for a month or so helping harvest and dry peyote. Mr. Loneman would come down in February for the meeting, and eventually he was charged with running the Saturday night meeting. It was during the February meeting at Amada's place in 1973 that an Anglo lawyer from Houston, Jerry Patchen, and his wife, Linda, met Mr. Loneman, after coming to Amada's house for that event by her invitation. The friendships that developed were enduring and deeply meaningful.

The Patchens first learned about Amada by watching a travelogue television program that aired in Houston. Mr. Patchen describes the events:

My first encounter with Amada, which is one of the happiest moments of my life, and one of the most unforgettable moments of my life . . . it was in 1972. Linda and I were watching TV here in Houston and the "Eyes of Texas" came on TV by Ray Miller. . . .

he did these little snippets for Channel 11, as I recall. And he had gone down to Mirando City, Texas, in February and recorded with TV cameras a Native American Church gathering. And we are watching TV and we see, I can still visualize that sign—Mirando City—and he is narrating, and with his cameras goes into Amada's place, starts talking about the Indians using peyote.

Linda and I both had a tremendous interest in peyote. And we wrote down the name Cardenas, and we rode down to Mirando City. And we were determined that we wanted to make contact with the Native American Church. And so some months thereafter we traveled down to South Texas, we went to Mirando City, and we started asking around, "Where does Cardenas live?" We were directed to this house in Mirando City. . . .

So we went down, drove down the road, pulled in the driveway and we could recognize it because I had this visual image from Ray Miller's TV special. . . . So we pulled up at Amada's house, we knew we were at the right place. We rather timidly walked up on her porch, knocked on the door, not knowing what to expect. Amada came to the door and it was "heellllooo"; it was the most wonderful, remarkable greeting that I have ever experienced in my life before or since.

And so we went in and we talked to Amada, and told her about our interests and asked her questions and looked in her home . . . at the pictures, the relics, the peyote license. She took us out to her drying boards—back then you didn't even need a fence around, they hadn't yet passed that regulation. And it was just a phenomenal experience for both Linda and I.

And so it was a wonderful, magical moment in our lives. And there are just so many people, hundreds of people, literally thousands of people that have had that same greeting from Amada. And we drove away in just this giddy, happy, blissful state for having met such an openhearted, sweet, nice person. That prayer, you know, she said that prayer for us and made . . . the sign of the cross. And that moment, that greeting, that encounter launched, fused, created, one of the most enduring, one of the most important, one of the most beautiful relationships in my life, and Linda's life, to this day. And so that's how we met Amada Cardenas.

> Amada was just so genuinely thankful and appreciated the fact that we were interested in her, that we were interested in Indian people, that we were interested in peyote. And she said, "You must come back in February when the Indians are here." And we said, "Oh gosh, we were shy about doing that." Oh, she insisted and said, "You can be my guests." We said, "Well, we don't know these people, and we are not sure that they would want us here." And she said, "You can be my guests." [Interview, April 29, 2004]

Mr. Patchen describes what transpired upon their return to Amada's place in February:

> Well, we came back in February, at her invitation. We were very excited about that, and I can remember driving up to her home and parking outside on the perimeter of the property. And this one Indian took note that we were getting out of the car. We were again timidly going to walk up to her house. This one Indian, a big smile on his face, took note of us and started walking towards us. And we got another good greeting. It was Rutherford Loneman. "Hi, how are you? What you doin' here? What brings you here? Let me show you in the tepee. Let me introduce you to some people."
>
> And we got to meet some of the Indians, we got to watch them go in the tepee, and I swear this was the coldest night that ever occurred in South Texas. We sat on the north side of the tepee, on an old railroad tie. . . . And Rutherford, I remember he told me that after that first year at Amada's, that first meeting that . . . he could feel us out there through the whole meeting . . . He was impressed that we were interested enough to stay up all night sitting out in the cold with no fire, no peyote, just our tremendous curiosity about the goings-on of the Native American Church. He told me, "I want you to come back next year, and I want you to come in." So we did. We came back the next year, and I went in. And he told me, Rutherford told me, he said, "You just sit there and you just watch." He said, "When they put that chief peyote down, you will be sitting down and you don't get up until they take that chief peyote off that hearth. You sit there with that chief peyote." And that was the way the Indians were trained in his era. . . .

But Rutherford went out west and he invited us. He said, "I want to show you something." I guess he had not experienced that until he went out west. But there was a wonderful group of Indian people out there, Taos Pueblo Indians, and there were Cheyenne Indians from Oklahoma also. But it was the American Church of God group that had become involved with the Native American Church up there, and here were these non-Indians that could sing these beautiful songs, that could hit drum, that could take care of fire. And he took me out there to see that. And you know, until that time I always felt that it would be disrespectful for me as a non-Indian to participate, to sing, to participate directly except as an observer. [Interview, April 29, 2004]

So began the Patchens' journey, as they became more involved with the NAC. Amada had helped initiate their involvement, and she remained a steadfast influence and friend to the Patchen family. Rutherford Loneman brought other people to Amada's. Margaret Behan, Arapaho/Cheyenne, describes how she met Amada and the experiences she had at her place:

It was in 1982. And my uncle, Rutherford Loneman, came out to New Mexico where I lived, in Taos. And he had asked me to come and participate in the Native American Church because he was running a meeting. He is a roadman, so he had asked me to bring the water in for him in the morning. And our custom is that when our own parents die, our aunts and uncles become our parents. Well, they already are, extended. So he said, "Now I am your dad and you are my daughter, so you bring in the water for me."

So I came down with my two children, the youngest was maybe four and [the other] six. . . . I carried water in. He was so proud, you know, that I was willing to do that. He said, "You know you need to learn, to participate in this ceremony that I am conducting." And so he introduced Amada, and he told me she was his mother, that she adopted him. So she would be my grandma. So he came in and told her I was his daughter, and that adoption took place right there as he introduced me.

And so immediately she accepted me because she really liked

Rutherford. You know I could just see it in her eyes when he walked into the room, her eyes would just sparkle at him.

And so she thought it was really sweet, she said that "the daughter could come and help her father in the ceremony."

... Yeah, this was my first time down here. ... [when bringing in the water and praying] the main thing that kept coming to me was the peyote. I ate peyote all night, so I was peyote-affected. So I started talking about the fire, and the fireplace, that it is the process of life and it led up to the peyote. And we came over here for the peyote. And the prayer just came out and it linked. You know, it related to the whole altar there. And then to my dad. . . . I prayed, and then I prayed for the people, and he said, "I never thought I would hear this. That my own kid would tell me about this fireplace. She really listened to the fireplace; it's the process of life. 'Til you get up to the chief peyote on the altar."

They brought Amada in that morning. And she just stood there and they fanned her off. And she was just happy to see all in there, the condition we were in. And then she waved good-bye and they took her back out. . . . When we came up to the house, Amada was waiting for us with bread and coffee. She knew Rutherford liked coffee. So she was waiting for him. And she would wait on him with coffee and bread. And he was just thrilled. Like it really meant to be a real family. For just that one day he had a real family, a mother and a daughter, right there. . . . And then he would always, just like that was like his own mother, he would always call her. He would always send money, he'd put it in an envelope and send it to her. And he was poor, he didn't have that much money to offer. Anything like that he would receive, he would want to give something to Amada in appreciation. [Interview, February 23, 1997]

Renewal of the NAC–US Texas Chapter

Legal access to peyote for Native Americans continued to be foremost on the minds of many, including Amada. It had been decades since Claudio Cardenas Sr.'s arrest for selling peyote to NAC members resulted in passage of an amendment to the Texas Narcotic Drug Act in 1954 by the Texas Legislature. Then there was the arrest of David Clark for purchasing peyote from Amada Cardenas, for which an amendment to the Texas Dangerous Drug Act of 1967 was enacted. Yet possession and transportation of peyote by NAC members were challenging. Further complicating access to peyote was the threat to the protection guaranteed by the First Amendment right to the freedom of religion, including the use of peyote within the context of NAC ceremonies. This played out in various state-level cases in the 1960s through the 1980s and into 1990 in California (*People v. Woody*, 1964), Arizona (*State of Arizona v. Mary Attakai*, 1960, and *State of Arizona v. Whittingham*, 1973), and Oklahoma (*Whitehorn v. State*, 1977). The rulings in all these cases highlighted and reaffirmed protection of First Amendment rights for these NAC members (Botsford and Echo-Hawk 1996:129–133; Maroukis 2010:194–195). This was not true in Oregon in the case *State of Oregon v. Soto*, 1977, for which the Court refused to consider evidence that peyote was a sacrament and religiously integral to NAC ceremony (Botsford and Echo-Hawk 1996:133–134), and *Employment Division of Oregon v. Smith*, 1990, a landmark case that went before the United States Supreme Court and essentially "stripped the Native American Church of Constitutional protection altogether" (Botsford and Echo-Hawk 1996:135). Closer to home and the original mother church of the NAC, which was founded in Oklahoma, attorney Jerry Patchen explains the unease felt by Indians in Oklahoma. Represented by the NAC national officer, Frank Takes Gun, they "were concerned . . . that peyote was coming from Texas but they didn't have a presence in Texas. So they come down, Frank Takes Gun and Oklahoma Indians, and I have those old charters, they went to Austin, and Amada went with them, and she visited with her old friend Helen Holloway with the DPS. . . . she went to Austin and they filed that charter for the Native American Church of the United States" (interview, April 29, 2004).[2]

Over time, internal politics within the church had resulted in Frank Takes Gun stepping down from his position as president of the NAC–NA. Jerry Patchen continues,

> When Takes Gun got pushed to the side, it [the NAC–US had] laid dormant and then when I got up, when I made contact with Takes

Gun, he came down here to visit me in Texas, he went down to Amada's and visited with Amada. He said, "You know, there is just this one left, that Amada and I, we are the only ones left in that old Texas charter. I would sure like to see that continue."

So he enlisted me to update the old Texas charter, to change its name back [in 1987], because its name had been changed at one point to North America, to change it back to the Native American Church of the United States, and he continued on as president, Rutherford Loneman and Jerry Etcitty were Vice Presidents and custodians, Amada was Secretary, and I was Recorder. And I handled all the administrative files in Austin . . . [Amada's] address was the home address, or the PO box was the home address for the Native American Church of the United States.

In her elderly years, her position has become more a position of honor and history. But she was, in the early days, she was a spark plug for protecting the sacrament in Texas and giving it its legal, formal structure in Texas. [Interview, April 29, 2004]

Indians and Non-Indians in Meetings at Amada's Place

As the official NAC–US was reinstated in 1987 with Amada as one of the officers, more meetings were held on her property, and during the ceremonies, prayers were always offered for her. She would enter the tepee in the morning to greet everyone and share the communal space and sentiments as everyone greeted the day with good thoughts. On rare occasions she would have to remind participants about the importance of respecting and honoring everyone regardless of who they were or whence they came.

Loreta Cook and her husband, Tom, experienced Amada's sage actions in a meeting when she came into the tepee for morning water and breakfast. Loreta Cook relates,

> And I've even seen where there was a meeting at a particular time in February and Tom and I were also privy to be there. And there was a lot of political things going on that we never got involved in but, attending that service, we witnessed many things. A woman in there

getting jealous about her husband sitting next to another woman and beating the drum. You know, really odd things.

A man who was leading the service having to tell the people that it was okay because his adopted daughter, who is non-native, made the spiritual food and that her husband was also non-native, but he was indigenous because he was from South America, from Venezuela or somewhere. So, she came in the next morning and all of this stuff was chaos, kind of running underneath everything. Some of us had been sitting down since 5:00 p.m. that evening into the next morning. And the woman who got jealous spoke for two or three hours about the jealousy, about being jealous that her husband was sitting next to that other woman. And went on and on.

And then Amada comes in and she says, "These are earthly things, these are things that you all need to deal with, your own issues, at home. Right here is a place for peace; let's all sit together in peace." Boom, just like that, it straightened right out. And it took us; we sat there until noon that next day, Tom and I. The leader had asked that if we were not sickly or did not have the need to go springing out to go out to the bathroom to hold our place because we are praying on the grounds of a holy woman. And so, we did that. [Interview, July 16, 2005]

Up until the late '80s and early '90s, few non-Indians came to Amada's house and stayed for long. Even fewer participated in NAC meetings on her grounds. George Morgan and Jerry and Linda Patchen were exceptions, along with several whites who had married NAC members. Some Indians fervently believed that the NAC and the use of peyote were religious traditions that God had reserved only for Indians. The controlled substances laws, enforced since the '70s, which defined peyote as a Schedule 1 drug, contained an exemption clause that recognized the use of peyote by Indians, defined as anyone with 25 percent Indian blood quantum.[3] This definition for "Indian" is problematic and even more challenging when spouses or adopted kin are non-Indians.[4] The politics of race, cultural histories, drug laws, and religious freedoms sometimes played out at Amada's.[5] As far as Amada was concerned, everyone was welcome, and she treated everyone equally.

Bertha Grove shared similar sentiments in her thoughts about non-Indians involved in the NAC: "We have our friends that come in. They learn how to sing, white people, teach them how. Sometimes they are the only help we got. . . . So we got people; everybody's just people. Can't discriminate if you are to follow God's ways. You can't do that. Even the trees that drop all different colors, fall colors. Animals too, birds, insects, flowers" (interview, February 21, 2004).

On Amada's land the involvement of non-Indians became a contested issue. Regardless of Amada's unconditional love and generous hospitality, events arose at her place that worried and saddened her. Jerry Patchen describes one such occasion:

> One time at the Friday night meeting, there was an Arapaho Indian, Homer Black, that was married to a non-Indian—she was just a golden blonde hair, natural golden, Norwegian-looking, white, white skin. And she was in that tepee and North America [representatives of the NAC–NA] was down there and they didn't like a non-Indian being in that Friday night meeting and they called DPS and the DPS colonel—no, lieutenant—that came because they had put so much pressure on DPS down there to go into that meeting. And Amada calling me . . . Junior was leading the meeting. We would have been down there but a friend of ours passed away, and we had to go to the wake and then go on down to the Saturday-night meeting, and Amada being upset and crying because there was police there at her home, and were talking about entering the tepee, and Amada got me on the phone and . . . I talked to that DPS captain or lieutenant and I told him, I said, "You better not go in that tepee." Well, he understood there was a non-Indian in there, and I said, "Judge Kazen, he's been in that tepee." . . . But he didn't go in. And we agreed to meet there noon the next day and resolve these problems. He stayed around there for a couple of hours, and the Indians were debating about what was going on, and he finally decided, "You know, I think this is an internal church matter and I'm going to leave." [Interview, April 29, 2004]

This encounter deeply pained Amada, so much so that it played a part later on in her rethinking and revising her will regarding the disposition of a portion of her property upon her death, as is discussed in chapter 8.

The Media Arrive

In the late '70s, Richard Geissler, an Anglo photojournalist from Laredo, made his way to Amada's house, but not with the anticipation of attending a NAC meeting or trying to acquire peyote. Rather, he arrived to Amada's doorstep during the February meetings held over Washington's birthday weekend in the hope of writing a human-interest story for the *Laredo Times*.

> The first time was, I was a photojournalist, and it was Washington's birthday, and my editor wanted a story. He knew that I went out there because he knew that my best friend at the time had a ranch just down the road. . . . I knew of her before, I think I knew of her around '76, '77, because we would go by her house all the time, going to the ranch. And, we would know when the Indians were in and you'd see the out-of-state license plates in the parking lot. . . .
>
> They'd stay in the house, they'd bathe in the house, and then there was a little shed out there. . . . or, they slept in the cars or they popped little popup tents or a lot of them were in pickups with campers, so they slept in the back of the pickup. I think some left her a little cash, you know, after the weekend . . . to pay the water bills and that kind of stuff. . . . she had a special bond, she had a kinship with those folks, the way the house is decorated, you know, all those paintings different people give her. And, the Indians would use the kitchen and they'd cook, and then they built this little cookstove outside so that there would be two stoves going and a real communal feeling to the gathering. . . . people going in and out of the house constantly.
>
> . . . It wasn't until a couple years after that, probably more, three or four years after that, that I approached her about doing a story for

a local newspaper. And, she agreed, and they liked the pictures, and I gave some to her and relatives of hers, so they invited me back.

Mr. Geissler did return to Amada's for the February weekend. He recalls the "uptightness" that some Indians had about non-Indians being on the premises. But when "You greeted her and she greeted you, then that put out the vibe, so when you run into folks at Amada's they'd be different.... Before, the Indians would be standoffish.... once you connected, because you were both at her house, then it would be more cordial on all sides."

Over time, Mr. Geissler came to know an Indian family at Amada's home. He says he took them out to his friends' ranch to harvest peyote

> and made a connection with them, and they would always stay at Amada's. So, that is when I started seeing her a lot more, simply 'cause of these folks. Because I knew when they would come down, they'd call and I'd go visit her.... You know, I kind of, then learned a lot about Indians and who they trusted and who they didn't. And then, they would always ask me, "Are you a writer?" "No, I'm a photographer." "Oh. Okay."
>
> Then, when they come back the next time, and I took a photo of them or got an address, I always sent a photo to them. Nothing like a group photograph to open some doors. So, when they would come back, they were not uncomfortable with me taking photographs, and I kept it at that.... I was in the Army... and I saw how they treated Indians in Oklahoma, so it was certain, I don't know, solidarity in thought, you know. So I did everything possible not to be seen as trying to exploit anything.... And then that newspaper article I did landed on my lap.... I took a stack of... the newspaper and gave her [Amada] a bunch.... they got passed around... and so it got to be so I would say, "Hey, there is this reporter that wants to do a story." They like reporters because if they like what [I] wrote it would be positive PR. [Interview, April 20, 2004]

Richard Geissler goes on to say that Philip True, a reporter for the *San Antonio Express*, approached him about writing a story about Amada, and he helped True make the connections.[6] The story was "about Amada, the gathering, and the people coming to Mirando City, and everybody liked it. It was . . . a great little story, and different reporters from the San Antonio paper, they would come through. . . . Yeah, it was almost a ritual. . . . a picture of them [Indians] with Amada, or them around the tepee, or whatever, and the local newspaper, they were happy to get it, too" (interview, April 20, 2004).

Word of Amada and the peyote trade spread across the continent in the print world of newspaper media. From the 1990s onward, local and syndicated stories of this amazing woman and the activities at her place were published across the country every year. "Just Call Her Mom" (Lara 2001) was one of the catchier titles. Soon, newspapers in other countries picked up Amada's story, even as far away as Japan. They also began to cover other peyote dealers in telling the story of the peyote trade. In the last decade of the twentieth century, a dizzying number of local, national, and international people flocked to Amada and her humble home in Mirando City, deep in the heart of South Texas. Some visitors may have been motivated to come to Amada's out of mere curiosity, to meet this modest "celebrity"; others may have come seeking fulfillment in their lives in the "exotic" world that they imagined the peyote gardens to be. Regardless of people's reasons for coming to Amada's house, and irrespective of the cultural upbringing or personal life history each visitor brought along, most could sense that Amada and her place were intertwined, and they were special. Many visitors could identify from their own experiences that this was a place where wisdom, morality, politeness, and civility resided. The experiences and understandings non-Indians had of Amada and her place were different than those of Native American or local Tejano visitors, who held their own individual histories and sense of place here. Together her visitors shared, however briefly, time and space with her, and with all those who had come to the peyote gardens, the holy land, and the place she called home.[7]

Peyote given to Amada as a gift from a peyote dealer. Courtesy of Stacy B. Schaefer.

Peyote given to Amada by a peyote dealer in a pot on her front porch. Courtesy of Stacy B. Schaefer.

Peyote on Amada's property where people have prayed and left offerings of coins and the remnants of a tobacco cigarettes smoked during prayer. Courtesy of Stacy B. Schaefer.

Altar created for NAC members to pray in the backyard of a peyote dealer. The majority of NAC members do not have access to pray or harvest in the peyote gardens, which are on private property. Courtesy of Stacy B. Schaefer.

Fresh-cut peyote drying on platforms at the home of a peyote dealer. Courtesy of Stacy B. Schaefer.

Newly erected sign above the entrance gate to Amada's property, 1990s. Courtesy of Stacy B. Schaefer.

Typical scene at Amada's place during certain times of the year. Courtesy of Stacy B. Schaefer.

License plate of a large truck parked on Amada's premises. Courtesy of Stacy B. Schaefer.

Daybreak near the end of an all-night prayer meeting held at Amada's place on the sacred tepee grounds. Courtesy of Stacy B. Schaefer.

Amada exiting tepee after a prayer meeting to honor her and her family. Courtesy of Stacy B. Schaefer.

Amada in front of a tepee. Courtesy of Michelle Patchen.

View of an interior wall in Amada's house. Courtesy of Stacy B. Schaefer.

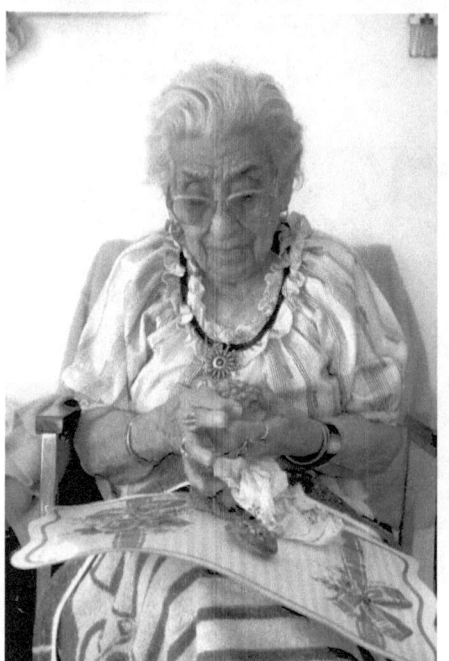

Above: Amada sitting on her front porch holding a pot of peyote, 1994. Courtesy of Stacy B. Schaefer.

Opposite page, top left: View of an interior wall with small altar by the main entrance to Amada's house. Courtesy of Stacy B. Schaefer.

Opposite page, top right: Amada and the Virgen. Courtesy of Michelle Patchen.

Opposite page, bottom left: Amada making peyote chiefs, 1995. Photo courtesy of Stacy B. Schaefer.

Opposite page, bottom right: Close-up of Amada making a peyote chief, 1995. Courtesy of Stacy B. Schaefer.

Close-up of peyote chiefs on miniature Navajo blankets, ready to give to their destined NAC recipients, 1995. Courtesy of Stacy B. Schaefer.

Amada's cedar box with the first peyote chief she made when she was young, her fans, cedar, and photos, 2013. Courtesy of Stacy B. Schaefer.

Author with Amada the morning after a prayer meeting on her property. Courtesy of Jim Bauml.

Author with Amada. Courtesy of Jim Bauml.

𝒲ell, you know there are some Indians that come down here, very old people, and they come in and [Amada says], "Oh, it has been a long time, I haven't seen you," and la la la la. And it is so amazing because she remembers them. And their names and where they are from. They call her Mom, they call her Grandma, all of them are her kids. There are even people who have their own kids and they name them Amada. . . .

A lot of mail . . . and a lot of pictures . . . Yeah, we put candles to protect herself, to protect all the people. . . . the Virgen de Guadalupe, San Juditas; San Juditas is traditional for your job, *que te vaya bien en tu trabajo* [so that your work goes well], and the *buena suerte* [for good luck]. Jesucristo, we put it, but she believes more in the Virgen de Guadalupe . . . We put the pictures on her wall, all those people . . . we hope to put all of them but there are so many of them, we would probably fill the whole house with them. And those are all the people that have been blessed. And we think of everybody, but it's hard because there are so many of them.

—Nora Martinez, Amada's caregiver, friend, and surrogate daughter, interview, February 25, 2004

ℋer blessings, you know, it's like she invokes the Holy Spirit, God Almighty, Diosito Santo, el Espíritu Santo, Jesucristo, la Virgin. She invokes the most powerful spiritual beings, entities, and then she gives you the sign of the cross, kind of touches your forehead. Holds your hand, it is like she is giving you some of her energy in a way. The way the *abuelitas* [grandmothers] and the moms do it in the Chicano [way], they try to . . . I guess they try to pat your forehead and hold your face in their hand. I see some native people that way feeling, kind of praying. You can almost imagine her saying a rosary the way she is saying the blessings that she gives you. That is a real traditional Chicano-type blessing.

—Manuel Kwautli Vásquez, Tejano/Coahuiltecan, interview, April 23, 2004

Chapter 7

Saint, Mom, and Grandma on Sacred Peyote Grounds

Nora

In the 1990s Amada entered her ninth decade of life. As she greeted every day with her prayers, she always felt thankful to be alive. The times I stayed at Amada's house, I found comfort and awe, hearing her praying out loud before going to sleep and again upon waking up in the morning. Amada continued to welcome everyone who came to her house with open arms. She also acknowledged that she was no longer able to get along on her own as well as she had in the past, and some of her friends from Mirando City helped out. Mrs. Martinez helped with cleaning her house, and Mrs. Maria Esquivel took Amada in her car to Laredo to run errands. Then one day Nora Martinez, daughter of Mrs. Teresa Johnson and sister of peyote dealer Salvador Johnson, entered Amada's life. It was an auspicious event that kindled a bright light for Amada and brought a deep richness to her personal life that provided her another decade of living life to its fullest. Nora's presence also enabled Amada to continue to live at her home and bless the people who came to visit with prayers for health, good life, and safe journeys.

Nora Martinez, a mother of two with a husband who works on the oilrigs and also plays in a local Tejano band, became Amada's caregiver.

She worked for a home healthcare service as a nurse assistant, in addition to operating her own small local restaurant in Mirando City. She recounts how she came to work for Amada:

> I've known Amada since—I was raised in Mirando—since I was a little girl, and we would respect her land because the Indians would go by in October, and one day she called me at my restaurant. She would order pizza, lasagna, and shrimp. And one day I answered and she said, "I have something to ask you." And I said, "What do you mean?" And she said, "I want to know if you will work with me." So I said, "Well, I guess I will." So I started to work with her; since then I have been with her.

On the first day of work, Nora remembers,

> I sat down with her in the morning and she told me, "You have to drink coffee." And I told her, "But I don't drink coffee." And she said, "Well, I drink a cup of coffee every day, and I would like you to have breakfast with me." So we sat there, and we drank coffee, and we ate our tacos. She likes tacos, *guisado* (simmered, seasoned beef) and with potato and egg. And she told me she used to make tortillas and tamales. [Interview, February 25, 2004]

Nora noted that because of the years of Amada living alone with modest means, her house needed some repairs and redecorating. She cheerfully helped Amada fix up the house and was savvy navigating county, state, and federal agencies, finding all the low-income senior citizens' programs for which Amada was eligible. In addition to health care, supplemental nutrition, and home maintenance, she also helped Amada enroll in the social programs for senior citizens at the Mirando City Civic Center.

Even with the number of people that came to her house, weeks could go by without a single visitor and the place would feel lonely. The senior citizens' program livened up Amada's days. Nora recalls, "Yes. She would go in the mornings to play bingo, *la chalupa*, she would go every morning, and she would play the bingo there, and then in the evenings, I would pick her up, or they would take her home. And she liked it."

Then, Nora brought even more sparkle into Amada's life when she started taking Amada from Mirando City to the outlying towns, to Laredo, as well as into the lower Rio Grande area on errands and visits with friends and family in her car. They would joke, saying that they were *callejeras* (street women). Nora remembers,

> When I started working with her . . . I would tell her in the mornings, "Let's go have breakfast." "Oookay, let's go. Let me get dressed." So she would dress up, and we would always be in the *calle* [street]. And I would tell her, "Mira donde andamos, en la calle." [Look where we are, in the street.] And to me that made her very happy and I liked it. Because I knew she was going to be happy. . . .
>
> One day, Mother's Day, I'll never forget, my husband Isidro had bought me a ticket to go see Tigrillos; it was a very Tejano band. And I told Isidro, "But we have no one to take care of Amada, so we need to take her." "Oh, we'll take her." And we did; it was Mother's Day, and they were giving corsages and everyone thought she was the most beautiful woman there because everybody came up to the table and told her, "Ay, how old are you? You are so pretty." And so she would feel special and she was like, "Oh man, everyone is coming to the table." I would tell Amada, "Are you ready to go home?" "Oh no, I am having fun." And it was about eleven thirty, and then finally the dance finished at twelve thirty, and so, "Are you ready to go?" "Yes I am ready to go." Because it was already over, *pero* [but] she could continue going.

Nora elaborates further:

> She was, I think, ninety-three. And then from there on, she was always going with me everywhere. And they would get mad at me at the Home Health because I am not supposed to travel with her. And I told them, "Well just fire me. I don't care." And they would tell me, "It's a risk because if anything happens and you have an accident, you know you are liable." "Ah, that's okay, God's there." And Amada would tell me, "Ah, let's go anyway." [Interview, February 25, 2004]

With all the excitement and flurry of activity traveling around with Nora in her car, Amada nicknamed Nora "Remolino de Suerte" (Whirlwind of Luck) after a Mexican game show on television in which contestants stand in a closed phone booth–like glass chamber and try to grab as many dollar bills as possible flying through the air at whirlwind speed. Nora's mother, Mrs. Johnson, sometimes visited or stayed with Amada at her house and was happy that Amada had the stamina and endurance to keep up with Nora. Mrs. Johnson comments, "Nora, sí, porque [Nora, yes, because] Nora—'Get ready because we are going somewhere . . . Y [And] we going over here, and we going over there. I get tired. I tell Nora, 'No, I'm gonna stay here. You can go and go wherever you want to go'" (interview, April 10, 2004).

Peyote, Healing, and Charity

Eventually, Amada began to experience the aches and pains that come with aging, particularly arthritis in her knees and occasional stomach discomfort. After spending time with Amada, Nora, trained as a nurse assistant, witnessed the healing power of peyote:

> Yeah, she heals herself, mostly with the medicine, with the peyote, and other ways. . . . And she told me, "Oh no, it's just medicine and I eat the little ones, the baby ones." "Uh-huh," and I told her, "You eat the little ones?" And she said, "Yeah, I eat the little ones." And I asked her, "What for? What does it help?" "Oh, whenever . . . I have phlegm, it cleans my chest," and it's true. She would start loosening up all her congestion, and I was like, "Wow," but you know it is amazing what that medicine does. . . . Well, she has never been complaining, since I don't know, I can't remember that last time we had brought her, she was complaining about her stomach and then from there on, you know, arthritis. Before she used to always complain about her legs, and it has been a while since. She has a saying, she says in Spanish, "No me duele nada, ni la uña me duele" [I don't have any pain, not even in my fingernail]. [Interview, February 25, 2004]

Nora also recognized Amada's powers to heal others. "I think she can heal people too, because a lot of people believe in her. To them, a lot of people think she is a healer, and a lot of people think of her, if they come to her it is going to be something big."

Amada's spirituality and healing powers were also manifest in the peyote chiefs that she made for others (as discussed in chapter 6). Nora recalls that Amada

> would tell me to call the dealers and tell them to bring the peyote because she would make the chief peyote. . . . And she would teach me but I never learned. She would show me how. She used to tell me, "You cut it up and there is a way to press on it. And then you put it backwards," and she would put them in the window to dry, for the sun to dry them. . . . then the following day, she pressed on it again until they would dry up and the little hair on the peyote, it would stand up beautiful. [Interview, February 25, 2004]

Another way that Amada shared her healing and generosity was in her charitable actions. One day she spoke to me about greediness, that some people think about *puro commercio* (only financial gain) and how much they will get. She told me she gives money to charitable causes such as the Mirando Civic Center, the Catholic Church in Mirando, the Bishop in Corpus Christi, and other people. Amada even gave money to a woman who lost her eyesight in an accident at a candle factory where she was working. The woman told Amada that she doesn't need the money because her husband works. But Amada insisted on donating money to her. As Amada explained it to me, it was her *promesa* (promised vow) to do all her life; it is her prayer and blessing. She also believed that by doing good that it will also be her own prayer and blessing (Amada Cardenas, personal communication, March 29, 1997).

Nora concurred with Amada's plentiful generosity and charitable actions:

> Oh, everybody respects her, everybody thinks of her, because they told me, there is this lady, Ms. Inocencio, she goes and gives Amada the hostia [holy wafer] every Sunday, and she says that everybody

loves her because she is always a good woman. If anybody needed anything they would ask her and she would give it to them. Donations, gifts, whatever anybody needed. She was there to help. . . . She doesn't have that much money, but it was all in her heart that she does it. . . . [She gives to] the Virgen of San Juan, and then for the children, the March of Dimes, and there's a lot of them, the sheriff department, the highway patrol, you name it. Everyone who calls, she'll say yes. [Interview, February 25, 2004]

Becoming the Mother of a Daughter

Within a relatively short period of time, Amada and Nora's relationship grew well beyond the boundaries of caregiver and patient and became much more than a comfortable friendship. Their feelings for each other evolved into a deep, familial tie, a kinship between mother and daughter. Nora explains,

> To me, she's like my mom. She's like my second mom. Because she is a very loving, caring person. And she kisses me and she tells me, "You know you are my daughter I almost had, and she went away, so you took her place."
>
> . . . I have been with her for so long and she is so special that everywhere I'm at, I am always thinking of her. I can leave out of town, and I still have to call her. And I have to make sure that she is okay. Because to me she is like my mom.

And like a dedicated daughter, Nora made sure that Amada was not left out when the holidays arrived:

> Well first, in October, we get ready for Halloween. And we give the kids candy. Kids come down to her house and we'll turn on the lights. We'll get a few, but they will come in. And then on Thanksgiving, we'll have her over for Thanksgiving and she'll say "Here we go, another pound to go." And then on Christmas, for the last ten, fifteen years she's been with me for Christmas. And we sit

down and my kids buy her little gifts. And we all open our gifts. And she'll tell me, "You didn't have to buy me anything. For me it is fine just to be here." And on the fourth of July, *pos* [well] . . . she likes to go to the park to watch fireworks. [Interview, February 25, 2004]

Amada's son, Claudio Jr., and his wife, Joanne, were immensely grateful that Nora was there for Amada. When they made their annual visit to see Amada, Nora was treated like part of the family. Together they would all go out to eat, take day trips to Nuevo Laredo, and visit Amada's nieces and visit the cemetery in Laredo to put flowers on Claudio Sr.'s grave and the graves of Amada's sisters. In a sense, Nora became like a sister to Claudio as well.

Open-Door Policy

One of Amada's habits that worried both Nora and Claudio was her open-door policy at all hours of the day and night. At times various trucks and campers would drive onto her property late in the night. Some of the occupants would come to pray, others to rest or reorganize their things before they headed back home. Amada said that some didn't even come into the house or say hello. One night I was staying over at Amada's house. It was filled with sleeping people, and I was asleep on the couch in the living room. During the night the phone rang a few times, waking up Amada, and at 4:00 a.m. I heard pounding on the front door that would not stop. I answered the door. It was an older heavyset Indian man who was blind, and a young, tall guy, who was introduced as his adopted son, accompanied him. The man wanted to know if Amada was there. I told him she was asleep, as were all of us. He wanted to know if he could take a shower. I told him in a couple hours; he would have to wait a couple hours. They then went to sleep in their car until sunrise.

I recounted this experience to Nora, who responded,

But she's not scared. And I told Amada, "One day they are going to try, you know you need to be careful and don't open the door to anybody." Amada—"Ah no, everybody is okay, they're good people." And I told her, "You never know. One day they are going to tie us down and who are we going to scream to?" And she just shrugs and says, "No, I don't think they are going to do anything." [Interview, February 25, 2004]

Amada's son, Claudio Jr., added,

> For a long time, my mother lived here all by herself. All by herself, nobody here. And she would get up at two or three o'clock in the morning, in the middle of the night, when somebody would come to the door, not knowing who was on the other side. She would open that door, and they would come in. And I would tell Joanne [Claudio's wife], "I don't like that at all." But she seemed to persevere. And something is watching over her because she's never been harmed or anything. And she could have very easily. I think about that a lot.
> ... Yeah. I don't think she ever figured out that she should be scared about anything. I don't know why. And you know, she's got a strong faith, a very strong faith; I think that is what has really kept her going a lot. [Interview, October 24, 2004]

Amada's friend Catalina Inocencio remembers Amada's attitude about living alone and opening her house to everybody:

> Todo el tiempo me decía ella que todo el tiempo había que confiar en Dios. Ella tenía mucha fe en Dios. . . . Ella era muy fuerte y ella tenía fe en Dios. . . . Ella dice "Estoy solita porque cuando está solita, ya está fuerte, por estar solita. Estoy sola pero no tengo miedo porque estoy acompañada por Dios." Y yo sé que es verdad de Amadita. [Interview, April 21, 2004]

> All the time she told me that I have to trust in God all the time. She had a lot of faith in God. . . . She was very strong, and she had a lot of faith in God. . . . She says, "I am alone because when one is alone, one is already strong, from being alone. I am alone, but I am not afraid because God is with me." I know it is true for Amadita.

Nora's entrance into Amada's life was part of a general turning point that took place at Amada's home in the 1990s; a synchronicity attracted more and more people from all walks of life to Amada's place. Her land and her legendary status created a kind of vortex, drawing people to the sacred peyote gardens, a crossroads where people's paths met. Amada was at the center of this matrix; her presence, friendship, and love forever changed the lives of many who ventured to her place to meet her.

Coahuiltecans

During this time a new contingency of people from Texas began to come down to Amada's, and they formed a special bond with her and with the gardens. They identify themselves as Coahuiltecans, Tejanos who are Chicanos. Coahuiltecans actively claim their Native American heritage from the Coahuiltecan Indians who inhabited the region along what is now the South Texas borderlands with northern Mexico, including the states of Coahuila, Tamaulipas, Nuevo León, and even into Zacatecas. This area includes the native desert habitat where peyote grows, and it was also the region where the peyote religion presumably formed an integral part of indigenous cultural traditions. In times past, when Spain controlled this region, Coahuiltecan-speaking Indians were moved to the missions in San Antonio.[1] One of the events early in the 1990s that unified people who considered themselves activists and Coahuiltecans was the repatriation of indigenous human remains from the San Antonio missions.

In honoring the dead by the reburial of these human remains, Coahuiltecans had come to know indigenous people who are members of the NAC and started to attend prayer meetings in the tepee with them. The emergence of this contemporary Coahuiltecan culture also came from the cross-pollination of the Chicano movement in the Southwest and the cultural florescence of the Mexican *danzante* cultural awakening in Mexico. One Coahuiltecan, Manuel Kwautli Vásquez, explains how he became involved with the Coahuiltecan chapter of the NAC, which was recognized by the State of Texas:

I started going to sweat lodges, Aztec dancing, the Sun Dance, carrying a pipe, and then medicine, which was a large part of that, learning the whole culture. . . . At first I was [involved with] the Native American Church Mexicayo, which had already been established in Arizona with assistance from the Lakota people. So it was kind of a joint effort between some Chicano roadmen, Chicano peyote people, and Leonard Crow Dog and the Lakotas, some of his nephews.

But after a couple of years, we decided here in Texas that we needed to establish our own chapter in order to conduct ceremonies here. So it was a Mayan person who was a Catholic priest; he was at Mission San Juan. His name was Father Jorge Piestra, He is from Mérida, Yucatán, and he invited us to go to the church and pray there. Since the church was originally established for indigenous people . . . He asked us to go to the church and I helped him move his altar down to where the pews were. He let us dance and pray in our own language and dance and pray during the mass ceremony. In other words, he kind of took a second seat to the native way of prayer during the Catholic mass. He was so supportive, so I asked him if we could set up our tepee and have peyote meetings there on the church grounds. He said yeah, that would be fine.

We wanted to establish the legality to be able to do that here. So we formed our own Native American Church Chapter, which is called Teocali Quetzalcoatl here in Texas. I was named as the custodian[2] for this chapter here. . . . we went and reintroduced ourselves to the peyote distributors. We explained to them that we had established our church chapter.[3] [Interview, April 23, 2004]

Mr. Vásquez tells of how he came to know Amada and to pray in the peyote gardens upon arriving in the Mirando City area:

I was in Mirando City, I went to obtain some medicine, some peyote for a ceremony we were going to have at the Mission San Juan. It was in the nineties; I don't remember the exact year, somewhere maybe '94, approximately. . . . And when I went there with the peyote dealers there at the time, Isabel Lopez and Salvador Johnson, they both directed me to Amada's house and said that I should visit her, to know her and pay my respects to her, to sign her little book, which she is very proud of. And so that was the first time that I made an entry into her log about our visit there. . . .

. . . she just seemed full of a lot of energy and a lot of supportive emotional love, I guess you would call it. She was very open, invited us into her house . . . offered us something to eat. She wanted to know where we were from and what church. She seemed like she was almost like the gatekeeper for the medicine activities there in Mirando City. I got that impression from her, she was an overseer or a guardian of everything that was taking place. And at the same time she began to tell us her story. About her and her husband. . . . It gave me the impression that they were some of the first peyote dealers that established themselves there. . . . She gave us a little education there, about the history and a little kind of up-to-date on what's going on. She is very knowledgeable of the whole national scene of the Native American Church and knew a lot of people in the church. She had pictures of them. [Interview, April 23, 2004]

From then on, Mr. Vásquez and other Coahuiltecan church members started coming to see Amada and participate in prayer meetings on her property, including the February meetings. In the same tradition as Claudio Sr., Mr. Vásquez and other Coahuiltecans sang songs during the ceremony in Spanish and English, but they also included Nahuatl (the language of the Aztecs) in their songs as well. He recalls a time when he was in Mirando City:

I was singing one of those songs, "Con el corazón, te canto." *Con el corazón, te canto. Con el corazón, te canto* [With my heart, I sing to you]. Which is a song that someone else wrote, but that we kind of adapted into different ways. . . . And when I was singing it someone mentioned that Claudio [Sr.] used to use those words in his songs. . . . That is the thing about those songs, they are out there, so to speak. They say you catch them. That is the way they explain it. It is like a language of the soul that is out there. [Interview, April 23, 2004]

Songs, like rituals, carry symbols that can transcend individual realities and cultural traditions. Mr. Vásquez elaborates on this, drawing upon the meaning people attribute to Amada and peyote when they speak about her in tepee ceremonies:

> Well, people from all-native families, nations in their languages, pay that homage to her. Most of them refer to her as Grandma or Mom. . . . For some people, the medicine, the peyote, too, is a kind of female or grandma. . . . Amada is like Grandmother Peyote. Like you are looking at her. They talk about her like that. They talk about her like they are talking about the medicine, in the same sentence. We understand the relationship of humanity with the other spirits; like they say, we are all one. So being one means that humans are in touch and connected to the Peyote Spirit. And it is in us, too, and we are in that spirit and she is. . . . So when they talk about her and they call her Grandma, and they see how the medicine has worked through her to bring about the things that we see. [Interview, April 23, 2004]

My Arrival at Amada's Place

As I described in chapter 1, in 1993 I appeared on Amada's doorstep. It was the second week of February 1993 when my student, Marly Moran, and I ventured out in my car from my home in McAllen, Texas, onto the back country roads that eventually led us to Mirando City. From that first encounter, Amada touched my soul, and I knew that whenever I had the opportunity, I wanted to spend more time with her and come to know her as a friend. Our relationship in the end evolved into an intimate one that blended mother-daughter and grandmother-granddaughter feelings.

I was also one who arrived at Amada's in the 1990s during this amazingly synchronistic period. Every weekend that I could get away, I drove to visit her, bringing gifts of flowers, her favorite dessert (pecan pie) or another sweet, and oftentimes take-out food, such as *botanas* (small dishes) of beef fajitas with rice, beans, and tortillas from a little Mexican restaurant in Rio Grande City. Preferring to drive the isolated country roads to Amada's house for a change of scenery, I was once stopped by border patrol officers who thought I looked out of place and suspicious with my California license plates on these lonely roads near the Mexican border. After I answered their questions and opened the trunk of my car for inspection upon their request, they allowed me to continue on my journey to Amada's home.[4]

Spring was always the most beautiful time of the year to drive the back roads, when the landscape was bursting with brilliant green grass; new shoots of tender green leaves on the mesquite trees; the fresh, sweet smell of golden blossoms covering huisache trees; white flowering stalks towering from the yuccas; and an array of eye-dazzling wildflowers that spanned the color spectrum from yellows to purples, red, orange, and white. Raptorial birds soared above the roads looking for roadkill, which, more times than not, was plentiful. On one of these memorable drives, as I cruised the desolate Texas Highway 649 to Mirando City, I ran over a snake. I clenched my teeth as I felt and heard the "thud, thud, thud." "Oh well," I thought, "what's done is done." When I arrived at Amada's I had a chance to tell her of the snake I had killed, fearing the worst of what folk beliefs might exist for my actions. It was a relief to hear from Amada that it was good luck to run over a snake, and this assuaged the dread I had of some kind of serpentine retribution.

From 1993 to 2005, I made sure to visit during the February NAC gathering, helping with whatever tasks I could, and often going into the tepee and participating in the Saturday night meeting. I also met many people at Amada's home: Mirando City community members, Amada's family, Amada's friends from other places in Texas and all over North America. I relished the stories they shared about her and enjoyed their company at this crossroads where everyone was made to feel at home. With Amada as our focal point, I became dear friends with some of these people. I also visited Amada over the holidays—Easter, Thanksgiving, and Christmas Eve.

An excerpt from my field notes on Easter weekend, March 1997, describes in snippets a typical visit we would have:

> I drive up to Amada's house just as she arrives in a car with her
> friend and hair stylist, Maria Esquivel. She had her hair fixed so nice
> for tomorrow and was happy to see me. I brought in a big Easter

basket of shiny gold with a large white Easter lily blooming and more blooms to open, and a delicate purple-flowered plant next to it. A big multicolored ribbon—pink, purple, blue, and white hues—was tied around the basket. I brought a bunch of pink, orange, and yellow snapdragons cut from my yard, a chocolate cake, and an Easter card and chocolate bunny for her. Amada excitedly tells me how we must be in tune with each other, arriving at the same time.

Since March 3 she has had a steady stream of Indian visitors coming through the house. She heated up refried beans and a beef *guisado* [stew] dish Nora made with tomatoes, onions, *calabaza* [squash], and flour tortillas. She had already eaten, but accompanied me drinking a cup of coffee and eating *galletas Marías*, cookies she proudly said are from Mexico. She loves those sweets. She told me all about the ending of her favorite telenovela, *María, la del barrio* (Maria from the poor neighborhood), and of the new one, *Te sigo amando* (I still love you). I watch them with her when I visit and find it endearing how involved she gets with the plots and characters, talking loudly, reprimanding the bad guys in Spanish, and congratulating the protagonists when justice is served.

It was hot and I lay down on the spare bed, noting seven new chiefs being made in the windowsill. Amada said she had sold the other ones and had many orders so she started on these. After napping we sit out on the front porch. It is much cooler with the late afternoon breeze. We watch cars pass on the highway; some are large tanker trucks, others carry heavy equipment to the oilrigs in the area. Next thing we know, several trucks with Arizona license plates drive up, pull onto her property, and she is ready to welcome the travelers and make them comfortable. With Easter tomorrow, she will be sure to make these visitors feel welcome and help them celebrate the day giving homage to Jesus Christ and the peyote gardens.

I wanted my family and people dear to me to meet Amada. I brought my nephew and sister from California to visit Amada on separate occasions, and when it could be arranged, my now husband, then boyfriend, Jim Bauml, would accompany me on my sojourns to Amada's, and they showered each other with love and attention. During summer break from my professorial duties at UT–PA, I would spend time in California with my family and friends and travel to Mexico to visit and conduct fieldwork among my Huichol Indian friends and family in San Andrés Cohamiata, Jalisco. Upon returning every fall to Texas, I would bring Amada up to date on my time with my Huichol family, especially with my compadres, Estela and Andrés, and my goddaughter, Cristalina.

My Huichol Family Meets Amada

On two different occasions, members of my Huichol family came to stay with me in McAllen, Texas. While there, they attended classes I taught, gave demonstrations on how they make their art, and sold art to people interested in their work. I made a special point of taking them to Amada's house and the peyote gardens of South Texas. I called these lands "Wirikuta del Norte," in reference to their sacred peyote lands farther south in the Mexican state of San Luis Potosí, which I had visited with them on peyote pilgrimages.

Their first visit with Amada and to the peyote gardens is described in passages from my field notes from March 17 and 18, 1996:

> We arrive at Amada's. She is alone. Then a truck filled with Indians pulls up and the adults sleep in the truck, several boys exit the truck and play in the yard. Before we go into Amada's house to greet her, I point out to them the peyote in the little gardens bordered with stones. . . . they exclaim that it really is peyote or *hikuri*, as they call the sacred plant. We go into the house and Amada had been resting but gets up to greet us. Estela and Andrés are very interested in all the things she has on her wall, artwork and photos. When I introduce them and get to Cristalina, Amada says in Spanish—"Oh, this must be the goddaughter who you bought the burro for." That dispelled whatever awkwardness there might have been when they realized that I had spoken of them often to Amada.
>
> It's hot, in the nineties and humid. We rest until it cools down. . . . I showed them the grounds where the tepee is placed when meetings are being held. There were still clear markings of

where the fire had been made and remnants of the red sand and crescent moon altar from the last ceremony. I tell them about the peyote chief in the middle of the altar that guides the roadman and all the participants. They recognize similarities in the roles of participants in their ceremonies.

We go out to eat. Amada comes along. . . . upon returning to Amada's, there are lots of people waiting for her. Later we go to sleep, my family in the spare bedroom, I sleep on the cot in Amada's. It is a windy night. . . . Estela dreams that she sees in the smoky haze a figure by the fire where the tepee is put up. She hears wind, and on the wind she ever so faintly hears singing in the distance. In the morning she tells me of her dream and interprets the figure to be the *kakauyari*, the god or deity of the place.

We visit Los Ojuelos . . . and upon returning, Amada has a meal ready for us. She prays, arms upraised over the food she has prepared, makes the sign of the cross, and passes a glass of holy water from which each of us takes a sip.[5]

. . . Estela had told me before we came here that she wondered if the *kakauyari* of peyote here is a woman like in Wirikuta. I commented that she would have to dream on it. . . . Now that we have visited "Wirikuta del Norte" and Amada, caretaker of the peyote and a woman, I wonder if her dreams will reveal to her the answer to this question. For in many ways, Amada is a reflection of Wuili Uwi, the goddess of peyote in Wirikuta in Huichol beliefs, and the woman who appeared to the Mescalero Apaches and told them of the wonder of peyote, according to Native American Church beliefs.[6]

My Huichol family returned with me to Amada's place in February 1999, during the Washington's birthday weekend meetings, at which time they displayed their artwork to sell. Amada, as always, was the consummate hostess, and my family was able to meet Native Americans from a number of different tribes. Although the language differences made it difficult to communicate, and my Huichol family felt more culturally familiar with Mexican and Tejano culture, they shared with NAC members a knowledge of and deep respect for peyote as expressed in my family's artwork that visually communicates metaphysical experiences they both see with the guidance of peyote.

Many Visitors from Different Walks of Life

Many more people entered Amada's world; some learned of her through the media or the internet, which was beginning to expand its range, linking people globally. Nora recalls that from the 1990s onward,

> Yes, she was walking, and . . . she was independent. . . . the Indians would go in and she would also give them their coffee. The house was always open, and she was the one who did everything for them. . . . Yes, we had some Japanese people also that came down, and we also had all kinds of people. You know, they see it on the internet and they read about her, I guess. So they show up. [Interview, February 25, 2004]

Her sign-in book contained the names of all these visitors. Some of the NAC visitors I remember meeting were two tall men who introduced themselves as Eskimos from Alaska as well as a Tewa family from the Hopi pueblos. The husband was a sergeant in the tribal police department and explained that there were additional police officers from the pueblos that were NAC members. A number of the Navajo elders, the women dressed in traditional velvet skirts and blouses, journeyed down to see Amada with their families. One or more members of the family would lavish silver and turquoise jewelry, or sometimes woven blankets or pillow covers, upon Amada.[7] Navajo men and women in the armed forces came with their families to Amada's place when on approved leave or vacation from their duties to visit and attend prayer meetings on her property. Taos, New Mexico, was represented by such visitors as Jasper Gomez and family from the Taos Pueblo, Anglo friend Peter Templeton and family, and Mrs. Eugenia Franco and daughters. Professor Steven Pratt, Osage from the Department of Mass Communication at the University of Central Oklahoma, also came to Amada's place for the February prayer meetings (see Pratt 2003).

Professionals who were not Native American in various fields of study came to meet and visit with Amada, such as Harvard medical doctor and researcher John H. Halpern, who later conducted important research that corroborated other findings on the therapeutic benefits of using peyote by Navajo members of the NAC (Halpern 2005). Darrel McDonald—former student of Dr. George Morgan—and Clarissa Kimber, geography professors at Stephen F. Austin State University and Texas A&M University respectively, came to know Amada and published scholarly articles about her, the peyote religion, and the cultural geography of the peyote gardens (Kimber and McDonald 2004). Servando Hinojosa Jr., cultural anthropologist at UT–PA, who filled my position there after I had moved on to California State University, Chico, would visit Amada accompanied by his father, Servando Hinojosa Sr., a junior high school art teacher in nearby Alice, Texas. Servando Jr. reviewed the status and health of peyote populations in South Texas (Hinojosa 2000), while his father sketched scenes of people who attended the February weekend meetings at Amada's place.

Judge Kazen, his wife, and his daughter made a visit to Amada's home from Laredo during one February weekend meeting. Judge Kazen proudly wore the NAC prayer shawl and held the prayer staff that the NAC had given him years ago when they had made him an honorary member of the church. Judge Kazen's niece, Cathy Kazen, and Jackie Geissler visited Amada more frequently, as did Austin residents Barry and Patti Hamrick and Houston-based Jerry and Linda Patchen. From San Antonio the Coahuiltecans frequented Amada's place, including Manuel Vásquez, José Zepeda, and occasionally his brother Zep.

Among the more notable visitors at Amada's place was a female rabbi who had been living in New York. She had flown into the Laredo airport and arrived at Amada's home by taxi at 11:00 p.m., insisting that she should be allowed to attend the tepee meeting. She wore a yarmulke and *tallit* (prayer shawl) and urgently requested she be part of the meeting because she had gynecological health problems that she openly discussed; she hoped that she would be healed here. Another colorful group of visitors were Japanese Hawaiians who had come to meet Amada and reverently left in one of her peyote garden beds a ceramic statue of a buxom topless black woman in a sensual dance pose. Amada confided in me that she really didn't like it, but because of her nature she just could not say no. She and everyone around were jubilant when the statue eventually disintegrated from the elements.

A more controversial visitor who came to visit Amada was James "Flaming Eagle" Mooney, who claimed to be the famous anthropologist James Mooney's grandson. He also claimed to be at least one-quarter Seminole and a medicine man. He and his wife Linda founded the Oklevueha Earthwalks Native American Church of Utah, Inc., in 1997. Mr. Mooney and his wife made several visits to South Texas to obtain peyote and search for land to purchase. They also met Amada, and several of Mooney's church members accompanied him to Amada's property to film clips for the video *Chasing a Good Day to Die*, directed by Paul Larsen and produced by Terry Holland.[8] The Mooneys were arrested in 2000 and charged with distributing peyote during ceremonies at their church. The Utah Supreme Court ruled that, although the Mooneys were not enrolled members in a federally recognized tribe, the term "members" of the NAC was in compliance with the exemption in the Federal Controlled Substance Act that allows the use of peyote in religious ceremonies. Needless to say, NAC members who oppose non-Indians participating, let alone running meetings—even worse if they purportedly charge for the performance of the meetings—were outraged by the decision.

Another video filmed at Amada's place was *Amada of the Gardens*. With support from the Texas State Historical Commission and the Texas Foundation for the Arts, as well as the City of Austin Cultural Arts Contracts, Susan Maynard teamed up with Aida Franco, Bill Daniel, and Alan Pappe to film and produce this video to honor Amada and her unique role in Texas history and culture.

And of course, more "hippy" visitors made their way to Amada's as well. Nora remembers,

> Ah, we get all kinds, we get hippies. One day I will never forget, Jerry Patchen had come down to visit, close to Christmas, I remember, and I had gone shopping for my Christmas gifts. And he called me on my cell, and he told me, "Nora, you know I saw Amada down there in her living room sitting with a hippy. And I am kind of worried, I need to head back." And then my brother Salvador called me again, and he said, "Jerry stopped by and he said he was kind of worried." So we got

back to Mirando, and I told my daughter and my son-in-law, I told them, "Let's go by Amada's." And she was by herself. She had given the hippy permission to sleep outside on the tables, on the picnic tables. And that hippy was covered with rugs all over. And I told them, "Where is he?" And Gracie told me, "Mom, he is laying over there, on the picnic tables there." We woke him up, and I told him, "Can I help you?" "Well Mrs. Cardenas told me I can stay out here." . . . we gave him blankets and everything and the next day he had left me all the blankets on the porch of the house. [Interview, February 25, 2004]

As courteous and appreciative as most of the visitors were to Amada and her property, there were always a few who took advantage of her and were disrespectful of her property. Geri Arviso comments,

She opens her doors for anybody, she allows people to come regardless, even taking advantage of her. . . . [One time] my mother sat with her, and I was standing there, and she was crying, so I left and I asked my mother later why Amada was crying. She said, "She's crying because she said that she opens her doors to these people, and people take from her, her dishes." My mother said she cried too, and I thought, "Oh, my goodness." So my mother went and got some dishes . . . and she brought them back and gave her some food. Amada was really happy about that. And by the time we returned later on during that visit, I don't know how she did it, but she had cake for us. [Interview, February 16, 2004]

The sacred peyote, thoughtfully planted in Amada's gardens for people to commune and pray with, and sometimes their offerings of coins and tobacco, were occasionally targets of theft. Bertha Grove comments,

A lot of them didn't respect, I guess. That peyote that used to be around, but it disappeared as time went on, it disappeared. Used to be a lot of money going through, you know, where there was the peyote. People would put money there, quarters, dimes, nickels, a lot of money on top of them. Pretty soon they started to disappear, too. And soon the peyotes disappeared.

Through the years there has been a lot of things here that she's sad [about]. She's generous to a fault, you might say. She doesn't say anything. She just feels bad about it.

. . . She's like a rock. A lot of people can get to know her. It's getting better. Used to be a lot of people would throw trash all over. Before we left we'd clean up the place for her, pick up all the trash. That's what I told them this morning, "You people who smoke, pick up your [cigarette] butts." [Interview, February 21, 2004]

Amada's friend Catalina Inocencio reflects upon Amada's quiet strength, even when she and her property had been violated:

Ella nunca se queja de nada. . . . ella es muy paciente. . . . ella es muy optimista, piensa muy positivo, muy bien . . . muy bien de los demás también. Siempre piensa bien de la gente, nunca piensa mal. . . . estoy muy orgullosa de ella y de que ella me vea como su amiga. [Interview, April 21, 2004]

She never complains about anything. . . . she is very patient. . . . she is very optimistic, she thinks very positively, really well . . . really well of everyone else. She always thinks well of people, she never thinks badly. . . . I am very proud of her and that she sees me as her friend.

The Hogan

During the 1990s there were notable changes to Amada's property, which, in turn, brought further changes. The old stone house on the property where Amada, Claudio Sr., and their son had lived for many years prior to Amada moving into her wooden house in 1967 was torn down with Amada's permission. It had been falling apart over the years and had become a safety hazard. In its place, Amada allowed Navajos from the NAC of Navajoland to build a wooden hogan, or ceremonial building, where the old house had stood.

The cement foundation had been laid for the hogan by April 1994. Good quality wood was erected to make the frame and walls. It even had glass windows and a fancy beveled glass door that faced east toward the highway and beyond. The hogan was a much more ornate structure than the modest stone house that previously stood in that spot. When the hogan was completed by December of that year, the Navajos who had built it gave Amada a key to it.[9] Amada told me that the hogan would be for everyone who needed a place to stay, that it was not just for Navajos.

Upon completion of the hogan, select members of the NAC of Navajoland held an inaugural peyote meeting there. As they prayed, they also spoke of how this hogan was their umbilical cord to the sacred gardens and to Amada's place. Use of the hogan was in high demand after that. In the month of December it was reserved every weekend. Prayer meetings by members of the NAC of Navajoland were held at various times of the year, including Valentine's weekend, to coincide with the spring NAC business meetings; this one took place at the Civic Center in Mirando City.

Earlier, in February 1994, Lillian and Jerry Etcitty, Navajos from Aztec, New Mexico, had brought a canvas tepee measuring twenty-seven feet in diameter that Lillian had made, decorated with sixteen stars appliquéd in red and blue fabric surrounding the doorway. It was commissioned through a donation and was made to leave at Amada's place for anyone who needed a tepee for a prayer meeting on her property. Jerry Patchen brought the poles made out of pine trees from a forest located north of Houston to support the tepee. The tepee and poles were intended to help reduce the hardship for people who would otherwise have to transport a large tepee and long poles with them from far away in order to have a prayer meeting on Amada's property. Even so, Roadman Alden Naranjo and his wife, Juanita, who ran the Friday meeting in February, chose to bring their own Ute tepee decorated with bear paw prints from their home in Colorado to Amada's place.

It wasn't long until misunderstandings and tensions led to heated conflict about hogan and tepee meetings on Amada's property. In 1996 during the traditional February meetings on Washington's birthday weekend, there was an explosive blowup over scheduled peyote meetings. According to some elders of the Ute and Oklahoma NAC traditions, it is sacrilegious to have more than one meeting going on at the same time;

doing so constitutes the crossing of and an invasion of one's hearth or fireplace. They were under the impression that, due to the history and protocol of the February weekend meetings, the Navajos had agreed to not run a meeting during that weekend. This had been discussed in advance and they thought there was no problem with this arrangement. Yet, according to some Navajos and their church traditions there is nothing wrong at all with having more than one meeting going on at the same time. The parties involved brought the conflict to Amada for arbitration. Amada was quite upset about having this issue fall on her shoulders; she just wanted everyone to get along. As one might expect, Amada was so concerned about the disharmony on her property that she became ill, and it took days for her to regain her good health and high spirits again.

Amada continued to maintain her open-door policy regardless of the disagreement a few NAC members had about non-natives participating in meetings on her property. She also left it to the roadmen to resolve their differences of ideas about holding more than one meeting on her property on the same night. Eventually she chose her son Claudio to stand in for her when she was no longer able to deal with the conflicts that arose.

In February 1997, the NAC–NA approached Amada to fund the construction of a covered wooden shelter with picnic benches near the hogan. She agreed, and local peyote dealer Salvador Johnson built the shelter and tables. When this project was completed, the NAC–NA placed a plaque of recognition below the awning. At least 150 people came to inaugurate this space over the February 14 meeting weekend. The following weekend there were three instead of the usual two meetings, every night of the weekend, including Sunday.

Following the construction of the covered picnic area, Amada was asked, and again gave permission to members of the NAC of Navajoland, to install a chain-link fence around her property, including a gate topped with an ornate arching metal sign with the words "Native American Church, Spiritual Residence, Hope, Love, Faith, Charity" and a tepee, the emblem for the NAC. Some people were concerned that the construction of the fence and gate might be a foreboding sign of future attempts by some NAC groups to lock up the property, limiting or restricting access to it by other groups. Fortunately, to this day, the gate has never been closed and locked.

Alden "Junior" Naranjo, the Ute roadman who has run the Friday night meeting during the Washington's birthday weekend for many years, comments about these changes:

> It's kind of become a tradition, I guess, you know, Friday night and Saturday night around the third weekend of February. People have come here from different places and I guess there have been times when there have been some misunderstandings, but everything kind of worked out good, you know. And, all the people that have been here have really been for the most part respectful of her place there. And, some of the Navajo folks have built this round house here to be used for a different meeting time, maybe when it is cold weather or whatever, use it for a church house. And, I think that she appreciates that also, and some of them have built this fence around here too, and the gate she has over here, and they built that. Donations made by different people, they help build these things. If they can do that, still a lot of people still come down and utilize some of these things built here. [Interview, February 22, 2004]

Amendment to the American Indian Religious Freedom Act

Into her nineties, Amada stayed informed about national issues that concerned the NAC. She was even interviewed for the short film *Peyote Road*, which detailed the legal status of peyote use by church members.[10] The video rallied support for a bill with amendments to the American Indian Religious Freedom Act. Grounded in the First Amendment of the US Constitution, which protects the free exercise of religion, members of the NAC chapters were permitted to use peyote for ceremonial purposes. Despite this recognition by the federal government, state laws and court decisions driven by anti-peyote sentiment eroded the federal law that guaranteed Native Americans religious freedom and the right to use peyote in their religious practices.

This all changed in 1994, with the momentous ratification by the US Congress and President Clinton of federal law HR4230, which was an amendment to the American Indian Religious Freedom Act. This law provided specific federal legislation that directly states, "the use, possession, or transportation of peyote by an Indian for bona fide traditional ceremonial purposes in connection with the practice of a traditional religion is lawful and shall not be prohibited by the United States or any State."[11]

Everyone who came through Amada's place around that time expressed elation about this new legislation. The meeting of the National Council of Native American Churches held in Mirando City in February 1995 was unusually well attended. I arrived with Amada who occupied a place of honor at the table with other officers of the NAC–US, in which she still held the position of secretary.

The Texas Department of Public Safety (DPS) did not share such a positive reaction to the new legislation. Representatives from the DPS explained to NAC members of the council and delegates from affiliated chapters such as NAC of Oklahoma, NAC of South Dakota, NAC of North America, and NAC of Navajoland that there were some gray areas in the interpretation of the new legislation; one major concern was the definition of "Indian," which no longer specified a 25 percent blood quantum. This important detail was later resolved in the Department of Public Safety Drug Rules subchapter on regulation of peyote (Section C 13.50 and 51) in which dealers can only sell peyote to Indians with at least 25 percent Native American blood. Furthermore, sales in person require travel permits issued on official stationery of the NAC chapters with the appropriate names, dates of permit, and signatures of church officials. Representatives from some of the church chapters assured the attending DPS officials that they would abide by these rules. Attendees who strictly believed that peyote was given by God only to the Indians and that non-Indians had no right to use it added that they would be willing to help DPS prosecute non-Indians who obtained and used peyote in Texas. Upon conclusion of the business meeting, many delegates and officers from the NAC arrived at Amada's house and conducted prayer meetings. Representatives from the NAC of Navajoland held their meeting in the hogan, while those from the NAC–NA and some delegates from other chapters concurrently held their meeting in a tepee erected on Amada's property.

A New Tradition: Amada's Birthday Meeting

A new tradition to celebrate Amada and her life began when she turned ninety years of age in 1994, with a birthday meeting in October, followed the next day by a bountiful meal and a birthday cake. An Anglo couple from Austin, Patti and Barry Hamrick, who had met Amada in the early 1990s, later assumed an important role in sponsoring this birthday meeting.

Patti and Barry, or "Bear," as many know him, had a friend in Laredo whose family owned a portion of Rancho los Ojuelos down the road, the same rancho where Amada had been born and raised. In the early 1990s, they participated in a peyote meeting in the countryside near the rancho with some of their Native American friends who knew Amada. In the afternoon of the following day, Amada was invited to lunch with all of them in Los Ojuelos. Amada described this event:

> En marzo [1993], corrió un meeting muy grande en Los Ojuelos. Jasper Gomez [de Taos Pueblo] me llevaba para que yo comiera con ellos . . . y mira tanta gente que no me conocían, y qué cariño y que me saludaron allí en Los Ojuelos. . . . Tanta gente que había allí, habían tantos anglos. [Interview, November 27, 1993]

> In March [1993], a very large meeting was run in Los Ojuelos. Jasper Gomez [from Taos Pueblo] brought me over there to eat with them . . . and there were so many people that didn't know me, and how friendly they were and they greeted me there in Los Ojuelos. . . . there were so many people, so many Anglos.

The next weekend all of them went over to Amada's for the February meeting. Patti explains,

> So we had gone down there and done some meetings on their ranch. And over a period of time after we'd gone up to New Mexico, gone to some meetings up there, and met Jimmy Reyna and [his father] Tellis Good Morning, we started feeling like we might be welcome to start staying, being a part of the community more [at Amada's], because we are not Indian, and with certain concerns about the

appropriateness of being involved in all that. But, over a period of a few years, we started feeling comfortable with it and Jimmy and Tellis would come down to the meeting. And it was like, it was almost like this patron saint of people who were in the peyote [religion]. And, it was, yah, a little bit intimidating to walk into her house and have this elderly lady with all these people surrounding her. And, I guess one of the surprising things to me was that she was very kind and generous and open for hospitality and she told me she wanted me to come back and I just thought she was being hospitable. And, I didn't realize it until the next year when I came back, that she was very upset that I hadn't come back sooner. [Interview, April 25, 2004]

Bear Hamrick elaborates:

And so I sat in on one of those meetings with them, and we saw Amada again, and it was just beautiful the way she remembered me and appreciated me and talked good to me and asked me to come back and prayed for me whenever I had to go home in the beautiful way that she does with the sign of the cross and put her hands together and made sure that I called her when I got home and let her know that I was home safe. For someone who had just met me to basically start treating me like her own beloved son was quite remarkable.

For a while at the beginning, I was just seeing her at the February meetings. And then they started up the birthday meetings in October and then I started going down there and cooking for people, for her, and for whoever came to see her for her birthday, and then I was beginning my massage therapy practice at that time, and I didn't have it well established in Austin, so I was going down to Laredo quite often and working down there so that I could maintain financial stability. And when I was going down there I would go visit her, so at that time I was going to see her quite often. [Interview, April 24, 2004]

Patti and Bear visited Amada more frequently. However, six years after they first met Amada, they separated and eventually divorced. Afterward each would visit Amada separately. But when they were still a couple, Patti explains, "So when we started coming down to Amada's, it's one of the things we did. . . . my ex-husband and I ended up sponsoring four meetings down there, and the last meeting was Amada's birthday" (interview, April 25, 2004). Bear recounts,

> Jerry Etcitty and his wife Lillian were running the meeting, the first one for Amada. And they invited me to sit in there with them, and they needed help cooking in the kitchen, and I enjoy cooking, and there is always a lot of work to be done, and so I volunteered to help. And others would sit around and talk and visit and do what they do down there, and I enjoy helping and so I volunteered to help, that first meeting. [Interview, April 24, 2004]

The birthday meeting to celebrate Amada's ninetieth birthday was such a joyful, momentous occasion that many participants agreed to make this a tradition. The weekend closest to October 26, Amada's birthday, would be when they would hold an annual tepee meeting to honor Amada. Patti informs,

> And during the spring and summer I would ask Amada about who would sponsor the next meeting and Jerry [Etcitty] had gotten thyroid cancer. And so they weren't going to be able to run it and every time I would go down there to ask Amada, "Well, what are they going to do for your meeting?" And she would keep saying, "I don't know. I don't think we'll have a meeting this year." And so finally it got to be September and I was asking her, "What are we going to do for your meeting?" She said, "No one is coming forward to sponsor a meeting for us." And I was being real reluctant, in terms of being non-Indian, and sponsoring a meeting, considering all that political stuff going on down there. And so finally, we had talked about it, and so I asked her, "Well, you know, if nobody else wants to, you know, wants to step up to do it, Barry and I would be glad to do it. We'd like to sponsor that." [Interview, April 25, 2004]

Bear continues,

And I called Jerry Patchen to find out if it would be all right with him and the church hierarchy, for me to sponsor a meeting for her. And got permission to do that . . . and got the president of the Native American Church [of the United States] to run the meeting for us, Anthony Davis at the time, and everyone came together, and everyone showed up even though there was no invitation, and there was a full tepee meeting and a full tepee of people there. And everyone was fed and there was plenty of food for everyone to take home and it was a very joyful occasion. Everyone was happy, and Amada was extremely happy and it worked in all the ways. It was no trouble at all, and from that point on I made a commitment that I would cook for her for her birthday meetings until God called her home. And it was a very special opportunity for me to serve God by serving her and her family and friends on her birthday. [Interview, April 24, 2004]

And so began the tradition of Amada's birthday meeting in October. As in the February meetings, Amada would come into the tepee in the morning to greet and be greeted by everyone with the morning sun. She would go in with her son, Claudio Jr., and his family, and with Nora, her dear friend, caregiver, and adopted daughter, to be fanned off with cedar, offered peyote, morning water, and breakfast.

Manuel Vásquez described this part of the ceremony and how he saw and understood Amada's spiritual essence:

The Native American ceremony has a particular time in the morning where the female energy of the universe is revered. It is symbolized with the water that is brought in, in a decorated water bucket. It reminds us of the fact that life brought us into the world when we were in our mother's womb, in a container of water, you know, the placenta, in the sack that we are in. At that moment, the people in the ceremony acknowledge that all life came from a mother, and if it wasn't for a mother, none of us would be here. And the fact that the way the native people understand it, this whole universe was born of a mother. That God has a mother, that everything begins with the mother, different from some theological understanding where God is a male persona. Most native people understand that life comes from a woman. So when Amada comes in the morning, she emanates that mother-spirit. Because of her age, because of the way she lives, because of her spirit, she is kind of the Mother Creation in person. [Interview, April 23, 2004]

Bear Hamrick reflects upon this moment and the wondrous experience Amada brings into the tepee in the morning:

In the night people are sitting up and they can't lean back and relax and get comfortable, and it is usually tight quarters in there because so many people want to be in there in a limited amount of space. And, your back would be tired and you kind of wish that you could be outside and move around and stretch your legs. Maybe you've been having some hard time with something that you weren't willing to deal with in your life, and maybe you kind of felt crowded in there tonight. Maybe it was hot in there; maybe it was smoky in there. And they'd bring Amada in, in the morning, and she was like this beautiful flower of the medicine. This beautiful orchid in the desert would come in there. Just seeing her, just seeing the joyful look on her face that she would, she would look us all right in the eyes and say, "Thank you very much for being here," and, "Good to see you," and just [be] so thankful that you are here and so happy to see you. It would just be like two days' worth of sleep in just that one look that she would give you. She would just completely refresh you like a cool, cool splash of water in your face, and [it was] just so refreshing to see her so happy that it just made it all worthwhile for the sacrifice of sitting up all night, forgoing sleep and forgoing your comfort in the heat and lack of comfort things that we enjoy as human beings just to see her happy like that. It just brought you into that space of "I'm so thankful that I had this opportunity to sit and pray for this woman." [Interview, April 24, 2004]

Amada's birthday meeting in October was different from the February meetings in that it brought together Amada's family members from near and far. Visitors included her son, Claudio Jr., and his wife, Joanne, from

Minnesota, sometimes Claudio's children, Alan and Cheryl, and always the grandkids—Alan's daughters, Ally and Alison, and Cheryl's little daughter, Rachael. Every year family pictures were updated, often in front of the tepee where the meeting had taken place the night before. Members of the community also came to celebrate Amada's birthday; they would visit together, sometimes sitting alongside other visitors, be they Native Americans, Anglos, or foreigners from distant lands.

Amada's comadre Guadalupe Lira tells of attending the fiesta and recalls that the picnic tables were so full of people that some attendees had to get creative about where they sat:

> Well, when they had this fiesta for her birthday, my *nuera*, my daughter-in-law, we would go to her fiesta and take her a *maceta* [flowerpot] with flowers for her birthday; we would take her that. There would be a lot of people, lot of people, we would sit outside with our plates in our lap . . . because there were no tables, no nothing. We would sit on the bench, and we would eat and stay there with her . . . then we would come inside and talk to her; she would see the flowers on the table in her kitchen. . . . We would stay there with her for a while and we would eat cake, and then we could come home for the night. . . . There were fiestas for her very often, every year . . . every year they would do that. . . . I believe Amadita, she's something very special to these Indians. [Interview, April 21, 2004]

Amada's friend Catalina Inocencio remembers,

> Su cumpleaños, muy bonito que fue. Estaba el tipi grande allá. Yo nunca he visto un tipi ya cerca. . . . Yo recuerdo que vi a Amada muy animada, muy bonita y con mucha gente toda rodeada de todos los indios donde estaban dándola mucha atención, muy bonito. Es lo que recuerdo allá, que la pusieron allá muy arreglada, con sus collares y sus joyas hechas por los indios. [Interview, April 21, 2004]
>
> Her birthday was very nice. The big tepee was there. I have never seen a tepee so close up. . . . I remember that I saw Amada very lively, very pretty and with many people, all of the Indians

surrounding her, paying their respects to her, it was very nice. That's what I remember there, that they placed her there all dressed up with her necklaces and jewelry made by the Indians.

Jerry and Lillian Etcitty, the roadman and his wife, were able to attend Amada's third annual birthday celebration. Jerry had recovered from thyroid cancer, and he and his wife ran a number of birthday meetings to pray for Amada and celebrate her life. They explain how they came to know Amada:

> My name is Jerry Etcitty and I come down . . . I believe it was about 1964 or 1963, that's when I met Amada, that's when I start coming around here. I really found out the first time I come down and see her, this beautiful, beautiful woman. How beautiful a mother, she is, that's what I found out. That's why I really [like to be] around her. I'm happy, the way she cares about you, no matter what skin it is, what color it is, we are all her children. And that's the way that God is, her mind is set up that way. So the way she loves her relatives, her children. So I started coming around, this beautiful country. I see there is a beautiful flower around here, it's beautiful, seeing it that time. So that's how I see her love.

Lillian adds,

> Jerry had already been coming here and he told me, "Let's go down." That's how I met Amada. She just became my mom, just like that. She's done it before, you know, bless [us] when we are leaving. She's really a special person, you know, really, really special. And she made me feel really welcome. That's how I met her. And then Rutherford Loneman, he's the one who talked to us and asked us to bring a new tepee down here, so we did. We brought a tepee down here. And later I learned to start making tepees. . . . So that's how we got started. . . . And I had all these uncles, all the different tribes that we met here, that really helped . . . so she's a very special person. I try my best to be loving and kind, like her. She's really got a big heart. To see her today, it put tears in my eyes. [Interview, February 19, 2005]

A Full Life

With the progression of time, Amada's health was no longer as robust as it had been all of her life. Nora relates, "When she fell one day, because she had gone to the Civic Center for the Senior Program, that is when she broke her ribs, she had fell [sic] on them. Or else she would be walking *todavía* [still]. She got scared." Amada's knees caused her more pain, sometimes agonizing pain in the morning as she awakened, and she was no longer able to walk any distance on her own. She became wheelchair bound, yet resolute to remain at her house to greet and offer her hospitality to all who might come to visit. Nora arranged for her aunt, tía Ana, from Monterrey, Mexico, to stay with Amada and assist her. The two became close companions, and Amada welcomed the company.[12]

Not one to be deterred or feel sorry for herself for being confined to a wheelchair, Amada continued to live life to the fullest, always happy to have people come to her house. Now, when her visitors left, she wheeled herself to the open front door and sat with her arms outstretched, bestowing blessings upon them and praying for their safe travels. She still accompanied Nora as she ran errands or went visiting. For a while, Nora took Amada to the Laredo flea market on the weekends. In one area of the market there was live music. Amada learned and became adept at certain dance moves she could make, sometimes quite lively and animated, from the seat of her wheelchair. Needless to say, she was the "hit" of the market and adored by many who happened to see her there.

Amada's One-Hundredth Birthday Party

A long-awaited moment arrived when Amada reached her one-hundredth birthday. Nora and Amada's family had been planning the celebration for almost a year. Keeping with Tejano traditions, it was a gala event that lasted several days. Nora took care of most of the arrangements. She reserved the Mirando City Civic Center for the party and took care of every detail, including the white tablecloths, lavender napkins, and party favors of candy wrapped in lavender mesh bags tied with pieces of delicate white ribbon with the word "love" repeated in purple ink along its entire length. The balloons and colorful rows of crepe paper adorning the walls and ceiling and a riveting sound system, complete with pulsating lights and DJ, were in place for the event. The meal of Tejano-style Texas brisket, kept just below a simmer in the serving trays, welcomed the guests with its delicious piquant aroma. As described in the introduction, this was a celebration not to be forgotten, for Amada was now a centenarian.

Eloquent words were spoken to honor Amada. Heartfelt expressions of love and appreciation for her, her acts of kindness, and how she has come to symbolize the goodness of humanity graced the atmosphere. Seated at the table of honor, she peered over, capturing the movements, the sounds, the lights, the exuberance. Amada was wheeled down to the dance floor, where she joined the others who danced to the music, showing off the moves she had practiced at the Laredo flea market. A birthday cake, brightly lit with candles, was placed in front of her, and, with a little help, she managed to blow out the candles. Proudly and gracefully with the swoop of her hand she acknowledged everyone's good wishes for her one-hundredth year of life.

That evening Jerry and Lillian Etcitty ran the prayer meeting to honor Amada. Jerry explained, "Maybe we started around thirteen years ago, her birthday meeting. And then my wife, we got together and we would talk about the way she is, and we appreciate her." Lillian added, "For my part, she was always the mother that I never had. I had a mother but she passed on when I was two years old. When I met Amada, I felt like I knew her forever. Like she was the mom, she was there to fill that position. So it made me feel like what I could do for her with love. And try to help her in any way I could as my mother." Jerry continued,

> That's how we always start our meeting for her. This year was our thirteenth year; she's a hundred years. . . . We told them at that time that we were going to run a meeting for you, for your birthday, until Claudio [Sr.] calls you back, then we are going to stop that meeting. So we can be with her that time, that is why we are doing that. We are really happy, we've been doing this every year. That's how we know, that's how we feel alive. [Interview, February 19, 2005]

Prayers for Amada

The tepee grounds on Amada's property, already filled with the energy and prayers of so many who had come on pilgrimages to find answers, to be healed, and to heal others, was charged with the renewal of Amada's life when she was still among the living. In tepee meetings across North America, people would speak about Amada and pray for her health and long life, and they thanked her for all the blessings she had bestowed upon them and the NAC. Salvador Johnson exclaimed,

> Oh yeah, they always talk about her, pray for her, pray for the gardens, her grounds, herself, her health, and everything there is. Probably in a weekend like this, there is usually between ten, fifteen, twenty thousand tepees set up . . . all over the United States and Canada. And I can guarantee you that 95 percent or better of every tepee that is up there is praying on her. . . . and it's something she has earned, and something that only by being involved with the NAC can someone understand the reasons that go behind everything that they owe . . . and devote . . . to Ms. Cardenas, how much love is there. [Interview, April 21, 2004]

Those who knew Amada remember her in their hearts and thoughts, and they pray for her spirit.

Whenever she would sleep, she would hear the drums coming; the Indians were going to come in the morning. She would hear them at night because they would leave the reservations, wherever they were traveling from, and they were always praying and beating the drum. And it would wake her up. And then in the morning we would have Indians out there . . . like magic.

—Nora Martinez, Amada's caregiver, friend,
and surrogate daughter, interview, February 25, 2004

You know, she's a good person, she's a good woman. The time comes, what's going to happen then? . . . Amada, she looks happy this morning. . . . "One more year," she told me, "I don't know after that, I may get old, I guess."

—Bertha Grove, Ute, interview, February 21, 2004

More than anything I think she symbolizes the virtues humans aspire to have. I guess the most evident is that of love. You know, her name in Spanish . . . translates into love, the loved one or the one that loves. I think she symbolizes the attainment of a human who can love . . . unconditionally.

—Manuel Kwautli Vásquez, Tejano/Coahuiltecan, interview, April 23, 2004

Ya la vemos como está . . . como . . . un ejemplo a seguir. Porque ella nos da un ejemplo de ser mejores personas. . . . ella dice que las palabras ayudan, pero el ejemplo arrastra la gente con su ejemplo . . . mejor que las palabras. . . . Ella hace el ejemplo de amor de los demás. Eso es Amada, tan cerca a Dios.

We see her as she is . . . as . . . an example to follow. Because she is a role model of how to be better people. . . . she says that words help, but example leads the people, example . . . [is] better than words. . . . She is the example of loving everyone. That is Amada, so close to God.

—Catalina Inocencio, Amada's friend, interview, April 21, 2004

Chapter 8

Amada's Love

Nora's Care

Although it seemed Amada would never fully experience the mortal effects of aging, it finally became apparent that her body was getting old and frail. No longer able to attend Sunday mass at the local Catholic church, her friends Catalina Inocencio and her husband Oscar came to the house to visit and bring Amada the hostia. Amada told me that eating the wafer made her feel good; it cleansed her of any sins or bad thoughts or deeds, even if she was unaware of them. It made her feel pure.

Once she became wheelchair bound, Amada started having more severe intestinal discomfort. With care from her longtime medical doctor, Dr. Figueroa, and friend and massage therapist Barry "Bear" Hamrick, who healed through body work, she was able to feel some relief from her bodily pains. Nora's aunt, tía Ana, who was Amada's companion and housemate for some time, began to have health problems, too, and returned to Monterrey to be with her family. On top of this, Nora and her family decided to move to Laredo. No longer able to live alone, Amada faced the decision of moving to a nursing home in Laredo or traveling to Minnesota to live out her final days with her son, Claudio Jr., and his family. Desiring to be as independent as possible in a familiar environment, neither of these options appealed to her. Nora, unable to bear the idea of Amada moving away and adamant that she not be put into a seniors' home, generously invited Amada to come live with her and her family in their new home in Laredo. Nora's mom, Teresa Johnson, explains,

> Y Nora, la que tiene, con toda la gente, tiene amistad. Y para que Amadita no la echan por locura, de que le iban a echar a la casa de los viejitos a Amadita, dijo Nora, "No. Por eso la tengo conmigo. A que le echan a la cárcel de los viejitos." Es que Nora se pone muy *attached*. . . . Y le dijo este doctor, le dijo que, "Ya está que tiene que estar en un hospital para los viejitos." Y Nora dice, "No, que no, señor." Dijo, "Me la tengo yo. Mejor me queda ella conmigo en mi casa." [Interview, April 10, 2004]

> And Nora, she forms a friendship with everyone, and in order that they didn't do something crazy and put Amada in a senior home, Nora said, "No. That's why I have her with me. There's no way they are going to put her in a prison for old folks." It's because Nora gets very attached. . . . And the doctor said, "She has to be in a hospital for old people." And Nora said, "No, no, sir." She said, "I will take her. It's better for her to stay with me in my home."

In November 2002 Nora helped Amada relocate from Mirando City to her home in Laredo, where she received love and care from Nora, her husband, Isidro, and their children, Abel and Gracie Martinez. Indians continued to come to Amada's house in Mirando City and were surprised to not find her at home. Some of them had known Amada for many years, others had heard of her and wanted to meet her. Nora received phone messages from her brother and sister-in-law, Salvador and Vicenta Johnson, that Indians wanted to see Amada, and she helped arrange such meetings. Nora realized how important it was for these visits to take place, because many of the Indian visitors saw Amada as a healer and had brought people who were sick. They would place their hands in Amada's and she prayed over them, finalizing her prayers when she made the sign of the cross with her hand. Eventually the visits tapered off because her energy was fading.

Mirando City and the Peyote Gardens in the Twenty-First Century

The Mirando City that Amada left behind when she moved to Nora's house in Laredo has the feel of a ghost town. Wooden houses that line many blocks are abandoned or in serious disrepair. Boarded-up businesses bear only faint traces of signs that identify the services they once offered. After the oil boom, the town went bust. One of the large oil companies, Magnolia, relocated and people had to commute to work. Eventually Exxon bought the company and the operations were moved even farther away.[1] But some of the old-time residents still felt Mirando City was their home.

Amada's friend, Maria Esquivel, recalls that twenty years after the oil boom "everything started going down, down, down, down. Almost gone. Yah, it is such a nice town and people come here don't appreciate [it], but we do. We do, because we live all of our lives here. . . . you leave the door open . . . you leave the windows so you can get fresh air; you don't need to be afraid" (interview, April 21, 2004). Guadalupe Lira, Amada's comadre, voices similar sentiments: "I loved the place, I still do. I don't want to go nowhere else. Die here and be buried. . . . it was good to be living here. You could run and be happy. . . . uh huh, that's what I remember. Running and jumping and having a good time. When you are older you have a lot of problems, but you know there were no problems for me" (interview, April 21, 2004).

Los Ojuelos, the rancho where Amada was born and raised, is sparsely populated on weekends and holidays by families associated with some of the original founding families; in recent times the Texas Historical Commission and the National Park Service have recognized Rancho los Ojuelos as a National Historic District associated with El Camino Real de los Tejas.[2]

The land of the peyote gardens has also changed from the 1990s to the present. The consequences of a full-scale war on drugs can be felt throughout this border area. A high-tech blimp, tethered in a large clearing along an isolated highway, is dramatically lit at night. Known as the Tethered Aerostat Radar System, this hybrid airship provides data to federal agencies to interdict the flow of drugs reaching the US border.[3] Since March 2013 the US government has implemented the use of drone flights to patrol the border with Mexico "under the strategy, known internally as 'change detection.'"[4]

The trafficking of undocumented immigrants also occurs throughout this area. The route that once served to smuggle tequila into the United States during Prohibition is now used to bring people into Texas and beyond. The route passes near Amada's place, and Mirando City serves as a holding site for immigrants waiting for official documents or as a jumping off place for those who will be transported beyond the checkpoints located further from the border.[5]

Nora's mother, Mrs. Johnson, remembers many of the people who lived in Mirando City in the past. Her son adds, "Like when I was in school, there were a lot of people. We didn't have people from outside like now. You don't even know who lives here now. We got too many illegal aliens." Mrs. Johnson exclaims that now, "We are just about ten people that used to live here" (interview, April 10, 2004).

Another potentially catastrophic change to the peyote gardens where Amada was born and lived her entire life is the declining peyote populations. Old-time dealers remember certain areas that were so replete with peyote cactus that it was like walking on a living carpet. Richard Geissler tells of a story he heard about a border patrolman who says early in his tenure he remembers "that along the cliffs, then called the 'peyote road,' it looked like a big green serpent, and when he flies by there now . . . the serpent is gone. You can't tell that there is peyote; before it was the color green, and in the summer it was like a serpent along the cliffs" (interview, April 20, 2004).

Fencing large ranches where peyote grows has made it difficult for dealers and their harvesters to find land where they can gather peyote. If they are able to obtain a lease from the landowners, it is costly, and access is often limited to off-season, when the property is not leased to out-of-town weekend hunters. The degradation of the brush with plows that rip peyote out by the root so it can never grow again is encouraged through Texas Department of Agriculture programs that promote seeding the newly plowed land with buffelgrass to feed cattle and other livestock.[6] The difficulties of access to peyote and the alarming decrease of peyote populations is compounded by the dramatic rise in membership in the NAC, and hence increased demand for peyote for prayer meetings. These concerns were addressed in the 1970s and 1980s by George Morgan, and echoed by botanist Edward Anderson in 1995. The situation has become so difficult for the dealers that their numbers have diminished to three, sometimes four dealers for any given year, down from twenty-seven registered in 1974 with the Texas State Board of Pharmacy and the Texas Department of Public Safety (Morgan 1976:99). Amada remembered the days before dealers had to be licensed and the time when she became one of the first to apply for and receive a distributor's license to sell peyote.

Amada's Good-bye

Living in Laredo with Nora and her family, almost a month shy of her 101st birthday, Amada let out her last breath of air and her heart beat for the last time on the morning of the first day of September 2005. She died peacefully in Nora's arms. It seemed clear to those who knew her well that she was ready to join her husband, Claudio Sr., all her siblings and other family members, and so many Native American friends who had passed on before her. Now, she was finally going home.

That afternoon I received the call from Linda Patchen sharing the news of Amada's passing. I was in my office at California State University, Chico, and with a heavy heart I closed my door, canceled my office hours and classes, and started making plans with my husband, Jim, to travel to Texas to attend her funeral. It seemed like a long journey to the place that I had considered my real home when I lived in Texas not so very long ago. We departed together on Wednesday, September 7.

Nora's home shrine was brightly illuminated with the glow of many votive candles burning day and night. These beacons for the spirits were accompanied by statues of the Virgin. Pictures of Amada and Nora's mother, who had passed away a few months earlier, were illuminated by the candlelight in the center of the altar. It was comforting to see and experience such awe and reverence for their lives, and now for their ethereal presence.

Always attentive to the end, Nora helped Claudio Jr. and his wife, Joanne, take care of the many details involved in sending Amada off well to her next destination, from the dress she would wear to the rosary she would hold in her hands. Amada would look elegant wearing her lavender dress. Nora helped select the coffin itself, flowers for the church display, and an extraordinary blanket of living flowers to grace Amada's coffin. One of Amada's nieces and her husband produced a video made from photos of Amada during many eras of her life. A wake and rosary would take place Friday evening, September 9, in St. Agnes Catholic Church in Mirando City. The little church was filled with mourners from Mirando City, Laredo, and other cities in Texas and across the nation. Indians from Arizona, New Mexico, Colorado, and Oklahoma made the long journey to be there, as did non-Indians from Texas and California, Coahuiltecans, Tejanos, and Mexicans. Their languages and physical and cultural features varied greatly, but what brought them all together was this occasion to honor the life of this tiny centenarian with such a big, generous heart: Amada, the beloved one.

That same evening Alden Naranjo and his wife, Juanita, ran a prayer meeting for Amada on the tepee grounds at her place. All who attended prayed, sang, and drummed to Amada; her spirit was present. It felt as if she came into the tepee with the first rays of the sun for morning water and to be "cedared off." By 9:00 a.m. the next day, everyone from the prayer meeting rejoined those at the church for Amada's funeral mass. By then the church was fragrant with the vast flower arrangements and bouquets that lined the altar. The priest, with purple fabric adorning his robe, was from Mexico. Spanish was his first language, but he delivered much of the mass in English. Friends and family had a chance to express themselves. Jerry Patchen spoke on behalf of Claudio Cardenas Jr. and family. David Clark, the Navajo who was arrested in 1968 upon leaving Amada's property after she willingly sold him peyote for the legal test case, spoke as well.

The mass was followed by the somber funeral procession from Mirando City to the cemetery in Laredo, where Amada would be buried alongside her husband. The line of cars stretched as far as the eye could see. At the gravesite, the priest, now dressed in a brown robe, conducted the Catholic funeral service. Alden Naranjo prayed and purified Amada's coffin with the smoke of burning cedar. Mariachis stood by, and when it was time they sang soul-felt songs such as Juan Gabriel's "Amor eterno" (Eternal Love). It was all so beautiful and so fitting for Amada's good-bye.

The Future of Amada's Place

> Her son, Claudio Jr., has made a statement that these meetings, annual meetings, our traditional meetings, or whatever you call them now, will continue. That's what he said. That people come down and still make those prayers, not only for himself, but also for the memory of his mother. . . . A lot of people have been here to help themselves or come down here and maybe buy some of it [peyote]. And it's been good that they can do that, and hopefully there might be others that follow that road, but Amada's been one of those people who has really contributed to the influence of the Native American Church. Hopefully . . . she could be remembered like that, as a person that has really helped . . . a person that has really contributed to our [national] spirituality. So, hopefully the children will continue to remember that, maybe through photographs or maybe through stories, maybe through materials that are written, whatever, these things really, she'll continue to help people like that. Hopefully we are going to carry these meetings on.
>
> —Alden Naranjo, Ute roadman, interview, February 22, 2004

February 2011
In Laredo, it was George Washington's birthday the third weekend in February 2011. Six years had come and gone since Amada passed away and since I had been at Amada's place for the February meetings. Although I have been back various times since with my husband, Jim, this first return visit to Amada's place for this special weekend meeting tradition with the knowledge that she was really gone was most impressive and memorable. On this visit, Jim and I arrived at her home and found a tepee standing majestically on the traditional spot on the property. The tepee was already full of people, and the entrance flap was closed, signaling the beginning of the prayer meeting. People were milling around on Amada's property; cars and trucks bore many out-of-state license plates, and you could tell that a little bit of Indian Country had come to Amada's again to celebrate the annual February meeting tradition.

The next morning everyone was coming out of the tepee with broad smiles on their faces, with blankets, pillows, and cedar boxes in hand, and expressing good morning greetings to everyone they saw. Claudio Jr., and his son, Alan, also exited the tepee. Alan had flown from California to his dad's home, and together they had driven from Minnesota in time for the Friday-night meeting. The two Cardenas men were surrounded by well-wishers. Jim and I walked into Amada's house. The furniture was in its usual order, and the many photos that had adorned her walls were still in the same places they had been when she was alive. The kitchen was bustling with activity as the women worked together to prepare the midday meal. Gary Perez, the caretaker of Amada's property, and his wife, Debbie, warmly greeted us.

Gary Perez: Caretaker, Keeper, Coahuiltecan

I had been following the events since Amada's passing, and I had met Gary, his wife, and his children, Autumn and Cameron, various times. During this visit to Texas, I was able to speak with Gary in order to document how he had come to be the person overseeing Grandma Amada's place. Here is what he had to say:

> I first learned about Amada from the folks that I started to hang out with back in the early '90s. The Coahuiltecan movement of the Missions' descendants. . . . that kind of took me back to my roots growing up in my hometown. My parents were a part of the Raza Unida movement, and then I started hearing them talk about Grandma Amada, Grandma Amada, we're going to Grandma's house this weekend. Or it's Grandma's birthday. All through the '90s, and I thought it very curious that they talked about this lady so warmly, and I thought, this is interesting, this is what's going on. And I also understood that there were peyote ceremonies taking place on the property with American Indians, federally recognized Indians, and so that was somewhat intimidating.
>
> Like wow, that's special. And at that time in my life, I never sought it out, I thought it was just intimidating enough to say, "You

know, maybe I shouldn't go down there and find out what's going on because it's really none of my business. I haven't been invited."

Mr. Perez's children, who were in their late teens, were invited by a friend of the family from Austin, Cristala Mussato-Allen, to meet Amada and people who came to her house for the prayer meetings. On one of their visits, they helped celebrate Amada's one-hundredth birthday party and meeting. Autumn and Cameron insisted that their father needed to come meet Amada. Gary made an unexpected visit to Mirando City in September 2005.
He continues,

> Before the end of her 101st year of her life on Earth, she passed on and my children said, "Well, now you have to take us. We want to go to the funeral."
> So it was on that day that I arrived in Mirando City, Texas. We didn't know who to talk to. We really didn't recognize anyone, except maybe an elder of mine, Dr. Mario Garza. And we were there for the rosary, and we walked up to the building and there was a man standing outside to our right as you enter the church, the Catholic Church there in Mirando City. And my family walked in first, and he nodded at me and I nodded at him the way we do here in South Texas—it's an acknowledgment—and my kids went inside and I stood behind with my wife, waiting for them to pay their respects, and they went and sat down and I walked up to her. That was the first time I had ever laid eyes on her, ever. It was an open coffin. . . . And I talk about this in the ceremonies when I tell folks about when I first met her, and that was Claudio Jr. standing outside the front door when I walked in.
> When I met Claudio that day, I expressed my condolences, as a matter of fact, the day after the funeral we went back to Grandma's . . . and I noticed he needed some electrical work done, that there were problems. I could see immediately there were problems inside the house with electricity. The plugs looked burned out or unattended. So I said, "Claudio, you know, I am an electrician. Do you need any help with your electrical here? I'd like to contribute somehow. It's a little late, but that's the least I could do."

> And he says, "Yeah, come on back. I'm kind of busy right now. Come back in February, can you come back in February?" I said, "Sure." . . . And I came back in February during the Friday, Saturday-night Washington birthday deal, and I drove up. It was freezing, I will never forget that day; it was so cold. And I walked onto the property and I was looking around at the house, looking at the property seeing what else on the outside, looking at it, what else could I do? How else could I help here? And I noticed that the wires from the house to the transformer, from the pole to the house, were removed and rolled up at the post. And I said, "Man, these guys have got no power."

Mr. Perez waited for Claudio to come out of the tepee, and when he did, Mr. Perez remembers that Claudio had a disconcerted look on his face. Mr. Perez greeted Claudio and they talked about the lack of electricity. Claudio explained that in order for the power company to continue service to Amada's place, they needed to upgrade the service to national electrical code standards.

> And I said, "Well, I am very familiar with those standards. I'll build you a new service. A big one, so that it takes cares of all five lots because that's a pretty big property." And he says, "Well, I really appreciate that." He says, "Look, I want to sit down and have a cup of coffee next door at the Little Red Barn restaurant." So we sat down and we talked. And he sat down and I said, "Well, how you doing? How is everything else?" And he said, "Well, man, I just walked out of that tepee and promised everybody the world. And now I don't know how I am going to deliver it." And we talked about other things. At the time it seemed too much of a personal issue for me to get into. And we had a cup of coffee and we visited and talked about growing up in South Texas and laughed a bit, and even shared some slang. So we were getting a feel for one another. And we realized that we understood the same *plática, el ritmo* [talk, rhythm], or however it is you want to say it. And I said, "Well, you know, Claudio," I said it, I am the one who said it, I understood his need. He wasn't going to say it, absolutely no. Not in that culture.
>
> I said, "You know what, Claudio, do you need somebody to

come check up on the place, every once in a while, every month, every month and a half or so?" And he says, "Sure. You know, Gary, that would be a really nice idea." And I said, "Well," and there I go volunteering my wife, too. And I said, "Well, I don't think my wife would mind if we came down here." And that "Sure, we would be happy to do it." So he reached over and shook my hand, and I said, "No problem." And I felt his shoulder, this relief, just dropped and I recognized that, also.[7]

So we went back into the house and he says, "I want you to sit right here on the couch." . . . So I sat down and he went into the back bedroom, I guess, and he brought out his parents' gourd boxes. And he introduced them as such. He said, "Gary, this is my mom and this is my dad." And he sat down on the couch to my right and he opened both boxes up, and he was sharing all the beautiful things in there, beautiful, beautiful, beautiful things. I had never seen such beautiful rattles and such beautiful fans, and I didn't know how this Native American Church looked, I guess there were images, I didn't have very good images, but I saw this beauty, these plain old cedar boxes open up and this beauty comes out. It was just amazing. . . . He took everything out and gave me his dad's rattle. He says, "Here Gary, hold this." And I held it, and then he put [that rattle and] everything away. . . . he said, "[I am grateful] for all the things that you are going to do here for us and for my family."

Then he closed those boxes and he put them away. Then he came back into the living room with another box filled with correspondence between his mother and the Native American Churches and attorneys. And he said, "Gary, I don't know why I am sharing this with you now," his exact words, "but, here is some of the correspondence that has taken place in the past." He says, "This is a heavily, politically charged piece of property. I just want you to know that I am the boss here, and everything needs to go through me. And if you ever have any questions as to what is going to happen, just call me, ask me, and I will coach you through it." And I said, "Okay."

. . . And then we went outside and he introduced me to everybody as the person who is going to be his eyes and ears here on the property. . . . Of course at that time no one was really greeting me warmly because I was a stranger and like, where did this guy come from? [Interview, February 24, 2011]

Amada's Place: Sacred Grounds, Common Grounds
Amada had steadfastly supported her open door policy to all who came to her place, but the hegemonic actions of a few politically driven members of the NAC brought a change of heart, as reflected in the will she had drawn up. This related to the three lots on her property that were used for NAC gatherings, the lots where the hogan, the picnic tables, and the tepee grounds were located. She had always wanted her property to be welcoming, a gathering place for her family and friends from all walks of life. It had been a meeting place for members of the NAC, a holy place for over fifty years. Of the five lots that made up her property, these three had been highly contested among some politically ambitious members of the churches.

Amada had hoped that the NAC would return to being one unified church with its various chapters, but that was not to be. Instead, the three major churches under the umbrella of the NAC had evolved over time to be the NAC–NA, the NAC of Oklahoma, and the NAC of Navajoland, now known as Azee' Bee Nahaghá of Diné Nation (ABNDN). Over the years Amada had patiently tolerated the bickering and posturing from a few members of the NAC–NA and NAC of Navajoland over her property and the meetings that took place on it, but she finally had enough when one year, during the February weekend meetings, several members of these churches called the Department of Public Safety to interrupt the meeting and arrest a non-Indian, the wife of an Arapaho man, while the meeting was taking place on her property. Fortunately, Jerry Patchen intervened as her lawyer to prevent any such arrest (see chapter 7).

That incident and subsequent conflicts spurred by less than a handful of politically motivated members of the churches of Navajoland and North America concerning roadmen from other churches and non-Indians prompted Amada to revise her will. Gary explains, "Delegates of North America and Navajoland had come and interrupted that Friday and Saturday night meeting in February. They interrupted it. And after that interruption, she wrote a letter and asked them to 'Come to my house and pray, come to the peyote gardens and pray. Leave your politics at home'" (interview, February 24, 2011).

Amada then asked lawyer Jerry Patchen to help her draft a new will that addressed her property and its disposition upon her death. These three lots were to become a land trust for the entire NAC and they were referenced with great sincerity in her will as "Amada's Gift of Love." Mr. Patchen explains,

> Yeah, that was the "Gift of Love." . . . I didn't know her for very long at all, and she started telling me, she's generous, she wanted to leave a portion of her land . . . of the five lots . . . three lots . . . that the house was not on, she wanted to leave to the Native American Church so that they would always have a place to come in Texas to rest, to pray, to put up their tepee together, and so she asked me to help her with that. . . . her gift was not controversial at all, how to make everybody happy, with how it was handled and who was going to control it became a point of conflict. [Interview, April 29, 2004]

Several years before Amada passed away, she, her son, Claudio, and his wife, Joanne, met with an attorney in Laredo. Amada deeded to Claudio the two lots associated with her house with the understanding that she could live in her home until she passed away. Claudio would also be the executor of the land trust of the three lots on Amada's property that she wanted to be shared among all members of the NAC. Claudio Jr. has subsequently strived to honor his parents' wishes. He does not want to show favoritism or special treatment to any one group; rather, he works to keep the gates open to the property so that all NAC members can come to pray (Claudio Cardenas Jr., personal communication, November 23, 2014). Nevertheless, upon Amada's passing, some NAC members were not pleased with the manner in which Claudio Jr. chose to administer the property.

Gary goes into further detail about this:

> When she passed away, there was all this unsaid, this unfinished business between her and the conferences [churches], the major conferences [churches]. And unfortunately it reared its ugly head

soon after she passed away in the form of pressure on Claudio, and the property, and myself. And it was understandable, it really, really was. It's understandable, and now when I look back on it, I think gosh—well the property is still here, you still have access to it. Everything's going to be all right. They didn't feel that way for all those years. They felt disenfranchised. . . . last year, what was the Native American Church of Navajoland, now known as Azee' Bee Nahaghá of Diné Nation . . . had an exodus from the property. . . . it was something that got started by the Billy brothers, Johnny and Tommy Billy. Johnny was the one who initiated this, was my understanding. I don't know what's been written, I don't know their story. I hear it, but I don't know what is concrete. I can only repeat what I heard.

. . . they started this by looking for property further down the road near Hebbronville, for their own, for themselves. And they started this fundraising program and halfway through the fundraising program, Johnny Billy passed away; he died of a heart attack. And they kept on; his brother was going to see it through because he had lost his brother and they had had these plans and Tommy was the one who was really pushing all of this to get through. And he was very proud and very successful, he raised the money.

These representatives from NAC of Navajoland had one last ceremony in the hogan at Amada's place and wanted to present Gary with a blanket to honor the Cardenas family before they left the premises.

Gary continues,

I said, "God bless you." And I shook his [Tommy Billy's] hand and he walked off. They all left. The following day I went to go receive the blanket. About three weeks later I get a phone call from this young man in Albuquerque. He told me that Tommy died of a heart attack, also. . . . And of course, that shocked Claudio and I; we were shocked that Tommy Billy passed away, followed along, you know his brother started it, his brother ended it. Now they are both gone. I mean, that needs to be said, that is shocking. And scary, even . . .[8]

. . . So at some point I felt that I needed to separate this issue of

Grandma and her will because that was some bad taste in their mouths over the way that she changed her will.... And some people are just very unappreciative of the effort that she made to keep it from becoming a mess, a political mess....

And I called Claudio one day and I said, "If you wanted to sum up to these folks what your mother's intentions were, what would you say to them, or how do you want me to express your thoughts about the property?"

And he said, "Well, as long as they are willing to come down, I think we need to be there for them, to keep the gates open. That is what I feel we are obligated to do, to serve them if they continue to come down." And that was a level at which it seemed, I don't know, maybe Claudio was trying to be very pragmatic about this. But it wasn't until years later that I realized about how these meetings began. These meetings began, the main ones, with Amada and Claudio Sr., and it was just their relationship with the Native American Church in the '30s, '40s, and '50s. But it goes further back than that. It goes way back, when Grandma was fifteen years old or sixteen. It was 1920, 1921, 1922, when she made her first peyote chief.... So I am the keeper of those things now... I am the keeper of just that.

But what I learned was that these prayers that were put down both with her parents, then later on here in Mirando City with her and her husband, those prayers by the folks that were born in the 1860s, 1880s, 1890s, the turn of the twentieth century, those prayers that were put down with her folks and then with her and her husband were prayers that were put down so that generation after generation, their grandchildren, their great-grandchildren, their great-great-grandchildren—folks they'll never be able to see, will be able to come back and pray there, in her company, or her and Claudio Sr.'s company, or in the care of the Cardenases' home, however it is that you look at that. That they would always be able to return. And that's what a lot of those prayers are. The first thing that really fascinated me about that place is that folks are so grateful for being able to have a place to come to, to put down their prayers and sit right next to where their fathers sat, right next to where their grandmothers sat, or their great-grandfather, in some cases their great-great-grandfather in Mirando City at the house.

I said, hey, this is huge, this is so that those prayers continue on. So those prayers continue to be answered. If we shut those gates, if it ceases, those prayers stop getting answered. And we cannot, we cannot, we cannot allow that to happen. So we have to defend, we defended specifically for that purpose. Which covers us with Grandmother's intentions. I've told in Arizona a couple of years ago, look, we haven't seen [the NAC of] North America down there in a couple of years. We want to invite you back. And I am not asking you to come back because Grandma made a place for you. We're asking you because your parents, and your grandparents, and your great-grandparents put their prayers down there for you. So that you could come. So that they would be there for you when it's your time. And pray for them, remember them, and then pray for your great-greatgrandchildren. That's what it's for. [Interview, February 24, 2011]

Now, without Amada's presence to keep peace and unity, Gary has worked closely with Claudio Jr. as the executor of the land trust to keep Amada's wishes and dreams alive as well as viable. Gary has visited the officers of Azee' Bee Nahaghá of Diné Nation in Arizona, and with the officers of the NAC of Oklahoma to reiterate that they are all welcome to come to Amada's property to pray and hold peyote meetings.[9] Claudio Jr. also traveled to his mother's home over the years since she passed on, making sure that the timing of his trip coincided with the business meeting of the NAC–NA in Mirando City in April, where he has talked at great length with the officers, ensuring them that they are welcome, as are all the other Native American Churches and their members, as well as non-Indians, to come to his mother's place. The idea that Amada's place, a special land of religious and historical importance, could be used by everyone, NAC members and non-Indians alike, continues to be a source of conflict among some who feel that peyote should only be available to Native Americans. The ability to document one-quarter Indian blood quantum and official tribal recognition by the federal government are both required for membership in the NAC–NA (Maroukis 2010:210).[10] Add to this the growing scarcity of peyote in South Texas, noted earlier in this chapter, in order to better understand these emotionally charged issues that are part of the complex mix of legal, political, religious, and cultural dynamics (Maroukis 2010:210–212).

But there is also a spirit of openness and a desire to honor Amada's wishes. Donations from NAC members, friends, and anonymous donors, in money or in kind, help pay for the property taxes, utilities, and modest repairs and upgrades to the house, structures, and grounds. Mr. Perez has worked hard to keep the gates open and to serve as caretaker of the property. His thoughts on this are:

> I think "custodian" is more realistic. Some people have called me groundskeeper, custodian; some of the natives have called me their keeper, because it is their holy place. "Our keeper here," you know, which is kind of neat. But those are just descriptions that I hear; I don't know what they're calling me back home [laughing]. But I do know probably that if they are calling me anything back home, they're calling me a brick wall. Because I don't let anything get past what Grandma's intentions were. We project it in one direction and if anyone tries to change that, then they are going to meet this brick wall. [Interview, February 24, 2011]

Honoring Amada and Her Wishes

Although he never met Amada when she was alive, Gary has learned quickly and makes the utmost effort to emulate her ways.

> Related to Amada, the very first order of business is to make folks feel at home, welcome them with a smile and some warmth and ask them how they have been and thank God that they made it there safely. I know that is always a part of prayer in ceremony that thank God, that they ask God, or the Lord, or Christ to look after them on the way home and that they find everything back the way they left it. And so I know this journey takes quite its toll, and they concern themselves very much with this journey. So I have made it a point to develop this rapport, this language, about their arrival, about their stay, about what's going on at home, everything

will be all right. About their travel back home, everything will be all right.

They've taught me the language, they tell me through their prayers, or I listen to them. I don't know how that works, really; I hear it and I see that's what I need to pay attention to. And so the conversation and the prayers dictate what it is I am going to say, how I am going to handle things, what Grandma used to do. How Grandma was. Or really, not even make a decision, just sitting down and listening to somebody telling me a story about Grandma. Which is very, very, very enlightening. And I judge my behavior and my character and my actions there by what they tell me. It could be a story or some anecdote that is pertinent to my work there. [Interview, February 24, 2011]

The traditional February meetings over Washington's birthday weekend continue at Amada's place, as does her birthday meeting in October. Additional meetings have been added to the annual ceremonial cycle; in 2010 there were seven. In 2011 two more were added; one meeting run by the Comanches who, years ago, were part of the February meeting when they initially began with Claudio Sr. and Amada, and another meeting held by Lipan Apaches. It seems more than fitting that in the twenty-first century, Gary Perez, who identifies himself as a Coahuiltecan, has become the caretaker, the custodian, and the keeper of Amada's property. After all, South Texas was part of Coahuiltecan lands, and they were most likely the native people who shared the peyote religion with the Comanches and Lipan Apaches before the twentieth century, who, in turn, spread the beliefs and practices to other tribes in Oklahoma and beyond, across Indian Country in the United States and Canada.

As word spreads, Amada's place has the potential to become much more of an international gathering place, a crossroads for native peoples who know and revere peyote to meet and pray together. More than fourteen years ago, I brought my Huichol family to meet Amada and NAC members who were at her place. In more recent times, a delegation of Huichol Indians traveling through Texas to bring awareness to the impending destruction of their sacred places in the peyote desert came to the Mirando City Community Center to attend an international convention of the NAC. They also went to Amada's place and participated in a peyote meeting with NAC delegates, who shared their own concern about the diminishing peyote populations in the United States.[11] With the impact of globalization, Amada's place could emerge as a vortex that continues to bring people near and far together in the peyote gardens of South Texas.

Following in Grandmother Amada's Footsteps
Amada would be proud to see this come to pass. Her wishes for all people who visit her house to be treated with respect may also unfold in wondrous ways she may never have imagined. Her only grandson, Alan, the son of Claudio Jr., comes from an entirely different way of life; he works for Apple near Sacramento, California.[12] He is next in line to keep the Cardenas legacy going.

Gary Perez is generously willing to help make this so. He explains,

Claudio told me, he says, "You know, Gary, tuck him under your wing." And I said, "Yes, sir." He said, "Show him the ropes." I said, "Well, I had to earn this, and he's going to have to earn it, too. Because I appreciate the legacy, the blood line, so forth and so on, that's a given." What a privilege to say Grandma Amada was my grandmother . . . what a privilege. But it's a lot of responsibility, that's all I can say. [Interview, February 24, 2011]

Alan accompanied his dad to the February meetings in 2011. The last time he had been down to South Texas was also the last time I had seen him; it was at Grandma Amada's funeral in 2005. I had a chance to talk with him again after the Friday night meeting, and he shared his thoughts about Amada's place and her legacy:

I had not met Gary before. Yeah, and Gary was, we were just, like, drawn to each other. Really, very, very, very seriously. And this place has moved him.

 . . . I guess I didn't focus again on the land until after Grandma passed away. Because it became a concern to me; there was a point when there was some question about the land. . . . what would happen to it?

What I then realized was that what goes on here is my family's responsibility. We are the stewards of their way, we give them a place to exercise this tradition, and keep it alive, to teach it to the children and keep it going. . . . You go in a meeting and you see the joy, and you can see the elders, they go way back. They talk about when I was here with my daddy, and I remember your grandpa and so that whole lineage that ties people to the past. It's almost like my grandmother is a religious icon. . . . Yes. She really is. . . . she is the water woman.

. . . When my late wife passed away . . . I asked God, what am I stuck here for? What am I supposed to do? . . . the extraordinary thing about the meeting last night was knowing that, "Okay, you asked me long ago why you couldn't come home and this is why—because you have something important to do. And you can't come home until you do it."

Well, you know, I feel sad for people that don't see the blessings in their life. And, I mean sometimes I just get choked up, just thinking about it. All the things that have come my way. . . . But I think it really brings what my grandma is all about here. And that's the thing, Grandma's heart, Grandma's heart. And that's what's important to me because her heart is her will and that's what we want to do here. [Interview, February 9, 2011]

Shortly before this book went to press, I spoke with Alan Cardenas again about his thoughts regarding Amada's land. He confirmed much of what he had expressed to me in February 2011. He feels that it is a "distinct privilege to host his grandmother Amada's place" to ensure that the peyote traditions are kept alive and practiced.

We [the entire family] are very fortunate to have Gary to look after the place and be so invested in its spirituality. Gary helps us to carry on the traditions there—Dad cannot make it out there as much as before, and I and my sisters are one generation removed [from South Texas and the peyote traditions], and so I am very happy and grateful that Gary can keep the spiritual nature and traditions going. [Personal communication, April 23, 2015]

I also stay in contact with Claudio Jr. and Gary, who communicate frequently with each other. Alan's sentiments, Claudio's wise judgment, and Gary's passionate commitment make me optimistic, even enthusiastic, about keeping Amada's legacy alive, and I feel at peace. Amada's wishes for her property are being honored. All that she and her husband, Claudio Sr., had contributed to the wellbeing of the NAC and all its kin will live on. And for me, what matters the most is knowing that Amada graced the lives of so many people and that the memory and teachings of this remarkable woman through her example—about humanity, generosity, kindness, and unconditional love—will live on into the future. It is for these reasons that I have written this book. Many blessings to you Amada, as you shine brightly upon everyone in your beloved peyote gardens.

Conclusion

Amada's Legacy

At the funeral and celebration of Amada's life, her family handed out these printed words in appreciation of everyone who had come to see Amada one last time:

> ¡Mil Gracias! We, the Sanchez-Guadiano Family, have been overwhelmed by your display of love for and friendship to our dear Amada. Your kind gestures are heart-warming and greatly appreciated. Thank you for helping to keep her Spirit alive.

Amada's Spirit

In order to keep Amada's spirit alive, I present some sentiments people have expressed about what Amada means to them.

Aging with Dignity

> She was a very independent lady. And, I used to say, if I ever grow old, I want to be as independent as Amadita. . . . I want to be like . . . Amadita, an independent lady.
>
> —Maria Esquivel, Amada's friend, interview, April 21 2004

She has influenced me in showing me how to be a graceful old lady. . . . if you are going to get old, and of course we all are going to get old, it is better to be a happy old person than a mean, grouchy old person, and be receptive. Where I see a lot of old people shut down, she did the reverse. So, yah, she influenced me in trying, in making me a better person, by the observations that I had. She is very graceful, uncomplicated.

—Jackie Geissler, Amada's friend, interview, April 20, 2004

A Teacher in the Peyote Trade and More

To me she is an . . . angel and saint, [something like] Mother Teresa . . . a very special person. She gave me a lot. And I learned a lot from her. Probably because I do what she used to do, I harvest peyot [sic] and I sell peyot to the Native American people. And probably I've tried to be as dedicated as she was to the sacrament, peyot, and to me it's something I would call it, not special, but I'm trying to find the word for it, great teacher. You know, how dedicated she was to the church, and the peyot is something very special. You have to be very special, it's hard to find words.

—Salvador Johnson, peyote dealer, interview, April 21, 2004

Her Prayers and Good Thoughts

It has always meant a lot to me to know that my presence is honored and to know I am in her thoughts, and that I have been in her thoughts and prayers for the past ten, almost fifteen, years. It means a whole lot to me. . . . those are the things that have helped me continue my path and opened the doors for me to be where I am now. . . . it's really influenced how I am as a therapist . . . finishing up my doctorate and going to work with an Indian reservation or with American Indian people. . . . And I really feel like Amada's thoughts and prayers and intentions will carry me on into the future whether she is here in that physical form or has passed on to the other side.

—Patti Hamrick, Amada's friend, interview, April 25, 2004

Mother, Grandmother, Abuelita and Comadre

> [Amada is] the mother to all the Indians. Yah, they love her, I know they do, because they come to her home every year. And sometimes more, I don't know. But they come to her house and they are welcome. She loves them all. She is a mother to them all, young and old. I think she is a great person, Amadita, for them and for me, too, because she is my comadre. She will always be *mi* comadre Amadita. . . . She is a very good, sweet, and kind person and she loves everybody, she loved everybody.
>
> —Guadalupe Lira, Amada's comadre, interview, April 21, 2004

Amada exemplifies that kind of love that brings that kind of peace amongst all people. I think she even voices that, she voices that "Everyone is my children." She is that motherly figure that everyone can relate to. If the pope is the fatherly figure for Catholics, then Amada is that motherly figure for the Native American Church. . . .

She is an example for the Chicano people who are in limbo, in terms of being recognized as a native people. There is a big struggle now for Chicano people for themselves to recognize their native roots. Amada has done it in a very natural way. She did not do it by politicization . . . it just came to her in a very natural way. She is an example of how the Chicano people . . . are going back to their native roots. So when I see her, it gives me hope and it gives me a lot of encouragement to keep that going. Amada . . . she is a Chicana, she is an *indígena*, she is a *mexicana*. It gives me a lot of hope that other Chicanos and Mexicans will embrace their native culture, as a way to live a better life. To live a life like Amada, to be more giving, to be more of a human and not so much caught up in the material world. But to strengthen their links to what you would call the spiritual aspects of life. . . . She is like a saint, that someone would pray to, to ask for assistance. So she will be around for a long time in our hearts.

—Manuel Vásquez, Coahuiltecan, interview, April 23, 2004

Wise Lessons Amada Emulated

Amada inspired people, and through her actions, she also sent powerful messages that continue to remind others how to be a better person.

Compassion and Service to Others

> Well, I think my mom . . . just her being, having the idea that she is just an ordinary person. And that she wants to help where she can or who she can. And that's been her philosophy, throughout. . . . and you know she has always been a special person for me all my life."
>
> —Claudio Cardenas Jr., Amada's son, interview, October 24, 2004

> Amada calls me son. . . . the kindness that she has . . . she enjoyed always waiting on us, especially me. You know my vision—I can't see, I'm one hundred percent visually impaired. So she knew that, she was always waiting on me. . . . she would sit all the way across the table from me and make sure that I eat. I think she enjoyed doing all these things for everybody that comes here, all these years. . . . That's the kind of lady she is, kind, and she has that strength, that compassion for human beings. . . . all these years that's how she's been.
>
> —Danny Sandoval, Navajo[1]

> You know, Amada is the heart, Amada's spirit, that caring, sharing, open-hearted, the wonderful nature of Amada is the heart of the Native American Church. And of course her name, Love, she represents love, in the deepest, purest sense of the word. . . . She represents unselfishness, just her service, her unselfish service to others, her doting about to get her coffee pot to serve people. She is delighted in serving people. And in accepting people of all stations in life—poor people, humble people, Indian people, non-Indian, black people, people from all over the world have come, from foreign countries—and she is just open-hearted to everyone. She

knows no distinctions. She represents the true spirit of the Native American Church and what it hopes to stand for. What it, in its ideal way, is or should be.

—Jerry Patchen, Amada's friend and lawyer, interview, April 29, 2004

Respect Others, Work to Resolve Differences

Well, if they never met her, they really lost knowing somebody. People would learn how to be humble. Respect, honor other people. Respect themselves, too. You respect yourself, then you respect other people. That's the way she's been, like that, humble, respects people, she honors them, too. Like I said last night in the prayer meeting, she's been my role model since way back then. It's hard to be that kind of person. Open spirit, open heart, open mind, open home. She's, gosh, the most gracious woman I have ever met. I've never heard her say anything mean towards anybody, I've never heard her say nothing to turn people away. No matter what culture or what race they were. They are all welcome to her house.

—Bertha Grove Davis, Ute, interview, February 21, 2004

Number one, she does not choose or take sides, like the different color skin of people. She accepts everybody, and it makes her very special that she can do that. She welcomes everybody, any one in her home, she makes them feel at home. Being able to come over here, all our relatives to come over here and feel that kind of love would help us in return know how to love and how to understand, and how to be patient, just be careful of what you say and what you do. She's never judgmental, I don't think I have ever heard her say anything about anybody, she just wishes that we all get along.

—Lillian Etcitty, Navajo, interview, February 19, 2005

Have Faith in God, Believe in the Holy Creator

We can't measure up, but Linda and I have tried to integrate that warm hospitality, that warm caring, sharing, greeting, in my own life and in my own home. So, in that way, and in many other ways, she has, she certainly influenced my life. Her steadfast, faithful belief in God, and the Creator, and the wonderful way, humble way . . . a very humble lady. When I would say, well, you know we will see you again, and she would always say, 'God willing.' Never taking anything for granted. Always reminding us in a very subtle and powerful way that we don't know what's going to happen next in our life. And we have to be prepared to just accept God's will. But so, in many, many ways, Amada has taught us so much, and influenced our lives. We are better people, Linda and I are better people because we met Amada, so because we got to see her example. . . . Amada Cardenas is the Mother Teresa of the Native American Church. She has, she has just been a tremendous blessing in our lives.

—Jerry Patchen, Amada's friend and lawyer, interview, April 29, 2004

It is important to know that there are people on this planet that willingly offer themselves to reflect God through their life and be an exemplary reflection of God through unconditional love and that it doesn't have to be someone of a great powerful position, that it could be a sweet humble little woman out in the middle of the desert that can touch thousands of people just by her gentleness, her sweetness, her offering of whatever it is that she has in a loving way that they too can choose that and reflect that through their lives.

—Bear Hamrick, Amada's friend, interview, April 24, 2004

Amada and the Native American Church

An ever-present goal for Amada was the unification of the NAC as a single church that emulates the spiritual principles on which it was founded.

One Church

I remember her telling us . . . this was when I was twenty, I think.

She said that Navajoland should all go back under one church, the North America, the North, I called it. The bigger one, the North America Church. . . . It should all go back under and not separate; it should always be under one, is what she was saying. I don't remember why she was saying that. It seemed to be a major concern for her at that time.

. . . One church, one membership affiliation rather than separate ones. And this is years ago, you know, and now we see it on Navajoland, the concerns there for segregating it. And they have their own beliefs. So way back she had that kind of concern and now we see why that concern was there. There is a need to protect a lot of the originality, I guess, of the faith and love and hope and charity and not to expand on it too much with politics, the new political science, you know.

—Geri Arviso, Navajo, interview, February 16, 2004

Politics Have No Place in the Peyote Way of Life
Along with the sentiment of a unified church, Amada firmly believed that politics had no place in revering peyote and living the true beliefs of the peyote religion. Others echo Amada's conviction and leave politics out of the peyote way of life.

We brought the tepee poles and we left them here [at Amada's]. People started coming over here and having tepee meetings. Kind of been rough years, you know how it is. Caution sometimes. But peyote, the way I see things, spirituality don't mix with politics. Once you get politics in, you're going to get trouble.

—Bertha Grove Davis, Ute, interview, February 21, 2004

We were blessed to have known this woman in those ways, in the holy ways, because what better way to promote peace in the world and become one of those who does everything in peace and speaks peace, and grants peace to those of us who travel that way to make that pilgrimage? And it's through her efforts that we have seen miracles happen.

. . . Amada doesn't see medicine in a political arena; rather, a spiritual arena. And you need to differentiate between the political part and the spiritual part. And that's where she showed us that you can be an ambassador of good will at all times, it doesn't matter, she has that gift.

—Loreta Afraid of Bear Cook, Oglala Lakota, interview, July 16, 2005

She has been the record keeper for the people coming down and buying the medicine, taking back to their tribal homelands, for their own meetings. . . . And in a way, trying to be a peacekeeper so that, like in many church situations, trying to keep the politics out of it so that the people are not arguing about this, that, and the other. Even though it rises up at different times and they try to override her, she is still, because of her grace and her dignity, somehow has kept unity through the church, and her basically standing up for that creed of love, hope, faith, and charity, which the church is established on. And she has been the gatekeeper to the sacred medicine gardens down there, through her basically sitting on that gate altar.

—Bear Hamrick, Amada's friend, interview, April 24, 2004

Amada's Place: Common Ground, Sacred Land

NAC members who knew Amada and her husband Claudio saw them as the caretakers of the peyote, watching over these plant beings. Amada's longevity and her association with the peyote made her a living legend. For the nearly four decades that Amada remained at her home after Claudio's passing, she was a beacon of welcoming light for visitors and friends. She became synonymous with the peyote gardens and the peyote way of life. Her home was, and continues to be, a central gathering place, a common sacred place for all people who follow the peyote road.

Well I guess that is kind of how I was molded. . . . The belief in peyote that these are sacred plants. We believe that Mrs. and Mr. Cardenas watch over these beings here, you know, [they really are alive]. . . . I kind of thought of it that way, you know, all these years. And I still do [think that].

—Geri Arviso, Navajo, interview, February 16, 2004

The nerve center of peyote trade and heart of its tradition in South Texas is at the home of Amada Cárdenas. . . . She has brought the Peyotero tradition, from its probable point of origin at Los Ojuelos to her place . . . [which] has become the Native American Church's religious center in Texas, a place considered sacred by many and, in a sense, the "Peyote Gardens of Texas."

—George Morgan, Amada's friend and geographer,
Man, Plant, and Religion

People are aware [of Amada]. Even if they haven't met her, she is kind of a legend. She is a legend. You do hear people praying for her when they talk about the gardens. Sometimes people pray for the medicine for the garden and for Amada. She is associated with . . . as a guardian, as a protector, as a person that you can relate to when you pray about the gardens. When you are paying reverence to the gardens, you pay reverence to Amada, too.

You know, the tepee grounds there, they [Indian families] give her thanks for being the foundation of a lot of activity that takes place at her home. They see that as kind of a safe haven, as an oasis in all of this madness. Amada's home as a place where you can go . . . as a place of sanctuary. It is like a sanctuary for all native peoples. Regardless [of] the language you speak or what part of this continent that you come from, they acknowledge that she is a unifying force for all native peoples. She is like a grandma for all native peoples. She has that status or stature that, irrespective of your nation, you acknowledge her as the grandma or as the elder woman, the elder for that society, the peyote way of life.

—Manuel Vásquez, Coahuiltecan, interview, April 23, 2004

Amada's Blessings

Anyone who was fortunate enough to have met Amada will forever carry the blessings she lovingly bestowed without a second thought upon all her visitors.

> I recall what a wonderful old lady she is . . . kind-hearted, she had a heart for everyone. And she is loved by everyone. Everyone could see that when they walk into her home. She is right there with her open arms. Always happy to see everybody, and when they leave, well, she stands outside and gives us her blessing, and I miss all of that. So, I just wanted to talk about her like that and I know that she is a real, real blessed lady. She is like a saint. She prays for people, and people get healings, and she prays for our trip over and back, and we always make it over there safely and make it back safely.
>
> —Mrs. Weasel Bear, Oglala Lakota, interview, July 16, 2005

> I don't think anyone will forget the blessing that they had to know this person and good work and good spirit that she expressed.
>
> —Darrel McDonald, Amada's friend and professor of geography, interview, April 27, 2004

With Amada's passing, it has been a bittersweet time for many, a time filled with treasured memories as well as a profound sadness that she no longer walks this Earth. But if you happen to come to her place and walk into her house to be greeted by all the smiling faces in photos of her friends and family, you just might hear from the tepee grounds the distant sound of the water drum, the gourd rattle, and the impassioned songs to the peyote, the Holy Creator, and Amada. If you listen hard enough, you may even hear on the wind Amada's prayers and blessings as they gently embrace the living in the peyote gardens of South Texas.

Mis oraciones que tengo de la antigüedad .. . . . yo rezo mis oraciones . . . para todo el mundo, para todos los vivos, para mi hijo y su familia, todos los que vienen en el camino por acá. Que Dios les dé su mano, les cuide en el camino . . . para todas mis amistades, para todo el mundo.

My prayers are ancient. . . . I say prayers . . . for all the world, for everyone who is alive, for my son and his family, everyone that is traveling on the road to get here. That God lends them a hand, that he watch over them on the road . . . for their families, all of my friends, for all the world.

—Amada Cardenas, 1904–2005

Appendix

Legal Documents and Landmark Charters of Incorporation in Native American Church History

The Native American Church (NAC) of Oklahoma was granted the first official charter of incorporation on October 18, 1918 (Slotkin 1956:62). Membership in the NAC spread with the initiation of new charters; this was a strategy to protect the First Amendment rights of its members and, in the process, develop an organization that was recognized across the nation. In 1934, under the cultural pluralism program initiated under the presidency of Franklin D. Roosevelt, the Oklahoma peyotists amended their charter to permit other NAC groups outside of Oklahoma to be legally affiliated with them. This was implemented as federal Indian policy by anthropologist John Collier, commissioner of Indian Affairs (Maroukis 2010:122–126).

The rise in the number of NAC chapters nationwide prompted NAC of Oklahoma chapter officials in 1944 to amend the original charter and change the name of the church to the Native American Church of the United States (Stewart 1990:239) (see document A).

Some communities of the Oklahoma church later objected to being part of the national group. In 1949 they united and reinstated the original 1918 Oklahoma charter (Stewart 1990:239–240, Maroukis 2010:147–148). The group retained the name of the Native American Church of Oklahoma.

The NAC of the United States, wanting to reinforce its distinctiveness as a national group that was not part of the state-wide Oklahoma group, filed the official paperwork for reincorporation in 1950 (Maroukis 2010:148) (see document B).

The peyote religion eventually spread to First Nation communities in Canada. In order to accurately reflect the international level of membership in the Church, the Native American Church of the United States changed its name to the Native American Church of North America (NACNA) in 1955 (Stewart 1990:243). By this time the Cardenases were major suppliers of peyote to many NAC communities. After Claudio Cardenas' arrest in 1953 for shipping peyote out of Texas to NAC members (as discussed in chapter 4), an amendment was made in 1957 to the NACNA charter. Claudio and Amada became Delegates-at-Large for the NACNA in the State of Texas in 1957. They, along with Frank D. Bushy, were declared to be the "authorized supply agents" for the church (see document C).

More than thirty years later, Native American Church leader Frank Takes Gun, and others, saw the vital importance of regaining a strong legal presence in South Texas. In 1987 the charter for the Native American Church of the United States was reinstated (as discussed in chapter 6). The Cardenas' mailing address was also the address for the church, and Amada Cardenas was one of the officers (see document D).

A formal application process exists to obtain a federal license to sell peyote to members of the Native American Church. Under the umbrella of the Drug Enforcement Agency, the Texas Department of Public Safety (DPS) administers the licensing of peyote distributors. In the application for the Controlled Substance License, the peyote distributor must include the names of his or her employees. This 1977–1978 Certificate of Registration was one of Amada's last distributor's license before she retired from the business. I wish to thank Jody Patterson, DPS Supervisor of Controlled Substances Registration Regulatory Programs, Narcotics Service, for providing me with a copy of this document (see document E).

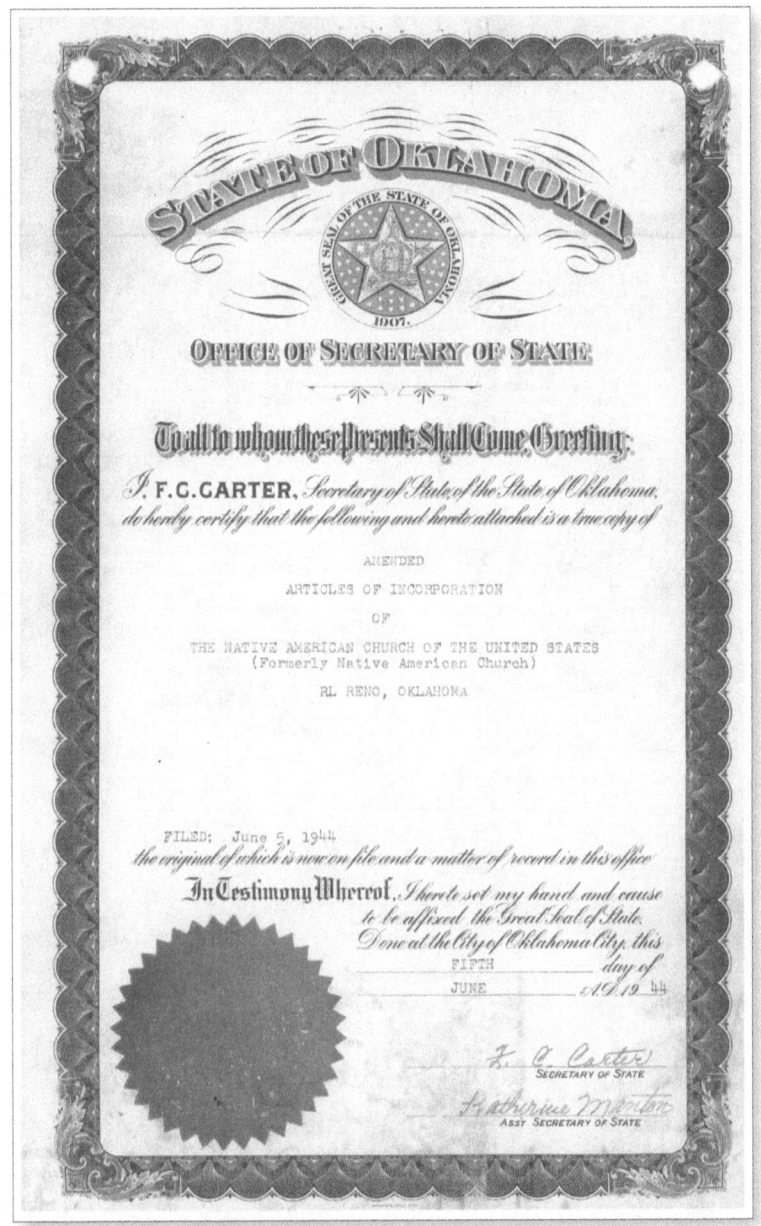

Document A. 1944 charter of the Native American Church of the United States.

AMENDED ARTICLES OF INCORPORATION

WHEREAS, The "human rights" of all citizens of our country are guaranteed and protected by Amendment I to the Constitution of our Country, and

WHEREAS, The Indians of the United States, we contend, are likewise protected by, and come within the meaning of and the protection of the Constitution, and

WHEREAS, They, the Indians, have their own native beliefs and religion known as "The Native American Church" the rituals of which require the use of peyote as a sacrament, the same as wine, that is used by the Catholic and Protestant denominations in their religious ceremonies, and

WHEREAS, These members of the Indian tribes of the United States belonging to the Native American Church, do by these presents declare and publish to the world that they too, in the exercise of their native religion, call upon all liberty loving people of our country for tolerance and that they likewise too, declare their inherent right to protection in the free exercise of their religious beliefs and in the unmolested practice of the rituals thereof, under Amendment I to the Constitution of the United States and in the further pursuance thereof, do hereby propose the adoption of the following, to-wit:

1. That the National name of our Church shall be "THE NATIVE AMERICAN CHURCH OF THE UNITED STATES;"

2. That we as a people place explicit faith, hope and belief in Almighty God, and declare full, competent and everlasting faith in our Church, through which and by which we worship God,

3. That as a people, we pledge our faith and our allegiance and our lives if need be, as we are now doing, to the protection of our new Common Country, its institutions and the Constitution and Government thereof.

4. That we further pledge ourselves to work in unity for, with and through the sacramental use of peyote and its religious use as such by "The Native American Church of the United States" to the interest of and the cause of religion and the cause of our fellowmen, whereupon, they may be, and in allegiance, to the Church to be Chartered and recognized by the United States of America as follows:

We, therefore, recommend that the original Articles of Incorporation of "The Native American Church" and the amendments thereto, now on file in the office of the Secretary of State of the State of Oklahoma, be amended to carry out the purposes set forth in this preamble and we, the undersigned, being all of the officers and trustees of the aforesaid corporation, do by these presents amend the aforesaid original Articles and amendments thereto in the following particulars, to-wit:

AMENDED ARTICLES OF INCORPORATION

ARTICLE I.

The name of this corporation shall be and remain

"THE NATIVE AMERICAN CHURCH OF THE UNITED STATES."
(formerly The Native American Church.")
ARTICLE II.

The purpose for which this corporation is formed is to foster and promote religious believers in Almighty God and the customs of the several Tribes of Indians throughout the United States in the worship of a Heavenly Father and to promote morality, sobriety, industry, charity, and the right living and to cultivate a spirit of self respect and brotherly love and union among the members of the several Tribes of Indians throughout the United States, with the right to own and hold property for the purpose of conducting its business or services.

Document A. (*continued*)

ARTICLE III.

That the place where the principal business of the corporation is to be transacted is at El Reno, Oklahoma.

ARTICLE IV.

The number of trustees of the corporation shall be five, and until their successors are elected and qualified, shall consist of one member of said Church, for each Tribe throughout the United States belonging to or incorporated as a member of said Church.

ARTICLE V.

That said corporation shall consist of as many subdivisions as are Tribes represented in its membership and which said separate tribes shall each in turn seek recognition in their respective States by applying for Charters in accordance with the laws of their respective States but that the name of the parent organization shall be "THE NATIVE AMERICAN CHURCH OF THE UNITED STATES."

In witness whereof, the undersigned, being all of the officers and trustees of the aforesaid Church, do hereunto subscribe our names this 2nd day of June, 1944, in the City of El Reno, State of Oklahoma.

Mack Haag, President — Address: Calumet, Okla.
Frank Takes Gun, Vice-President — Address: Crow Indian Agency, Montana
Truman W. Bailey, Secretary — Address: Red Rock, Oklahoma
Joe Kauleity, Treasurer — Address: Mountain View, Okla.
Alfred Wilson, Delegate-at-Large — Address: Thomas, Okla.

ACKNOWLEDGMENT

STATE OF OKLAHOMA
COUNTY OF OKLAHOMA ss

Before me, Lennie Baker, a notary public in and for said county and State, personally appeared Mack Haag, Frank Takes Gun, Truman W. Bailey, Joe Kauleity and Alfred Wilson, to me known to be the identical persons who executed the above and foregoing instrument and who, each for himself, acknowledged to me that he executed the same as his free and voluntary act and deed for the uses and purposes therein set forth.

Witness my hand and official seal this 2nd day of June, 1944.

Lennie Baker
Notary Public

My commission expires:
February 4, 1945

NO. _____

AMENDED ARTICLES OF INCORPORATION
of
THE NATIVE AMERICAN CHURCH OF THE UNITED STATES.

EL RENO, OKLA.

Formerly Native American Church.

SECRETARY'S MEMORANDUM
OKLAHOMA CITY, STATE OF OKLAHOMA
SECRETARY'S OFFICE.

This instrument was filed for record this 5th day of June, A. D. 1944, at 11:15 o'clock A. M.

Recorded in Corporation Record No._____
at Page_____

F. C. Carter
Secretary of State

By Horace Gettys

Fee $3.00 Charter
      1.00 Rec.
      9.00 6-Cert. Copies
     13.00

Delivered to

Judge Caruthers
Governor's Office
Okla City, Okla.

Document A. (*continued*)

240 | Appendix

Document B. 1950 reincorporation of the Native American Church of the United States.

Document 1

STATE OF ....
COUNTY OF.... Osage .... } ss

Before me, a Notary Public in and for said County and State, on this ....2nd.... day of ...March............19.50., personally appeared ...... Apache Ben ....

to me known to be the identical persons who executed the foregoing Articles of Incorporation and acknowledged to me that they executed the same as their free and voluntary act and deed for the uses and purposes therein set forth.
IN WITNESS WHEREOF, I have hereunto set my hand and seal the day and year above written.

.... *Jean Manan* ....
Notary Public

My Commission expires ..Juny 31st 1954......................

(S E A L)

Document 2

STATE OF OKLAHOMA
COUNTY OF..Craig........ } ss

County Clerk
Before me, a ~~Notary Public~~ in and for said County and State, on this ..20.. day of ..February...........195.0., personally appeared ..Allen P. Dale ....

to me known to be the identical persons who executed the foregoing Articles of Incorporation and acknowledged to me that they executed the same as their free and voluntary act and deed for the uses and purposes therein set forth.
IN WITNESS WHEREOF, I have hereunto set my hand and seal the day and year above written.

.... *Samuel Kraeger* ....
COUNTY CLERK, CRAIG COUNTY
VINITA, OKLA.

~~My Commission expires~~ ....

(S E A L)

Document 3

STATE OF OKLAHOMA
COUNTY OF................ } ss

Before me, a Notary Public in and for said County and State, on this ....7...... day of ..April..............19.50., personally appeared ......Woodrow Wilson..

to me known to be the identical persons who executed the foregoing Articles of Incorporation and acknowledged to me that they executed the same as their free and voluntary act and deed for the uses and purposes therein set forth.
IN WITNESS WHEREOF, I have hereunto set my hand and seal the day and year above written.

.... *Clara Jo. Bender* ....
Notary Public

My Commission expires .My Commission Expires Feb. 16, 1952......

(S E A L)

Document B. (*continued*)

Appendix

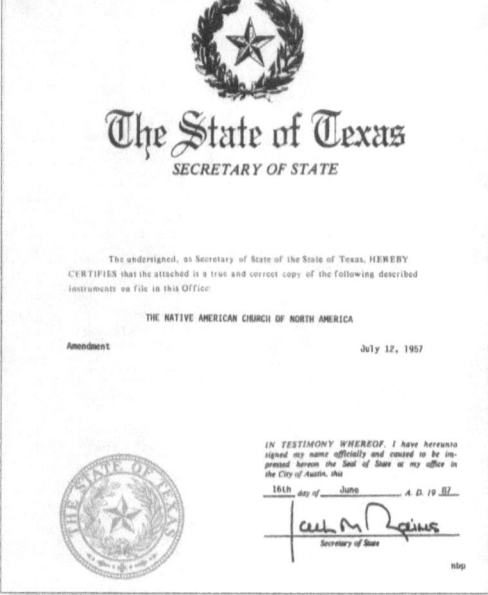

Document C. 1957 amendment of the Native American Church of North America to include Amada and Claudio Cardenas as Texas Delegates-At-Large.

Legal Documents and Landmark Charters of Incorporation | 243

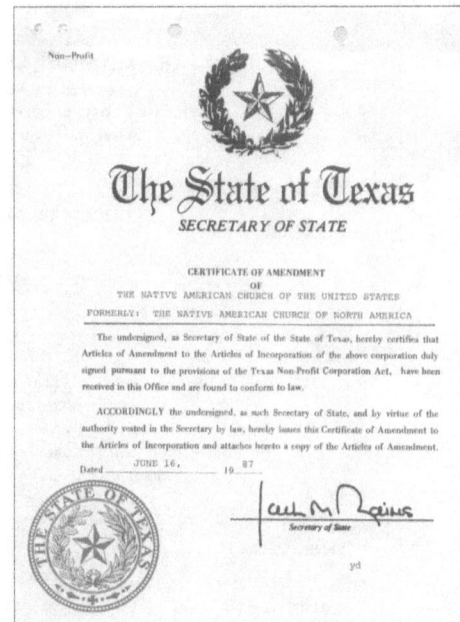

Document D. 1987 charter-reinstatement of the Native American Church of the United States, which appointed Amada as an officer; her home became the address for the church.

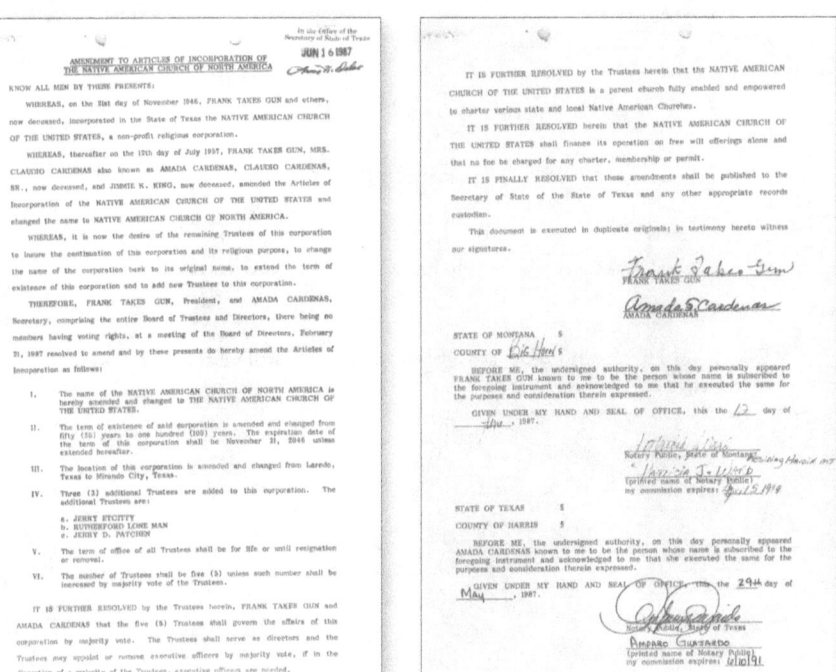

```
                TEXAS DEPARTMENT OF PUBLIC SAFETY
                           Narcotics Service
                    Criminal Law Enforcement Division
                         Austin, Texas 78773

    DPS Number 40029986                              Expires July 1, 1978

                        CERTIFICATE OF REGISTRATION

                             Amada S. Cardenas
                              Name of Registrant

                Highway 649 South, P. O. Box 302, Mirando City, Texas, 78369
                                       Address

                                     For
                             Peyote Distributorship
                      To Members of the Native American Church
                   with not less than 25% Indian Blood and with bona fide
                         membership cards and certifide credentials.

                                  Employee(s)
    Delfino Villarreal
    Ana Maria Villarreal
    Isaac Perez
    Esperanaza Perez
    George A. Chandarlie


         Amada S. Cardenas          has complied with the Provisions of the Texas Controlled
             Name of Registrant     Substances Act. Issued under the Seal of the Texas Department
                                    of Public Safety.
         This the  1st  day of  July                Wilson E. Speir
                                       19 77 .       Wilson E. Speir
                                                 Director, Texas Department of Public Safety

                   THIS PERMIT MUST BE DISPLAYED IN A CONSPICUOUS PLACE
```

Document E. Amada Cardenas's 1977–1978 Peyote Distributorship Certificate of Registration.

Notes

Introduction

1. Shortly afterward my student, Marly—a wife and a mother—graduated from UTPA and I then traveled alone to Amada's home.
2. At this point in time, I was well into work on the book manuscript *People of the Peyote: Huichol Indian History, Religion and Survival*, for which Peter T. Furst and I were editors and contributors. In one of the chapters that I wrote for this book, "The Crossing of the Souls: Peyote, Perception and Meaning," I mention taking Huichol Indian visitors to meet a few dealers in Rio Grande City and a trip to property where peyote grows (Schaefer 1996a:139).
3. Omer Stewart (1990), in his book *Peyote Religion*, briefly mentions Amada's husband, Claudio Cardenas (240–242), and incorrectly identifies Amada as "Amanda Cárdenas from Oilton, Texas" (286).
4. The film *Amada of the Gardens* was made possible with support from the Texas State Historical Commission and the Texas Foundation for the Arts, as well as the City of Austin Cultural Arts Contracts.

Chapter 1

1. "Republic of the Rio Grande," Texas State Historical Association, accessed Nov. 11, 2014, http://www.tshaonline.org/handbook/online/articles/ngr01.
2. Arturo Longoria, a Tejano native of the South Texas frontera, has written extensively in his book *Adios to the Brushland* about this distinctive geographic area and the ongoing threats to this natural ecological region that is so much a part of Tejano culture.

3. The Handbook of Texas Online, Texas State Historical Association, accessed May 1, 2015, Zapata County: https://tshaonline.org/handbook/online/articles/hcz01; Webb County: https://tshaonline.org/handbook/online/articles/hcw05; Starr County: https://tshaonline.org/handbook/online/articles/hcs13; Weather: https://tshaonline.org/handbook/online/articles/yzw01
4. The Handbook of Texas, accessed July 26. 2006, http://www.tsha.utexas.edu/handbook/online/articles/WW/hcw5_print.html.
5. Texas State Historical Association, accessed Nov. 11, 2014, http://www.tshaonline.org/handbook/online/articles/fsa19.
6. Estep 1960, accessed Nov. 10, 2014, http://www.tshaonline.org/handbook/online/articles/bzi04.
7. South of Los Ojuelos, from the late 1820s to the 1880s, steamboats on the Rio Grande were an important form of transportation for merchants and for military war efforts, especially during the Mexican-American War (1846–1848), the Juan Nepomuceno Cortina raids (1859–1860), and the Civil War, when Texas seceded from the Union from 1861 to 1865 (Thompson 1991:40–56). It does not appear that peyote was transported by steamboat.
8. The cattle industry reached deep into Texas. Drives moved cattle to market; later, with the establishment of the railroad, the animals were packed in train cars and transported north and east to stockyards and meatpacking houses.

> In 1868, Texas cattle were shipped to Illinois and Indiana in the early summer. This resulted in the loss of many local cattle. The cattle shipped from these states to Eastern markets died during transportation. This enormous loss in cattle prompted the study of the disease [commonly known as "Texas fever"], and established the danger of allowing southern cattle to be shipped north during the hot weather. In 1885, discussion began of the "infected district" and eventually, the establishment of the "Texas fever quarantine line" in 1891 by Dr. Daniel Elmer Salmon, head of the Bureau of Animal Industry (Mohler 1905:7–8). [Pasquill 2012:2]
>
> It was discovered that the disease was transmitted from one animal to the other by ticks (*Boophilus annulatus*). Upon direction of the Bureau of Animal Industry (BAI), and under a controversial statewide "dipping law" passed in 1918 and implemented in 1919, ranchers began to bathe their cattle, most commonly in dipping vats; the dips frequently were made from various

ingredients, some very toxic if not diluted, which included crude petroleum and arsenic (Pasquill 2012:15, 349).

9. The vaquero tradition continues today. The first vaqueros came to what is now the state of Texas from Spain and Mexico. Later on, Anglo settlers and contract workers learned the skills and traditions of the vaquero. The nearby town of Hebbronville, less than thirty miles from Los Ojuelos, hosts a Vaquero Festival every November to honor and celebrate the vaquero cultural heritage of this region (http://vaquerofestival.net/index.php/our-vaqueros, accessed Nov. 11, 2014).

10. Mario Montaño (1990, 1992) has written extensively on food traditions in South Texas and addresses the meaning of these foods and the ways that they symbolize and reinforce Tejano heritage and identity. His research highlights *barbacoa de cabeza* (barbecued beef head), its history, its preparation, and how this food represents a "cultural practice, one of resistance to and dissent against the values and way of life imposed by the dominant cultural order" (Montaño 1990:5), as it perseveres as a food enjoyed by many Tejanos today.

11. See also Arreola (2002:176–182) for a discussion of South Texas traditions.

12. Basilica of Our Lady of San Juan del Valle National Shrine: Our History, accessed June 17, 2011, and Nov. 11, 2014, http://www.olsjbasilica.org/web/static/history.

13. Many of his followers considered him to be a saint, and a shrine to "don Pedrito" was erected in Falfurrias, Texas; it is still visited today by the sick and by curanderos. The Texas Historical Commission erected a historic marker in 1971 in recognition of the legendary importance of this renowned healer (Arreola 2002:178–179). See Griffith, *Folk Saints of the Borderlands*, and Dodson, "Don Pedrito Jaramillo."

14. Although Texas was ratified into the United States after the Mexican-American War (1846–1848), it took several more years for the state boundaries to finally be delineated. Texas politicians who had governed the former Republic of Texas claimed ownership of eastern New Mexico, Kansas and Wyoming. These were slated to be "free states," whereas Texas, like other southern states, would remain a slave state. Eventually, a compromise was reached in 1850; Texas's state boundaries were reduced in exchange for the US government's agreement to pay the $10 million debt that Texas had incurred when it was the Republic of Texas (see Stegmaler 2012).

Chapter 2

1. I am grateful to Susan Maynard for sharing this interview with Robert Pedro recorded for the video project *Amada of the Gardens* (2006 Maynard/Pratt and Brown production).
2. Furst (1989) provides a radiocarbon date of five thousand BP for "peyote" samples at the Witte Museum in San Antonio, originally collected from the Shumla Caves in Val Verde County, Texas. Terry and his team determined a date of 5,200 years BP for the Shumla Caves samples and discovered that they were actually composed of a mixture of peyote with other plant material, and they appeared to have been intentionally made as peyote effigies (Terry et al. 2006). They also dated material from a string of dried peyotes from Shelter CM-79 near Cuatro Ciénegas in Coahuila, Mexico, at 835 years BP. Bruhn et al. (2002) determined that peyote's main active principal, mescaline, had a history of use for 5,700 years. A subsequent scientific paper included the details of the chemical and dating procedures (El-Seedi et al. 2005). Martin Terry, Department of Biology at Sul Ross State University in Alpine, Texas, is carrying out a population genetics study on peyote growing from South and West Texas into northern Mexico (personal communication, June 26, 2010).
3. Some scholars hypothesize that the mescal bean, which contains powerful toxic alkaloids that could cause nausea, convulsions, hallucinations, and sometimes death, was a precursor to the peyote religion and developed in Mexico and diffused north in ancient times to the southern borderlands of present-day United States. Later, it was proposed that peyote was combined with mescal bean ceremonialism. Omer Stewart (1990:4-8) and Edward Anderson (1996:32-34) point out that there has been a confusion of terms in which mescal was used to refer to peyote, and Stewart convincingly argues that the peyote religion did not arise from mescalism, for the mescal bean is so lethal that its ingestion carries severe consequences. Anderson acknowledges that Catholic priests in colonial Mexico and a few ethnologists in the United States reported that mescal beans were ingested in some tribes by medicine men and in dances associated with war and power. Mescal beans were also made into necklaces, bandoliers, and other adornments worn by peyotists.
4. In the George Morgan Archive (now the George Morgan Memorial Collection at Chadron State College) there is a manuscript written by Omer Stewart

titled "Peyotism in Texas." In this manuscript he provides more text from the correspondence between Gaitán and his superior. On page 10 of this manuscript, Stewart explains how he acquired the text that was published in his book *Peyote Religion* (1990:47). He writes that this "important reference which was supplied to me in March 1979 by Elizabeth A. H. John as a result of my short visit to the Bexar Archives in Austin provides the first data concerning Karankawa peyotism which has become known to anthropologists." The quotations are from Ms. John's translations from the microfilm of the Bexar Archives.

5. James Mooney (1896, 1897, 1898) believed that the Mescalero Apaches were the purveyors of peyote religion in the United States. Following his reasoning, my article "The Peyote Religion and Mescalero Apache: An Ethnohistorical View From West Texas" addresses this as I incorporate Weston La Barre's idea of "differential diffusion" (La Barre 1960) and provide a short history of Mescalero trading and raiding practices. From the evidence I present, I propose an additional route by which the traditional Mexican peyote religion was spread to the United States, from Chihuahua, through West Texas, and into New Mexico via the Mescalero Apaches.

6. Allan Bogue (1977:467) relates that this story comes from page 30 of Mooney's article "The Kiowa Peyote Rite" (1897) and that another of his informants named Häbä told him essentially the same story later. See Mooney 1896.

7. Since 1986 the annual total buttons sold officially and reported by the peyote dealers and recorded by the Texas Department of Public Safety are as follows:

Total of Peyote Buttons Sold 1986 to 2013

Year	Buttons Sold	Total Income to Dealers
1986	1,913,212	$149,307.52
1987	1,766,409	$137,046.30
1988	1,575,766	$129,051.01
1989	1,572,102	$129,618.72
1990	1,772,126	$156,607.29
1991	1,859,189	$182,544.02
1992	1,886,434	$192,695.25
1993	1,978,646	$210,247.60
1994	2,184,739	$246,632.94
1995	2,252,174	$234,750.20
1996	2,258,993	$278,579.50

Year	Count	Amount
1997	2,317,380	$274,500.62
1998	2,076,167	$277,119.71
1999	2,093,335	$335,823.02
2000	2,057,020	$310,722.10
2001	1,934,600	$360,676.00
2002	1,793,914	$404,859.50
2003	1,781,170	$416,727.00
2004	1,669,806	$393,572.50
2005	1,563,534	$407,789.50
2006	1,619,115	$463,714.75
2007	1,605,345	$474,321.80
2008	1,475,469	$463,148.00
2009	1,604,623	$493,834.00
2010	1,483,697	$459,699.00
2011	1,413,864	$466,590.50
2012	1,106.209	$434,609.00
2013	1,363,978	$530,230.00

Compiled from information provided by the Texas Department of Public Safety. I wish to thank Dr. Martin Terry and Keeper Trout of the Cactus Conservation Institute, as well as Leslie Peloquin, License and Permit Specialist 1, and Jody Patterson, Program Supervisor, Texas Department of Public Safety Regulatory Services Division Licensing and Registration Service. These are the totals that are reported by the peyote dealers to this office in the Department of Public Safety.

8. There are a few isolated accounts of Indians traveling through Texas in search of peyote. Stewart (1990:58-60) relates the story of two Lipan Apaches, Pinero and Chiwat (Chivato or Civato), who in the 1870s were reported to have traveled through Texas, consumed peyote, and who were instrumental in spreading the peyote religion.
9. My Huichol Indian friends and consultants who have made numerous pilgrimages to the peyote desert in the Mexican state of San Luis Potosí to gather peyote claim that dried peyote does not lose its potency over time. Martin Terry, botanist at Sul Ross University, comments that prehistoric "peyoteoid" specimens (made from peyote and some other plant material as effigies) from the Shumla Cave in West Texas and prehistoric peyote from Cuatro Ciénegas in Coahuila, Mexico, are the only specimens that have been dated and analyzed for alkaloid content with gas chromatography–mass spectrometry (Terry, et al 2006; El Seedi et al. 2005; Bruhn et al. 1978). Specimens from both sites were found to contain mescaline as well

as tetrahydroisoquinoline (THIQ) alkaloids. However the results are difficult to interpret. Terry writes, "Are we to infer that THIQs are less stable over time than mescaline? Are we to infer (as did Bruhn and Co.) that these two archaeological collections of peyote (and peyoteoid artifacts) are truly comparable. . . . It's hard to do much diachronic interpretation when you have only two data points and they are so far apart in time and the materials are inherently so different" (personal communication, August 2, 2011).

10. The spread of the peyote religion into Indian country and the acquisition of peyote buttons have been documented early on by various anthropologists carrying out fieldwork with specific tribes. Omer Stewart (1990:166) quotes Dr. Ruth Landes's work from her book on the Prairie Potawatomi. He discusses the Potawatomi and the influence of the charismatic Oklahoma peyotist Moonhead Wilson, writing "Ruth Landes (1970:303) provided additional evidence: 'In 1936, the band's cult pioneer, Bill Skishkee, was still around and was reputed to be in his late sixties. He had led the peyotists for some time after introducing the 'buttons,' a Christian-like cross, and dogma from the Oklahoma Osage to the Band's reservation, about 1910.'" Steward also writes that the Prairie Potawatomi, under the direction of William Skishkee, were involved in importing peyote from South Texas near Amada's town in 1901.

11. George Morgan writes that one of the dealers, A. Canales, "indicated that drying medicine on tables was rather recent in Los O. They use to pound caliche rock into powder then wet it and dry peyote. Canales' grandfather was a Peyote trader when he got married in 1870–72! Went into Starr Co. since 1945 because areas had less Peyote in the north and other areas were closed" (George Morgan Archive).

12. George Morgan (1976:74) writes that this event took place in 1908, the couple was from Omaha, and they drove a Model T.

13. From the early documentation of the peyote religion by James Mooney, Weston La Barre, and Omer Stewart, there are scattered accounts of Native Americans traveling to South Texas to purchase peyote. In 1914 a group of ten Cheyenne "peyote boys" traveled from Watonga, Oklahoma, to Laredo, Texas, a journey which at that time usually took nine days. Mooney reports that they purchased several suitcases full of peyote buttons, around 1,400, from a white dealer there (La Barre 1989:57). "Another time a Southern

Cheyenne, then President of the Native American Church, brought back a special trailer full of peyote from Romer [Roma?] Texas. The northern Plains tribes make infrequent pilgrimages for the plant depending largely upon supplies shipped from Texas or bought from Indians nearer the source" (La Barre 1989:57). In the 1930s a Washoe peyotist, Ben Lancaster (also known as Chief Gray Horse), made various trips to the southern border area of Texas to collect and buy peyote, which he then brought back to the Washoe and Paiute people in Nevada and California for ceremonies and to spread the peyote religion. An excerpt from Stewart's four-day interview with Ben Lancaster relates, "'I had cut and dried peyote near Sanderson, Texas, to bring to the Washo,' he said, 'for I knew these Indians needed it'" (Stewart 1984:71). Stewart goes on to say, "At the end of a successful year, during which peyote meetings had been started in three Washo and seven Paiute Indian communities, the 'peyote chief' again made the trip to the peyote fields. From December 1937, to April 1938, Ben Lancaster lived in Oiltown [Oilton], Texas, with his white wife, where he cut and dried peyote" (Stewart 1984b:75).

14. Voegler's narrative regarding Shawnee traditions in the peyote gardens continues, describing the dangers and "magic" of this land.

> The next morning, when the Morning Star comes up, the person goes to the patch where he put the tobacco and when he comes close he hears a rattler rattling. If he has the nerve enough to go over there, he grabs the rattlesnake (which is coiled up on the medicine) and takes it off and then he picks one peyote button from that place. Then he goes to another bunch and picks another button. . . . Perhaps at the fourth spot where he picks his fourth button, the snake is there again and he must remove it.
> [La Barre 1989:57–58]

A few of the peyote dealers I spoke with emphasized that in the spring one needs to be the most vigilant about rattlesnakes when harvesting peyote. From what I have been told, rattlesnakes are especially aggressive then because they have come out of hibernation and are hungry and looking for mates.

15. In my research among the Huichol Indians of Mexico, I have found that it is not uncommon for women to consume peyote during their pregnancies as well as when they are giving birth. From laboratory studies in the literature and anecdotal information I have collected, the mescaline from the peyote does cross the placental barrier to the fetus, and mothers can feel the babies'

responses, which they described as "dancing" in the womb. I have learned from a handful of members of the NAC visiting Amada's house that some NAC women also consume peyote while pregnant; one woman added that she thinks it makes the baby smarter. See Schaefer 2005, 2011.
16. In the NAC prayer meeting, water is ritually presented and consumed around midnight, when special prayers are offered. Often the person who takes care of the fire ritually smokes a tobacco cigarette, prays over the fire, and directs his prayers to everyone in the meeting. In the morning, water is also ritually consumed, frequently around dawn. In the early years of the peyote religion, some tribes excluded women from participating, as has been documented among Mescaleros, Lipan Apaches, and Tonkawas (La Barre 1989:41 n. 81). Over time, there has been greater inclusion of women in prayer meetings. One important female role in the ceremony is carried out by the "Water Woman," who is oftentimes the wife or highly esteemed relative of the roadman. The Water Woman brings in the special morning water, smokes a ritual tobacco cigarette, and directs her prayers to the fire, the roadman, the sponsors, and all the participants before the water is consumed.

Chapter 3

1. See LoneStarLandLaw.Com, accessed Nov. 16, 2014, http://www.lonestarlandlaw.com/Adverse.html.
2. Guadalupe Martínez Laurel (2001) writes that according to her family's reckonings, there remains great controversy in the transfer of ownership of Los Ojuelos from the Guerras to the García brothers who had married into the Guerra family, and that her side of the family continues to contest this appropriation of land with the hope they will regain title to at least some of it.
3. John Salmon Rip Ford was a Texas Ranger who earlier spent time in Los Ojuelos, defending it and the territory to the Rio Grande against Indian raids and wrote about his exploits in the United States' war with Mexico. Afterward, based in "Camp Los Ojuelos," he describes his encounters, battles, campaigns and efforts to pacify Comanches roaming South Texas and into Mexico (Ford 1987:168–184). As discussed in chapter 2, the house in Los Ojuelos where Amada, Claudio Sr., and Claudio Jr. lived had gun turrets on the roof, indicating that it had served as a defensive structure in the past.
4. Elvia Cristan remembers the services that her family's store provided for hunters who came to the area:

We used to have a grocery store and I remember when the Indians would come, they would. . . . camp out where the Cardenases were . . . and buy a lot of stuff [at the store]. Then in the wintertime, when it was season time we had a lot of people in and I recall, I used to help the butcher, Polito, we used to get all the deers and we used to dress them, cut them, it was money. I used to help cut the deer up and wrap it up and wrap up all the meat in portions, and then the skins and wrap them up and I would put them in boxes, and they would come pick them up, they were already dressed, ready to go . . . in the hunting season. [Interview, April 23, 2004]

5. For an excellent exposé of the history and impact of discrimination and corporal punishment on Mexican Americans in Texas that occurred in the segregated educational system, see the video *Stolen Education*, produced and co-written by Enrique Alemán Jr. and directed and co-written by Rudy Luna (2013), distributed by The Video Project (67 minutes). The film highlights the federal desegregation court case of Mexican Americans in the city of Driscoll, north of Kingsville, Texas.
6. For more information on Mexican American women and the roles they played in the war effort during World War II, see Santillán, "Rosita the Riveter," and Portales, *Women, Bombs, and War* and "Tejanas on the Home Front."
7. Tom DeLay was born in Laredo, Texas. According to Raquel Mendieta (personal communication, 2004), he lived the first few years of his life with his family in Mirando City. He later spent most of his childhood in Venezuela due to his father's work in the petroleum and natural gas industry (Wong 2009:17).
8. For information on Las Pastorelas activities in South Texas, see Pastorelas San Benito, Texas, accessed June 18, 2011, http://www.sanbenito.k12.tx.us/schools/bertacabaza/hssb/Reading_Homepage/Pastorelas/Pastorelas.html.
9. I am sincerely grateful to Dr. Nora Cantu for clarifying that "Levantar y acostar el Niño Dios" occurs on Christmas Eve, and for her helpful comments that elaborate on these narratives about Tejano Christmas traditions. For in-depth information on the Tejano tradition of La Pastorela see Cantu, *Offering and the Offerers*, and Flores, *History and Performance in the Mexican Shepherd's Play*.
10. The Tecolotes (Owls) was a baseball team in the Northern Division of the Mexican Baseball League. Founded in 1940, the Tecolotes were also known as

the Tecolotes de los Dos Laredos and the Tecolotes de Nuevo Laredo. The team's home baseball park for most of its existence was the Ciudad Deportiva Estadio in Nuevo Laredo. It was a unique team in that it played baseball games on both sides of the border and its fans hailed from the two Laredos. To the delight of its fans, the Tecolotes won the Mexican League Championship in 1953, 1954, 1958, 1977, and 1989 (Tecolotes de Nuevo Laredo, accessed Nov. 14, 2014, http://tecolotesdenuevolaredo.jimdo.com; http://www.baseball-reference.com/bullpen/Tecolotes_de_Nuevo_Laredo, http://tecolotesdenuevolaredo.wordpress.com/about/).

11. The song Guadalupe Lira referred to was "Sangre de indio," which was popular at this time on the Spanish-speaking airwaves of South Texas.

12. Elvia Cristan relates,

> As I recall, it must have been back in the early '50s or maybe in the '40s. I was sixteen when my father passed away and that was in 1952. And before then, well, my mother had been in the business for a long time. And my father used to work for Mr. Redcliff Killam in the oil fields. And at that time, in his spare time, he used to pick up the peyote and dry it out for the Indians, who came to town maybe once a year. They used to come once a year and have a powwow there. And he had been doing that for a while. And I recall, I must have been around ten or maybe younger, we used to ride down on the jig with him down to the oilfields and he would have us turn all the peyote over because it was drying, we were curious about it, we did not know what it was. But later he put them in burlap bags which were about one hundred pounds and saved them, and then they came and bought it from him. But back in 1952 he had a heart attack and he died. He passed away.

Even years after the Cristan family moved to San Antonio and established a restaurant called Cristan's, Elvia remembers,

> Yes, for years and years, and Dad used to do that [sell peyote] but, it just so happened that Dad passed away and we moved out. And I guess the tradition kept on because later in the years my sister met some of the Indians here at the restaurant [in San Antonio], and they came by because they knew our last name from Cristan's. And they talked about it and she was invited to one of their powwows. . . . I know now that maybe [it was]

the ones that were young at the time when their daddy used to go to the store, I know they [the elders] have already gone, but the children—I guess, the tradition keeps on. Because they still recall way back. . . . it was because we were families, it was an Indian family that used to go. And we got together, it was really nice. And that was a yearly thing that they would go down, and then Dad had all those sacks ready for them. . . . but the whole history stayed back in Mirando with Mrs. and Mr. Cardenas. [Interview, April 23, 2004]

Chapter 4

1. Few historical accounts can be found of such generous relationships between peyoteros and Indians. Frank Cortinas was one peyotero who was obliging to Indian peyotists. He began his career early in 1900 and, according to interviews gathered by George Morgan, Cortinas would guide Indians to the peyote gardens, allow them to harvest without charging a fee, sometimes gift peyote to individuals, and accompany Indians in their religious ceremonies (Morgan and Stewart 1984:282). Other peyote dealers planted home gardens associated with small shrines where Indians could pray and leave offerings during their visits.

2. Bertha Grove Davis's husband at the time of this interview was Vincent Grove. Omer Stewart (1990:292), in his discussion of the Southern Paiute incorporation into the NAC, refers to peyote leader Clifford Jake of Cedar City, Utah. He documents that Clifford traveled to Ignacio, Colorado, in 1972, where he was invited as a roadman to run a meeting sponsored by Southern Ute peyotist Vincent Grove. Stewart also writes,

   > Clifford had taken his family four times to Texas, to the peyote gardens. They visited the fields in Mirando City, Oilton, and Rio Grande City, as well as Laredo. During the last trip in 1968, a miracle happened. He had been searching some time before finding one small plant. He knelt down before it, rolled a cigarette of Bull Durham tobacco, and prayed, blowing smoke over the peyote plant from time to time. When he had finished, he discovered that peyote plants had come up all around him. He need search no more. After cutting some fresh buttons, Clifford bought five hundred dollars' worth of peyote at thirty-five dollars per thousand. In 1974 he still had peyote on hand from that purchase. [1990:292]

3. Allen P. Dale, Omaha, was elected president of the NAC–US in 1946. His tenure as head of the NAC endured for ten years (Stewart 1990:240). On various occasions Mr. Dale and his wife Chris hosted the Cardenases at their home in Oklahoma.
4. Botsford and Echo-Hawk (1996:126–127) point out the double irony of this legislation. For one, the peyote sacrament was referred to as "mescal" *(Sophora secundiflora)*. La Barre explains that "mescal" is a toxic bean that ranges from Coahuila to San Luis Potosí, Mexico, through southern and western Texas, and southern New Mexico. Known by various common names as the "mescal bean," (southern Plains), "*colorín*" (Coahuila, Nuevo León, Texas), "*frijolillo*" (Nuevo León, Texas), and "coral bean" and "mountain laurel" (southern New Mexico), the consumption of as little as one mescal bean can cause death from its narcotic alkaloid, sophorine (La Barre 1989:126). This misnomer for peyote was cause for a court appeal by a Native American. Secondly, peyote continued to be sold over the counter in drug stores as a therapeutic remedy throughout the United States into the 1920s.
5. There are abundant scientific publications on the benefits of peyote. See Schultes (1938), Anderson (1996), and Halpern et al. (2005).
6. Other anthropologists who testified or provided their expert opinion in statements against the bill include Weston La Barre, Vicenzo Petrullo, Franz Boas, A. L. Kroeber, Aleš Hrdlička, John F. Harrington, M. R. Harrington, and Elna Smith. Renowned Harvard ethnobotanist Richard Evans Schultes also made known his opinions about this bill (Stewart 1990:238).
7. In an interesting footnote, anthropologist Sydney J. Slotkin (1956:139 n. 24) states that "'The Native American Church of the United States' incorporated in Texas in 1946 was a clerical error; it should have been 'The Native American Church of Texas.'" I have not found the source upon which he bases this statement.
8. I am grateful to attorney Jerry Patchen for providing me with a copy of the original Articles of Incorporation for the NAC–US enacted November 21, 1946, and the amended Articles of Incorporation document enacted July 12, 1957, under the Secretary of State of the State of Texas, which changed the name to the Native American Church of North America (NAC-NA). Parts of this amended document are cited above in the text. Morgan and Stewart (1984:283) also refer to these Articles of Incorporation of the NAC charter.

Stewart (1990:243) writes that September 8, 1955, was when the charter was amended, changing the name to the NAC-NA during the annual convention of the NAC of the United States. This move was in response to the growing number of Native American groups recognized as peyotists and the incorporation of the Native American Church of Canada in Saskatchewan.

9. Frank D. Bushy was a NAC member from Oklahoma who may have set up residence in Rio Grande City, Texas, in order to ensure supply and transport of the peyote sacrament outside of the state of Texas (Melvyn George, personal communication, August 3, 2011).

10. Various individuals who regularly attended the February meeting related to me that around this time in February it had become a tradition for some NAC members to come to the Cardenases' house and the general area to obtain peyote to take home for future ceremonies. For some it was an ideal time to come to South Texas with the George Washington holiday: they had an extended weekend to make the journey. Additionally, the weather was usually warm and sunny in South Texas and this appealed to most NAC members, who at this time of the year endured the cold, snowy winter conditions in their homelands farther north. It is interesting to note that a number of these Native American pilgrims enjoyed seeing the Washington Day Parade in Laredo as well as going across the border to Nuevo Laredo for shopping and to watch the bullfights. It appears that in the early 1970s, perhaps earlier, the NAC-NA convention began to meet in February in Mirando City, Texas (see Stewart 1990:254). Over the years that I visited Amada in February, the NAC-NA commonly held their business meeting in February at the Mirando City Civic Center and would then hold a prayer meeting at Amada's house in the evening. This became cause for conflict if they held their prayer meeting over the special February weekend meeting at Amada's house on the property at the same time that the original meeting was being run. Some NAC members believe only one meeting should be held per evening, and the purpose of the meeting that falls over Washington's birthday weekend is to pray for Claudio and Amada and their family.

11. In 1898, nearly fifty years after Texas statehood, the Laredo chapter of the Improved Order of Red Men, local chapter Yaqui Tribe #59, chose George Washington as a symbol to reflect their patriotism as Americans; George Washington's birthday became a major cause for celebration with a parade. Over time the celebration has become a month-long event; additional layers of

elite display of legendary individuals combined with Tejano culture were incorporated into the event, such as pageants to honor Martha Washington and Princess Pocahontas, a colonial ball, a US–Mexico bridge ceremony, as well as a jalapeño-eating contest (*By-George, The Official Washington's Birthday Celebration Magazine,* January-February 2008).

"One highlight of the parade is a series of floats featuring the Martha Washington Society debutantes, wearing handmade colonial velvet and satin gowns that cost from $15,000 to $25,000. The society's founders were mostly Anglo women, but today's members and debutantes are mostly wealthy Latinas. Among the Laredo elite, intermarriage has been the rule rather than the exception, and Anglo newcomers still tend to assimilate into a bicultural, bilingual society. . . . We're patriotic Americans because we're Mexicans" (Salon.com, 2000, accessed July 6, 2012, www.salon.com).

I wish to thank Dr. Norma Cantú for bringing to my attention the film *Las Marthas*. In this documentary, filmmaker Cristina Ibarra provides a stunning exposé on the history, pageantry, and the social-economic context of Washington's birthday celebrations, especially the debutantes and the exclusive Colonial Ball that is hosted by the elite Society of Martha Washington (2014, 60 minutes, Independent Television Services [ITVS] in association with Laredo Public Broadcasting [LPB]).

12. I am grateful to Susan Maynard for sharing this interview with Archie Hoffman recorded for the film project *Amada of the Gardens* (2006 Maynard/Pratt & Brown production).

Albert Hoffman is mentioned in Aberle and Stewart (1975:17, 21; 1982:153, 157) in their examination of the spread of the peyote religion from Oklahoma to Utes and Navajos. Hoffman, among other Cheyenne "peyote missionaries" from Oklahoma, is documented as having visited Utes in Ignacio, Colorado, in the 1920s and 1930s and as having had contact with Navajos as well.

Chapter 5

1. Some Indians say that they helped Amada and Claudio buy the house. In actuality it is a matter of perceiving the way it was paid; yes, peyote and the sale of it paid for the house. The Cardenases over the years received donations of money trickling in from NAC members, but this became more common when Amada was a widow (Claudio Cardenas Jr., personal communication, October 24, 2004).

2. Joe T. Sierra is also mentioned by Omer Stewart (1987:243) as an important member of the NAC. In 1956 the annual meeting of the NAC-NA was held at his home in Scottsbluff, Nebraska.
3. Mrs. Weasel Bear continues, talking about her son at Amada's: "We went there in 1970, my son . . . was four years old then. We took him over there. And he found a cake knife in the peyote garden. He did, and he brought it back. We've had birthday meetings for him since he was one year old. . . . he's a leader in the Native American Church . . . he is a born leader."
4. Proper harvesting techniques allow peyote to regenerate. The tops of the peyote are removed with a sharp, flat knife, shovel, or other tool just below the soil line. Buds near the top of the thick taproot can give rise to new growth (interview, July 16, 2005).
5. Jerry Patchen elaborates on the life of Frank Takes Gun:

> Oh, he was a Crow Indian, it was in Montana territory and the Crow Indians were having a meeting and Frank Takes Gun was a young boy, a young teenager. And Big Sheep, there's a case on the books about it, was leading a meeting up there and the US marshals came in and arrested him and all these Crow Indians were, had been up praying all night, talking to God, . . . All night we prayed and all night we had good thoughts, and the US marshals come and they take Big Sheep, and they take our Road Chief away. So all these Crow Indians got together and they told Takes Gun, "You take his wife and you go where they took him and you bring him back." Because he was the only one who could speak English, he had gone to school some. So as a very young man, he got in the buckboard with Big Sheep's wife, went in and convinced the marshal to release him on bond, or whatever. And that began a career—I wish I had time to tell you all I know. [Interview, April 29, 2004]

6. In Kimber and McDonald (2004:194), the sequence of events is not quite correct. It states that Claudio Cardenas became ill shortly after this event and died not long after. Actually, Claudio Cardenas Sr. had passed away in October 1967. The arrest occurred in March 1968 (Stewart 1990:246). By this time Amada was a widow, and she, of her own volition, courageously agreed to sell peyote to David Clark.
7. At the time of Judge Kazen's ruling, the Penal Code of the State of Texas stated, "Peyote is an hallucinogenic drug, and the unlawful possession of same

is specified by Subsection 3 of Section 2 of Article 726-d as amended. The provisions of this subdivision, however, do not apply to unharvested peyote growing in its natural state, but no other exception is made by the statute" (Transcripts of *State of Texas v. David S. Clark* ruling).

8. The stipulation that required 25 percent Indian blood quantum in order to practice the peyote religion was problematic early on, especially for some Native Americans who lack the documentation to validate their ancestry, and for those who have non–Native American spouses and family members. This regulation also had implications for Mexican Americans who have Mexican Indian blood in their family history; the US government does not officially recognize Mexican Indian blood quantum in this formula. In the 1920s there was also a Negro peyote group documented by Elna Smith (1934). The leader of the Negro group, John Jamison, grew up among Indians, and according to his daughter he spoke various Indian languages and was most proficient in the Iowa, Pawnee, and Comanche languages. The meetings he led were held in a tepee and some followers were motivated to attend because of the healing and doctoring Jamison would perform. Evidently, upon his death, this group of Negro peyotists disbanded.

9. George Morgan (1976:104), in his fieldwork interview with rancher Jim Walker, writes, "One rancher insisted that he occasionally finds human skeletons on his land, which he believes are 'wet backs' bitten by rattlesnakes; and he was amazed that no harm had come, as far as he knows to any 'hippies,' since there were such a large number trespassing on his land in the late 1960s and early 1970s."

10. Morgan reflects upon his life and interest in learning about peyote and the peyote trade:

> The Peyote religion also advanced my formal education. One morning as I sat by the sacred fireplace I felt an urgent desire to journey to the land where Peyote grows and study the plant's environment and trade channels. That impulse was prompted by substantial price increases for the plant and occasional supply shortages which troubled the Indians. My university training in geography and plant ecology prepared me to study the biogeography and economic history of peyote. As there was a gap in the literature, I decided that this study would become my doctoral dissertation, and I felt that the knowledge gained from it would help Peyotists

to secure a dependable supply in the future. I spent several months over a period of 2 years in the Texas brush country studying Peyote. . . . I sincerely believe that Peyote guided in this study. [Morgan 1983b:99]

11. George Morgan was buried in the NAC graveyard on the Pine Ridge Reservation, a special tribute to his special status in the local NAC chapter, despite his being non-Indian. He had intended to write about his experiences and lessons learned among Native Americans and the NAC. His untimely death prevented him from completing the book. The chapter he contributed, titled "Recollections of the Peyote Road," in the book *Psychedelic Reflections* (Grinspoon and Bakalar 1983) is as far as he got in sharing his story.

12. A Washoe roadman describes the peyote chief that he keeps with his other sacred objects as follows:

> Here is the main things I got in there. This little box here got my Chiefs in it. When we get a load of Peyote I go through and pick out some of the biggest ones. They is the oldest. Them's the ones you can hear singing sometimes where they grow. This big one here is my special Chief now. When I put him on the Moon I put some sage under him . . . that's his mattress. . . . I keep my mind on my Chief button all through the meeting. Sometimes he tells me something . . . what I done wrong or how I can get over a tough spot. Sometimes that white hair sticking out of his head there starts to shine so bright it hurts my eyes. Like the sun. It gets bigger and bigger until everything is bright like daytime. I can see right out of the Tipi and all around. I can see everything going on.
>
> Some guys eat their Chief button when they got to have special help. I never did that. When they get dried up I put them in this little tin box where I keep the new Chief I'm using. That way the old ones see what's going on and help the new Chief along. [d'Azevedo 2006:10–11]

13. The protective powers of peyote chiefs have been described by various Native Americans. War Eagle, from the Delaware tribe, related to anthropologist Frank Gouldsmith Speck about a man who suffered from nerve gas in World War II and was deemed a hopeless case was cured by "Father peyote." Story has it that Comanche chief Quanah Parker carried a peyote chief hung to his chest to protect him in battle. And a Ponca tradition "tells of J.W. and his wife returning home as a cyclone was coming up; when they finally arrived the

house was destroyed, but in an undisturbed drawer they found four articles still intact: a 'peyote chief,' a bag of peyotes, a Bible, and a peyote drumstick" (La Barre 1989:25 n. 11).

14. From the earliest documentation on peyote use among American Indians, a number of reports describe the importance of its use for healing or medicinal purposes, "doctoring," as La Barre (1989:58, 85–88) refers to this intentional use. Even Schultes (1938:703–704) writes that from his observations, the therapeutic use of peyote, especially its medicinal value, "has been fundamental in the establishment, spread, and to some extent, the maintenance of the peyote cult." For some NAC members, often the reason for a meeting is for "doctoring," and among Mescalero Apaches, that was the primary purpose for having meetings (La Barre 1989:40, 85). Slotkin (1956:67) writes that peyote is said to cure invalids and that it also cures alcoholism. More recent studies (Halpern et al. 2005) indicate that peyote use in ceremonial context can have salubrious qualities. (See also Maroukis 2010:60–67.)

It is interesting to note that, in this account, Amada drew from the medicinal value of peyote in the healing ritual she performed. In the Texas–Mexico borderlands, *curanderismo* (folk healing) is a long-standing tradition that includes prayer, herbal medicines and healing rituals. In the book *Curanderismo*, published by Robert Trotter and Juan Chavira (1997), they describe this form of folk healing on the borderlands as a syncretic system that integrates early Spanish colonial beliefs and practices with local indigenous ones. As noted in chapter 1, not far from Amada's birthplace of Los Ojuelos lived a famous *curandero* (folk healer), don Pedrito Jaramillo, whom Amada's mother sought out for his healing powers.

Chapter 6

1. Alden Naranjo, also known as "Junior," commented to me in an interview why he continues to lead the Friday night meeting:

> I know there has been a lot of controversy on that though she's the one that asked me. I don't come down here because it's my thing. I come down here because of her. Because of her wishes, what she wants, what she wanted me to do. So that is what I have been doing, on her behalf. To me, she's still the sponsor, she still sponsors these meetings and I think that as long as she's able to be with it, I'll continue to do that. After she's

gone, I don't know what will happen. As long as she is here with us, I'll continue to run those meetings on Friday night. And honor her with that. It is an honor. It is not only an honor for me to come down here and do this for her, but I also come down here to honor her. Honor her, her life, her contribution, her hospitality, just to honor Amada Cardenas. [Interview, February 22, 2004]

2. As discussed in chapter 5, in an attempt to nationalize the NAC, a new charter was incorporated in 1944 under the name of the Native American Church of the United States, and it included many state churches as legal affiliates. The NAC–US came to be considered the "mother church" of the NAC, without replacing the Oklahoma Native American Church. Nevertheless, this move to nationalize the NAC into a single primary church, the NAC–US, did not sit well with some NAC members who favored their old state organization based in Oklahoma. For some NAC members, this was the beginning of a now decades-long schism between some members of the NAC from Oklahoma and others, particularly from the NAC of Navajoland (ABNDN) (Stewart 1990:239–240, 311–312).

By the 1950s the peyote religion was spreading, moving north beyond the US border to some First Nation peoples in Canada. In order to establish greater federal recognition of the peyote religion by these two nations, a new charter was incorporated in 1955 in which the name of the church was changed to the Native American Church of North America. (Stewart 1990:263). When the name was officially changed on the church charter, Amada and Claudio were trustee members of the board.

The original charter for the NAC–US was reinstated in 1987. When Frank Takes Gun passed away, Anthony Davis, Pawnee, became president, and Rutheford Loneman was the vice president/custodian. When Anthony Davis passed away, Jerry Etcitty took on the position of president. After Mr. Loneman passed on, Alden "Junior" Naranjo took his place. Jerry Patchen recounts, "And now since Anthony has passed, that left Junior, Jerry Etcitty, Amada, and I, and I have recently resigned. So, it is now Junior, Jerry Etcitty, and Amada" (interview, April 29, 2004). Since this interview, Jerry Etcitty and Amada have passed away, leaving only Junior (Alden) Naranjo as the sole member. As of this writing there is talk of again reinstating the NAC-US.

3. This law is known as the Comprehensive Drug Abuse Prevention and Control Act of 1970 (Public Law 91-513).
4. See Pevar (2012:17–27) for a discussion of the definitions of "Indian," "Indian Tribe," "Indian Country," and "Indian Title" in relation to federal laws.
5. From the time that the peyote religion was officially reported on the Kiowa, Comanche, and Witchita reservations in 1885, the Bureau of Indian Affairs officials and Christian missionaries worked in concert to prohibit the use of peyote, and hence the practice of the peyote religion (La Barre 1989:293; Stewart 1990:128). Throughout the twentieth century there were legal challenges to some members of the NAC, as mentioned in this and previous chapters. These cases caused great concern from NAC members. They feared that further prohibitive statutes at the state and federal legislative levels and unfavorable rulings in local, state and federal court cases could come next.

> There was also concern about non-Indian use of Peyote. The fear was that the use of Peyote by non-Indians, who sought the same legal right to possess Peyote on religious grounds that the Peyotists had, could result in the loss of such rights by NAC members. There was also a problem in the late 1950s and 1960s about the growing recreational use of Peyote by non-Indians that could . . . lead to restrictive legislation. [Maroukis 2010:184–185]

> NAC leaders such as NAC–NA Presidents Emerson Jackson (Diné) and Douglas Long (Winnebago) "argued that Peyotism is an Indian religion and others should not be allowed to join or partake of the holy sacrament. . . . Jackson is reported to have claimed that at the 1982 convention a resolution was passed supporting the one-fourth Indian-blood-quantum requirement for membership (It is not in the convention minutes)" (Maroukis 2010:201).

> Other reports of such crusade-like actions by Emerson Jackson and the NAC–NA have "gone as far as to report non-Native peyotists to police and urge their arrest. Many of the smaller NAC groups follow the lead of the mother church, which had White members on its executive board and believed that peyote came to the earth for all who want its help" (Epps 2009:170).

6. Philip True later died in the Huichol Sierra Madre of Mexico. This story is told in the book *Trail of Feathers: Searching for Philip True*, by Robert Rivard, Public Affairs Publishers, 2005.

7. I found Keith Basso's book *Wisdom Sits in Places* (1996), which views the idea of "sense of place" from the perspective of Cibecue Apache individuals and contemplates approaches ethnographers can follow in this line of inquiry, to be especially inspirational in understanding the meanings Amada and her place in the peyote gardens have for people. I wish to thank the anonymous reviewer of the manuscript of this book for bringing Basso's work to my attention.

Chapter 7

1. As Bancroft explains, before Coahuiltecans were eventually settled in the San Antonio missions, Indians from areas further south were relocated to the mission near Laredo, which eventually became known as the Presidio de San Juan Bautista (Stewart 1990:27). See chapter 3 for a discussion of mission Indians and peyote use along the Mexico–Texas borderland.
2. The term "custodian" refers to the person authorized by an NAC chapter to buy peyote.
3. Some of these contemporary Coahuiltecans are able to trace their family histories and heritage to the mission Indians of San Antonio, many of whom had been relocated there from their desert brush homelands, including San Antonio proper, that had been claimed and overtaken by Spanish settlers and clergy. Danny Hernandez and the Hernandez Pacheco family can trace their long Coahuiltecan lineage to the San Antonio River Missions; Ted Herrera also documents this cultural history in his family as do Ray Ríos and Isaac Treviño, to name some of these Coahuiltecan families from the missions. Dr. Mario Garza, however, states that his family of Coahuiltecan heritage were never missionized and he is deeply involved in the Indigenous Cultures Institute, a nonprofit organization founded by Coahuiltecans in Texas (Gary Perez, personal communication, November 18, 2014). Its website states, "The Indigenous Cultures Institute is . . . dedicated to the research and preservation of the culture including arts, traditions, ceremonies, and languages of this population. We present historical and cultural information on the identity and ancestral legacy of these original Americans—Native Americans who have millions of descendants still living in Texas and the U[nited] S[tates]." Programs include research projects, a library and archives, workshops and lectures, performances, speakers, a language program, the quarterly *Nakum Journal*, Powwow in the Schools, the Xinachtli Project, and an indigenous

community organizing program, Uniendo Nuestras Organizaciones (http://www.indigenouscultures.org/home accessed April 23, 2011).
4. During my tenure as a professor at the UT–PA, it was common to have students who were majoring in criminal justice in the general education classes I taught on cultural anthropology and Mexican-American culture. Some of these students, upon graduating, went on to work in law enforcement in South Texas, including working for the Border Patrol. I spoke openly about the peyote trade and the NAC in my classes, and through these efforts I would like to believe that my students gained greater cultural sensitivity to the dynamics and peoples involved in this Native American tradition.
5. My Huichol family is not Catholic, but they were vaguely familiar with making the sign of the cross and tried to be polite and follow along. Holy water, on the other hand, was something very familiar to them, as water collected on pilgrimages from sacred springs, lakes, and the ocean has an important role in their rituals.
6. There are various versions in the oral tradition of the origin of the peyote religion in North America. See Anderson (1996:25–31) for several of these stories. See Schaefer (2015:194–196) for a Huichol version of the origin of peyote and the peyote pilgrimage.
7. Navajos in the "old days" also gave Amada wool blankets and loose wool, which she used as stuffing for pillows.
8. While the film project was unfolding at Amada's place, my husband, Jim, and I spoke with members of the film crew, who told us that they had felt alienated from the Mormon Church. Their adolescent sons had been diagnosed as schizophrenics, and no treatments had proven effective until they attended NAC Oklevueha Earthwalks meetings run by James Mooney.
9. Lorenzo Max, some of his family members, and other officers of the NAC of Navajoland took charge of building the hogan.
10. The sixty-three–minute video *Peyote Road: Ancient Religion in Contemporary Crisis* was produced by Gary Rhine in 1996. The review of this video by the Berkeley Media LLC: Catalog is as follows:

> This widely acclaimed, landmark documentary was instrumental in the campaign to have Congress overturn the US Supreme Court's 1990 "Smith" decision, which denied the protection of the First Amendment to the traditional sacramental use of peyote by Indian people.

As timely and relevant today as ever, the film examines the history of European and American religious intolerance—especially toward indigenous peoples—and documents the centuries-old sacramental use of the cactus Peyote in the Americas, where it is integral to the beliefs and ceremonies of one of the oldest and largest Native religions in the Western hemisphere.

The film seamlessly interweaves live-action and archival film footage, historical photographs and paintings, and commentary by members of the Native American church, lawyers, and noted scholars of history, religion, and anthropology.

The film demonstrates how the Court's decision ultimately threatened the religious freedom of all Americans, and chronicles the successful efforts of the American Indian Religious Freedom Coalition, including the passage of the historic 1994 Amendment to The American Indian Religious Freedom Act that legalized sacramental peyote use.

The Peyote Road is both classic and utterly contemporary. It will engage students and will generate analysis and discussion in a variety of courses in Native American studies, religious studies and comparative religion, cultural anthropology, American history and studies, and legal studies. This version of the film includes a 1996 legislative update. It was produced by Gary Rhine and directed by Rhine and Fidel Moreno (Yaqui/Huichol) for Kifaru Productions. The film was written by Phil Cousineau and his eloquent narration is delivered by noted actor and activist Peter Coyote.

11. H.R.4230 text sec3(b)(1), www.congress.gov/bill/103rd-congress/house-bill/4230/text, accessed July 23, 2015.
12. Another crossing of religious beliefs and practices came with the arrival and extended stay of tía Ana's daughter, son-in-law Silvester, and his two daughters. Tía Ana's daughter and son-in-law were spiritualists, followers of the Niño Fidencio religion, and were curious about the NAC practices. Niño Fidencio, formerly known as José Fidencio de Jesús Síntora Constantino (1898–1893), was a folk saint from northern Mexico who was renowned as a healer; his career "spanned a critical phase of the Mexican Revolution during which the Church was openly persecuted" (Murray 2005:109). The religion that arose from Niño Fidencio, known as *fidencismo*, is a syncretic melding of

traditional Mexican Catholicism and nineteenth-century spiritism that continues to have a strong following in northern Mexico, especially in the state of Nuevo León, where Fidencio was born and lived much of his life (Murray 2005:109). Tía Ana's son-in-law, Silvester, participated in one prayer meeting at Amada's and marveled at the intensity of the songs and prayers, and the visual, physical, and spiritual impressions he took away from the meeting. It would come as no surprise if he found a way to integrate these into his own rituals, actions, and special implements, such as the feathered fan he made to use in the tepee meeting.

Chapter 8

1. Raquel Mendieta recalls that by the 1980s, Mirando City's decline had already begun.

   > Way back, all this machinery was still run manually and then it went to power, so then while this was being taken care of by say, ten, twenty men, one man could do the work. So that is the reason why a lot of the people moved out. I can still remember and I can still hear it, and when I first came here I didn't know what it was, but in the night when it was very still and early in the morning you could hear the *putt putt putt putt*. And I didn't know what that was. But it was the engines working, bringing the oil up. And you could hear the sound. [Interview, April 17, 2004]

2. "National Register Research," accessed July 10, 2012, http://www.nps.gov/elte/historyculture/national-register-research.htm.
3. "Broken Neighbor, Broken Border," created November 19, 2010, http://carter.house.gov/uploads/Broken-Neighbor-Broken-Border.pdf; "Rise of the Blimps," accessed April 26, 2011, http://thelivingmoon.com/45jack_files/03files/LTA_Rise_of_the_Blimps.htm accessed.
4. "Drones Patrol Half of Mexico Border," accessed November 18, 2014, http://www.chron.com/news/texas/article/AP-Exclusive-Drones_patrol-half-of-Mexico-border-5889614.php.
5. Richard Geissler explained that a retired Border Patrol agent once told him about the clandestine Tres Torres border crossing that passes near Mirando City.

   > There's three communication towers . . . a mile off the road on that high bluff. And, at night they have that little red light, the airplane warning light,

there's three, they look like a triangle, there are three together and . . . when you come off the river and you start walking through . . . and suddenly you hit a high hill and you get to the top . . . that is one of the few places that on both sides there is peyote. . . . so you are on a plateau and it is called Las Tres Torres [*The Three Towers*]. . . . And you are standing on that and you are looking down to the south and to the west and it just drops down and you can see Laredo dropping down, too, and that is one of the highest points out there, hence why those radio transmitters, those towers are there. So, when they come off the river . . . the illegal aliens, they see those three little lights and that's the beacon, that's your first thing, and then there are several others that are further out. So, there is a series of them, they run. When you get to one, you can see the other one, so you go from tower to tower and that is how you get to Hebbronville. From Hebbronville you are above the border patrol checkpoint and meet up with cars and stuff like that and there is no checkpoint there. [Interview, April 20, 2004]

6. Alden Naranjo explains,

> There are very few places where the peyote grows now, that it's hard to find. A lot of folks that harvest peyote for us are having a difficult time to find peyote. One of the things that . . . I would like to see, is that maybe there would be some kind of conservation of, not only for the plant, but also the animals, birds and animals, like that. So that's, you know, the place where it was, where there was a lot of movement of animals, birds, people, that came in, they're trying to block that off. . . . the habitat for the creatures has been destroyed. Habitat for the natural plant, the cactus, the peyote has been destroyed and it has just been disappearing. So, I talked to a couple of people in Boulder from the nature conservatory and maybe somehow we can get a hold of somebody down here who maybe find those people [who help] who could maybe buy places to help somehow to slow down the process of development in this area. [Interview, February 22, 2004]

In 1995–1996 the Peyote Foundation was established in Arizona by Leo and Raven Mercado, Patricia Byarlay, and Derek Westlund after the Mercados' peyote plants growing in their garden were confiscated by the Pinal County Sheriff's Office. The Mercados, who are not members of the NAC, but value peyote and its religious use as a sacrament, had the charges for peyote possession dropped by the prosecution on the basis of their rights to religious freedom as interpreted for the Arizona Revised Statutes 13–3402. The Peyote Foundation's mission has been to protect and promote peyote and its spiritual use, and intends to accomplish this through education, conservation, and inspiration. A document about the Foundation that Leo Mercado sent to me via fax (June 20, 1996) elaborates on these goals and objectives. For Conservation it states,

> To initiate conservation efforts for the peyote cactus itself. The Peyote Foundation will provide the facility to develop intensive propagation methods which will help insure the genetic safekeeping of the species, the sine qua non of the peyote religion. We will also seek to establish a land trust to provide a preserve on which the peyote plant and the traditional peyote pilgrimages would be protected.

In 1999 task force officers from Pinal County confiscated over eleven thousand peyote plants that the Foundation was growing in a greenhouse. The District Attorney acted on the ruling of a local judge that the Mercados were not protected by Arizona and federal laws regarding peyote and its religious use (http://stopthedrugwar.org/chronicle-old/074/peyote.shtm; http://www.cannabisculture.com/articles/1441.html, accessed July 10, 2012).

Martin Terry, Assistant Professor of Biology at Sul Ross State University in Alpine, Texas, has been dedicating his research efforts to peyote research and conservation, and is a founder of the Cactus Conservation Institute (CCI). CCI's mission is "the study and preservation of the vulnerable cacti in their natural range—starting with peyote and star cactus. To accomplish this vision the latest techniques are being applied to understand these vulnerable hunted species, from their DNA up. All interests are being respected: the regulatory agencies, the Native American Church, the ranchers, as well as the scientific community" (http//www.cactusconservation.org/CCI/CC_Home.html, accessed January 5, 2013).

7. In this part of the interview Gary Perez reflects on his own experiences:

> And then I remembered myself, that look, when I was a little kid and we would go across the bridge in Eagle Pass, and one day I looked up under the bridge and there were all these people living in these shanties underneath Eagle Pass. And I was wondering what was going on there. And I said, "Mom and Dad, why are those people living in such poor conditions?" And my Dad said, "Well, those are Indians." And I said,

"Why do they live like that? Why do they live underneath the bridge?" And my dad told me in Spanish, "Because nobody wants them." And I cried, I cried, and I cried, and I cried, and just couldn't believe that we lived in a world like that. This was in the 1970s—'72, '73, '74. Because we had everything, my folks, of course we had problems with money but, I mean, we had a lot compared to what they had. And so I grew up seeing that we had a lot and other people had so little. Migrant workers would stay with us when they came to pick watermelons or during that time of the year. My mom and my dad would open up their home to their folks, to the elders of that group of people of migrant workers. [Interview, February 24, 2011]

8. Another out-of-the-ordinary experience occurred around the time of the inaugural meeting on the newly purchased property in Hebbronville. Mauro Morales, who had driven up to provide the members with peyote, also had a heart attack near his home shortly afterward. Fortunately, he survived after quadruple bypass heart surgery (Mauro Morales, personal communication, February 10, 2011).

9. Upon the rescinding of the prohibition of peyote by the Navajo Tribal Council and the government of the Navajo Nation in the 1960s, the NAC of Navajoland became recognized as an official charted organization. This church was not affiliated with the NAC–NA. Other Navajo peyotists established charters elsewhere on the reservation. Some of these are the Native American Church of the Four Corners (which became affiliated with the NAC–NA), the Northern Navajoland Native American Church, and other smaller churches (Maroukis 2010:214). Early in the twenty-first century, the name of the NAC of Navajoland was changed to "Azee' Bee Nahaghá of Diné Nation." *Azee'* refers to peyote, and *Azee' Bee Nahaghá* is the peyote ceremony. By changing to this name, the coalition of local groups and chapters that are part of Azee' Bee Nahaghá of Diné Nation, have strived to have peyote and the peyote ceremony recognized by the Navajo Nation as "part of a traditional bona fide Diné Ceremony" (Maroukis 2010:215–216).

10. The membership requirements for the NAC–NA, which technically extends across Canada, the United States, and Mexico, stipulate that those outside of the United States be a member of the First Nations of Canada, or a member of an indigenous group in Mexico (Maroukis 2010:10).

11. In the San Luis Potosí desert, home to the Huichols' sacred peyote land of Wirikuta, the Canadian First Majestic Mining Company secured twenty-two concessions from the Mexican government to extract minerals. There are concerns about polluting the natural environment of this area. The sacred mountain known as Reu' unaxa, an inactive volcano near the colonial mining town of Real de Catorce, will be severely affected by mining activities. An excerpt from the article written by Tracy L. Barnett and translated by Yvonne Negrin on the Esperanza project website (http://theesperanzaproject.org/?s=mirando+city/, accessed July 11, 2012) reports on this gathering in Mirando City. During their visit to Mirando City to attend the International Convention of the NAC, the Huichol delegates and NAC members participated in a prayer meeting in the hogan on Mrs. Cardenas's property:

> MIRANDO CITY, TEXAS—It was an unforgettable meeting of cultures: Lakota and Navajo, Chippewa and Cree, Coahuiltecan and Chichimecan and more, joining hearts and minds with their Wixaritari brothers in a hogan in South Texas.
>
> "Never in my life did I imagine that this moment would come," said Efren Bautista Parra, a diminutive yet powerful marakame, or shaman, and the traditional governor of San Andrés Cohamiata, with tears in his eyes. "Just like the joy of this moment, our suffering brings us together in a bond of brotherhood." Around the fire, cradled in the curve of a crescent moon, the language of spirit transcended words to merge all souls into one.
>
> Efren was one of eight Wixarika leaders chosen by their communities in the highlands of Jalisco, Durango, and Nayarit to travel from their communities to this town in Mirando City, Texas. They were there to attend the International Convention of the Native American Church, a union of Native American peoples of North America dedicated to preserving the right to traditional use of the sacred peyote plant, or medicine as it is known.
>
> "Never did we imagine that there were others who, like us, use the sacred hikuri as we do in their ceremonies and prayers," he said.

12. Alan Cardenas elaborates further when I exclaim that his work is so different from his grandparents' as peyoteros: "I hear you. What I do for a living is that I am a support engineer for Apple Computer. I am a hardware engineer, and I support the consumer desktop line of products, which includes the iMac

computers, and the Mac mini computers, all of them in their various lovely iterations. And I have also taken on wireless peripherals, too. So I do Bluetooth crack pads and keyboards and mice."

Conclusion

1. I am grateful to Susan Maynard for sharing this interview with Danny Sandoval, recorded for the film project *Amada of the Gardens* (2006 Maynard/Pratt & Brown production).

References

Aberle, David F.
1991   The Peyote Religion Among the Navaho. Norman: University of Oklahoma Press.

Aberle, David F., and Omer C. Stewart
1984   Navaho and Ute Peyotism: A Chronological and Distributional Study. *In* Peyotism in the West. Omer C. Stewart and David F. Aberle, eds. Pp. 133–265. Anthropological Papers, 108. Salt Lake City: University of Utah Press.

Adovasio, J. M., and G. F. Fry
1976   Prehistoric Psychotropic Drug Use in Northeastern Mexico and Trans-Pecos Texas. Economic Botany 30:94–96.

Alemán, Enrique, Jr., and Rudy Luna
2013   Stolen Education. 67 minutes. The Video Project.

Anderson, Edward F.
1969   The Biogeography, Ecology, and Taxonomy of *Lophophora (Cactacea)*. Brittonia 21(4):299–310.
1996   Peyote: The Divine Cactus. Tucson: University of Arizona Press.

Arlegui, José
1737   Chrónica de la provincia de n.s.p.s. Francisco de Zacatecas. Hogel, México.

Arreola, Daniel David
2002   Tejano South Texas: A Mexican American Cultural Province. Austin: University of Texas Press.

Basso, Keith H.
1996   Wisdom Sits in Places: Landscape and Language Among the Western Apache. Albuquerque: University of New Mexico Press.

Bender, George A.
1968   Rough and Ready Research—1887 Style. Journal of the History of Medicine and Allied Sciences 23(2):159–166.

Black, F. Michael
1972   Mirando City: A New Town in a New Oil Field. Laredo: Laredo Pub. Co.
Bogue, Allan G.
1977   Routes to Rainy Mountain: A Biography of James Mooney, Ethnologist. Ph.D. dissertation, Department of History, University of Wisconsin, Madison.
Botsford, James, and Walter B. Echo-Hawk
1996   The Legal Tango: *The Native American Church v. The United States of America. In* One Nation Under God: The Triumph of the Native American Church. Huston Smith and Reuben Snake, eds. Pp. 125–142. Santa Fe, New Mexico: Clear Light Publishers.
Boyd, Carolyn E., and J. Philip Dering
1996   Medicinal and Hallucinogenic Plants Identified in the Sediments and Pictographs of the Lower Pecos, Texas Archaic. Antiquity 70(268):256–275.
Brooks County Historical Survey Committee
1990   Don Pedrito Jaramillo.
Bruhn, Jan G., J. E. Lindgren, B. Homstedt, and J. M. Adovasio
1978   Peyote Alkaloids: Identification in a Prehistoric Specimen of *Lophophora* from Coahuila, Mexico. Science 199(4336):1437–1438.
Cabeza de Vaca, Álvar Núñez
1999   The Narrative of Cabeza de Vaca. Rolena Adorno and Patrick Charles Pautz, eds. and trans. Lincoln: University of Nebraska Press.
Calabrese, Joseph D.
1997   Spiritual Healing and Human Development in the Native American Church: Toward a Cultural Psychiatry of Peyote. Psychoanalytic Review 84(2):237–255.
2001   The Supreme Court Versus Peyote: Consciousness Alteration, Cultural Psychiatry, and the Dilemma of Contemporary Subcultures. Anthropology of Consciousness 12:4–18.
Campbell, Thomas Nolan, and Tommy Jo Campbell
1981   Historic Indian Groups of Choke Canyon Reservoir and Surrounding Areas. Choke Canyon Series, 1. San Antonio: University of Texas Center for Archeological Research.
Campbell, T. N.
1983   Coahuiltecans and Their Neighbors. *In* Handbook of North American Indians, vol. 10: Southwest. Alonso Ortiz, ed., William Sturtevant, gen. ed. Pp. 343–358. Washington, DC: Smithsonian.
Cantú, Norma Elia
1982   The Offering and the Offerers: A Generic Illocation of a Laredo Pastorela in the Tradition of the Shepherds' Plays. Ph.D. dissertation, Department of English, University of Nebraska, Lincoln.

2002 Chicana Life-Cycle Rituals. *In* Chicana Traditions: Continuity and Change. Norma Elia Cantú and Olga Nájera-Ramírez, eds. Pp. 15–34. Urbana: University of Illinois Press.
2010a State–Federal Relations Concerning Latin@ Civil Rights in the United States. *In* Inside the Latin@ Experience: A Latin@ Reader. Norma Elia Cantú and María E. Fránquiz, eds. Pp. 23–36. New York: Palgrave Macmillan.
2010b Traditional Cultural Expressions: An Analysis of the Secular and Religious Folkways of Latin@s in the United States. *In* Inside the Latin@ Experience: A Latin@ Reader. Norma Elia Cantú and María E. Fránquiz, eds. Pp. 111–127. New York: Palgrave Macmillan.

d'Azevedo, Warren L.
2006 Straight With the Medicine: Narratives of Washoe Followers of the Tipi Way. Berkeley, CA: Heydey Books.

Dodson, Ruth
1966 Don Pedrito Jaramillo: The Curandero of Los Olmos. *In* The Healer of Los Olmos and Other Mexican Lore. Wilson M. Hudson, ed. Pp. 9–70. Dallas: Southern Methodist University Press.

El-Seedi, Hesham R., Peter A. De Smet, Olof Beck, Göran Possnert, and Jan G. Bruhn
2005 Pre-historic Peyote Use: Alkaloid Analysis and Radiocarbon Dating of Archaeological Specimens of *Lophophora* from Texas. Journal of Ethnopharmacology 101:238–242.

Epps, Garrett
2009 Peyote vs. The State: Religious Freedom on Trial. Norman: University of Oklahoma Press.

Estep, Raymond
1960 Lieutenant Wm. E. Burnett: Notes on Removal of Indians from Texas to Indian Country. Chronicles of Oklahoma 38(3):274–309 and 38(4):369–396.

Fikes, Jay C.
1996 Reuben Snake, Your Humble Serpent: Indian Visionary and Activist. Santa Fe, New Mexico: Clear Light Publishers.

Flores, Richard
1995 Los Pastores: History and Performance in the Mexican Shepherd's Play of South Texas. Washington, DC: Smithsonian.

Ford, John Salmon
1987 Rip Ford's Texas. Stephen B. Oates, ed. Austin: University of Texas Press.

Furst, Peter T.
1989 *Review of* Peyote Religion: A History. American Ethnologist 16:386–387.

Glazer, Mark
1982 Flour from Another Sack & Other Proverbs, Folk Beliefs, Tales, Riddles & Recipes. Edinburg, Texas: Pan American University Press.

Griffith, James S.
2003 Folk Saints of the Borderlands: Victims, Bandits and Healers. Tucson, AZ: Rio Nuevo.

Halpern, John H., A. R. Sewell, James I. Hudson, Deborah Yurgelun-Todd, and Harrison G. Pope Jr.
2005 Psychological and Cognitive Effects of Long-Term Peyote Use Among Native Americans. Biological Psychiatry 58(8):624–631.

Hinojosa, Servando Z.
2000 Human-Peyote Interaction in South Texas. Journal of Culture and Agriculture 22(1):29-36.

Ibarra, Cristina, dir.
2014 Las Marthas. 60 min. Independent Television Services (ITVS) in association with Laredo Public Broadcasting (LPB). Laredo.

Kimber, Clarissa T., and Darrel McDonald
2004 Sacred and Profane Uses of the Cactus *Lophophora williamsii* from the South Texas Peyote Gardens. *In* Dangerous Harvest: Drug Plants and the Transformation of Indigenous Landscapes. Michael K. Steinberg, Joseph John Hobbs, and Kent Mathewson, eds. Pp. 182–208. Oxford: Oxford University Press.

La Barre, Weston
1979 A "Retort Courteous" to Omer Stewart. American Anthropologist 81(1):113–114.
1989 The Peyote Cult. Norman: University of Oklahoma Press.

Landes, Ruth
1970 The Prairie Potawatomi: Tradition and Ritual in the Twentieth Century. Madison: University of Wisconsin Press.

Laurel, Guadalupe Martínez
2001 History of Guerra-Laurel and "Los Ojuelos." Archived material, Special Collections, Laredo Public Library, Laredo, Texas.

Long, Carolyn N.
2000 Religious Freedom and Indian Rights: The Case of *Oregon v. Smith*. Lawrence: University Press of Kansas.

LTA's Lighter Than Air Craft
2010 Rise of the "Blimps": The US Army's LEMV. http://thelivingmoon.com/45jack_files/03files/LTA_Rise_of_the_Blimps.htm, accessed April 26, 2011.

Lumholtz, Carl Sofus
1902 Unknown Mexico. New York: Scribners.

Madsen, William
1965 The Mexican-Americans of South Texas. New York: Holt, Rhinehart, Winston.

Maroukis, Thomas C.
2010   The Peyote Road: Religious Freedom and the Native American Church. Norman: University of Oklahoma Press.

Marriott, Alice Lee, and Carol K. Rachlin
1971   Peyote: An Account of the Origins and Growth of the Peyote Religion. Thomas Y. Crowell.

Maynard, Susan, et al.
2006   Amada of the Gardens. 33 mins. Maynard/Pratt & Brown. Laredo.

McCleary, James A., Paul S. Sypherd, and David L. Walkington
1960   Antibiotic Activity of an Extract of Peyote [*Lophophora williamsii* (Lemaire) Coulter]. Economic Botany 14(3):247–249.

Menchaca, Martha
1993   Chicano Indianism: A Historical Account of Racial Repression in the United States. American Ethnologist 20(3):583–603.

Mohler, J. R.
1919   Tick Eradication Plans for 1919. Journal of the American Veterinary Medical Association Index 54, n.s. 7:745–748.

Montaño, Mario
1990   *Barbacoa de Cabeza* Among South Texas Mexicans: A Research Note. The Digest: A Review for the Interdisciplinary Study of Food 10(1):2–5, 8.
1992   The History of Mexican Folk Foodways of South Texas. Street Vendors, Offal Foods, and *Barbacoa de Cabeza*. Ph.D. dissertation, Department of Anthropology, University of Pennsylvania.

Montejano, David
1987   Anglos and Mexicans in the Making of Texas, 1836–1986. Austin: University of Texas Press.

Mooney, James
1896   The Mescal Plant and Ceremony. Therapeutic Gazette, 3rd ser. 21:7–11.
1897   The Kiowa Peyote Rite. Am Ur-Quell, n.s. 1:329–333.
1979 [1898]   Calendar History of the Kiowa Indians. New York: Smithsonian.

Morgan, George
1976   Man, Plant, and Religion: Peyote Trade on the Mustang Plains of Texas. Ph.D. dissertation, University of Colorado.
1983a   Hispano-Indian Trade of an Indian Ceremonial Plant, Peyote (*Lophophora williamsii*), on the Mustang Plains of Texas. Journal of Ethnopharmacology 9:319–321.
1983b   Recollections of the Peyote Road. *In* Psychedelic Reflections. Lester Grinspoon and James B. Bakalar, eds. Pp. 91–99. New York: Human Sciences Press.

Morgan, George Robert, and Omer Call Stewart
1984   Peyote Trade in South Texas. Southwestern Historical Quarterly 87(3):270–296.
Murray, William Breen
2005   Spirits of a Holy Land: Place and Time in a Modern Mexican Religious Movement. *In* The Making of Saints: Contesting Sacred Ground. James F. Hopgood, ed. Pp. 107–123. Tuscaloosa, Alabama: The University of Alabama Press.
Newberne, Robert E. L.
1925   Peyote. An Abridged Compilation from the Files of the Bureau of Indian Affairs. 3rd ed. Lawrence, KS: Haskell Institute.
Newcomb, W. W., Jr.
1961   The Indians of Texas: From Prehistoric to Modern Times. Austin: University of Texas Press.
Opler, Morris E.
1938   The Use of Peyote by the Carrizo and the Lipan Apache. American Anthropologist 40(2):271–285.
Ortega, José de
1887   Historia de Nayarit, Sonora, Sinaloa y ambas Californias. México.
Pasquill, Robert G., Jr.
2012   Arsenic and Old Bovine Lace—History of the Cattle Tick Eradication Program in the South. http://www.fs.usda.gov/Internet/FSE_DOCUMENTS/stelprdb5396091.pdf, accessed Nov. 11, 2014.
Petrullo, Vincenzo
1934   The Diabolic Root: A Study of Peyotism, the New Indian Religion Among the Delawares. Philadelphia: University of Pennsylvania Press.
Pevar, Stephen L.
2012   The Rights of Indians and Tribes: The Basic ACLU Guide to Indian and Tribal Rights. Oxford University Press.
Portales, Patricia
2012   Women, Bombs, and War: Remapping Mexican American Woman's Home Front Agency In World War II Literature, Theater, And Film. Ph.D. dissertation, Department of English, University of Texas, San Antonio.
2014   Tejanas on the Home Front: Women, Bombs, and the (Re)Gendering of War in Mexican American World War II Literature. *In* Latina/os and World War II: Mobility, Agency and Ideology. Maggie Rivas-Rodriguez and B. V. Olguín, eds. Pp. 175–196. Austin: University of Texas Press.
Pratt, Steven B.
2003   Confessions of a *Road Man*: Being an Indian in Academe. Intercultural Communication Studies 7(2):146–155.

Prieto, Alejandro
1873 Historia, geografía y estadística del estado de Tamaulipas. México.
Ruecking, Fredrich, Jr.
1954 Ceremonies of the Coahuiltecan Indians of Southern Texas and Northeastern Mexico. The Texas Journal of Science 6(3):330–339.
Sahagún, Bernardino de
1950– Florentine Codex: A General History of the Things of New Spain. C. E.
1969 Dibble and A. J. Anderson, trans. Salt Lake City: University of Utah Press.
Salinas, Martín
1990 Indians of the Rio Grande Delta: Their Role in the History of Southern Texas and Northeastern Mexico. Austin: University of Texas Press.
San Benito, Texas
N.d. Las Pastorelas. http://www.sanbenito.k12.tx.us/schools/bertacabaza/hssb/Reading_Homepage/Pastorelas/Pastorelas.html, accessed June 18, 2011.
N.d. Basilica of Our Lady of San Juan del Valle National Shrine: Our History. http://www.olsjbasilica.org/about-us/history, accessed May 1, 2015.
Sánchez, Mario, L., and Aura Nell Ranzau Jr., eds.
1991 A Shared Experience: The History, Architecture and Historic Designations of the Lower Rio Grande Heritage Corridor. Austin: Los Caminos del Rio Heritage Project and the Texas Historical Commission.
Santillán, Richard
1989 Rosita the Riveter: Midwest Mexican American Women During World War II, 1941–1945. Perspectives in Mexican American Studies 2:115–147.
Santoscoy, Alberto, ed.
1899 Nayarit. Colección de documentos inéditos, históricos y etnográficos acerca de la sierra de este nombre. Guadalajara: J. Maria Yguíniz.
Schaefer, Stacy B.
1990 Becoming a Weaver: The Woman's Path in Huichol Culture. Ph.D. dissertation, Anthropology Department, University of California, Los Angeles.
1996 The Crossing of the Souls: Peyote, Perception and Meaning. *In* People of the Peyote: Huichol Indian History, Religion and Survival. Stacy B. Schaefer and Peter T. Furst, eds. Pp. 138–168. Albuquerque: University of New Mexico Press.
2011 Peyote and Meaning. *In Altering Consciousness: A Multidisciplinary Perspective*. Etzel Cardeña and Michael Winkelman, eds. Santa Barbara: Praeger Publishers.
2013 The Peyote Religion and Mescalero Apaches: An Ethnohistorical View from West Texas. *In* Big Bend's Ancient and Modern Past. Bruce A. Glasrud and Robert J. Mallouf, eds. Pp. 132–146. College Station, Texas: Texas A & M University Press.
2015 Huichol Women, Weavers, and Shamans. Albuquerque: University of New Mexico Press.

Schultes, Richard Evans
1938   The Appeal of Peyote (*Lophophora williamsii*) as Medicine. American Anthropologist 40:698–725.

Slotkin, J. S.
1955   Peyotism 1521–1891. American Anthropologist 57(2):202–230.
1956   Peyotism, 1521–1891: Supplement. American Anthropologist 58(1):184.
1975   The Peyote Religion: A Study in Indian-White Relations. New York: Octagon Books.

Smith, Huston, and Reuben Snake, eds.
1996   One Nation Under God: The Triumph of the Native American Church. Santa Fe, NM: Clear Light Publishers.

Smith, Maurice G.
1934   A Negro Peyote Cult. Journal of Washington Academy of Sciences 24(10):448–453.

Stegmaier, Mark Joseph
2012   Texas, New Mexico and the Compromise of 1850: Boundary Dispute and Sectional Crisis. Lubbock: Texas Tech University Press.

Sterling, William Warren
1959   Trails and Trials of a Texas Ranger. University of Oklahoma Press.

Stewart, Omer C.
1979   A Reply to La Barre's "Retort Courteous." American Anthropologist 81:114–115.
1984a Ute Peyotism: A Study of A Cultural Complex. *In* Peyotism in the West. Omer C. Stewart and David F. Aberle, eds. Pp. 1–42. Anthropological Papers, 108. Salt Lake City: University of Utah Press.
1984b Washoe-Northern Paiute Peyotism: A Study in Acculturation. *In* Peyotism in the West. Omer C. Stewart and David F. Aberle, eds. Pp. 47–127. Anthropological Papers, 108. Salt Lake City: University of Utah Press.
1986   Peyotism in California. Journal of California and Great Basin Anthropology 8(2):217–225.
1990   Peyote Religion: A History. Norman: University of Oklahoma Press.
[1987]
N.d.   Peyotism in Texas (manuscript). George Morgan Memorial Collection, Chadron State College, Chadron, Nebraska.

Stewart, Omer C., and David F. Aberle, eds.
1984   Peyotism in the West. Anthropological Papers, 108. Salt Lake City: University of Utah Press.

Stone, John E.
2010   Broken Neighbor, Broken Border. http://carter.house.gov/uploads/Broken-Neighbor-Broken-Border.pdf, released November 19.

Swan, Daniel C.
1999   Peyote Religious Art: Symbols of Faith and Belief. Jackson: University Press of Mississippi.
Terry, Martin, Karen L. Steelman, Tom Guilderson, Phil Dering, and Marvin W. Rowe
2006   Lower Pecos and Coahuila Peyote: New Radiocarbon Dates. Journal of Archaeological Science 33:1017–1021.
Thompson, Jerry D.
1991   Historical Survey. In A Shared Experience: The History, Architecture and Historic Designations of the Lower Rio Grande Heritage Corridor. Mario L. Sánchez and Aura Nell Ranzau Jr., eds. Pp. 11–71. Austin: Los Caminos del Rio Heritage Project and the Texas Historical Commission.
Tijerina, Andrés
1998   Tejano Empire: Life on the South Texas Ranchos. Texas A&M University Press.
Trotter, Robert T., and Juan A. Chavira
1997   Curanderismo: Mexican American Folk Healing. Athens: University of Georgia Press.
Underhill, Ruth
1950?   Modern Use of Peyote Among Cheyenne and Arapaho. George Morgan Archive, Chadron State College, Chadron, NE.
Vigil, James Diego
2011   From Indians to Chicanos: The Dynamics of Mexican-American Culture. Long Grove, IL: Waveland Press.
Weigand, Phil C.
1981   Differential Acculturation among the Huichol Indians. In Themes of Indigenous Acculturation in Northwest Mexico. Thomas B. Hinton and Phil C. Weigand, eds. Pp. 9–21. Anthropological Papers 38. Tucson: University of Arizona Press.
Weigand, Phil C., and Acelia Garcia de Weigand
2000   Huichol Society Before the Arrival of the Spanish. Journal of the Southwest 42(1):13–36.
Willis, David J.
2013   Adverse Possession in Texas. LoneStarLandLaw.Com. http://www.lonestarlandlaw.com/Adverse.html, accessed April 6, 2015.
Wong, Queenie
2009   Things you didn't know about Tom DeLay. U.S. News & World Report, August 17.

Newspapers

Geissler, Richard
1978   Indians Seek Peyote from S. Texas. Laredo News, September 13.
1979   Sacred pilgrimage ends in Mirando City. Laredo News, April 23.

Grothe, Randy Eli
1981   Mirando City: A Separate Reality. Dallas Morning News, March 22.

Harmon, Steve
1969   Sunday Dinner pays tribute to Mirando City's pioneers. Laredo Times, October 12.

Houston Post
1982   Severe peyote shortage threatens to put end to sacred Indian rites. March 21.

Jones, Jim
1996   Seeds of the Spirit: In the South Texas Brush Indians Use Peyote to Heal. Fort Worth Star-Telegram, March 3.
N.d.   Peyote—Indians: Plant Critical to Ritual Worship Ceremony. Fort Worth Star-Telegram.

Lara, Jerry
2001   Just Call Her Mom: Woman is Revered by Native American Church Members. San Antonio Express News, July 23. Metro page 2B.

MacCormack, John
1995   Peyote Prayers. San Antonio Express News, Sunday, March 12.

Paz-Martinez, Eduardo
1986   Peyote Ritual Highlights Indian Fete. Houston Post, February 24.

Spagat, Elliott, and Brian Skoloff
2014   Drones patrol half of Mexico border. Houston Chronicle, November 18. http://www.chron.com/news/texas/article/AP Exclusive-Drones patrol-half-of-Mexico-border-5889614.php, accessed November 18, 2014.

Tolbert, Frank X.
1972   Tolbert's Texas—Mirando City is Scene for the "Peyote Rites." GM Archives, March 22.
1974   A Good Peyote Crop Around Mirando City. Dallas Morning News, April 21.

Walraven, Bill
1975   Indians prepare for religious rite. Corpus Christi Caller, February 22.
1975   Walraven's World—Peyote No Laughing Matter. Corpus Christi Caller, February 24. GM Archives.

Interviews

Afraid of Bear-Cook, Loretta
2005   Interview by the author, July 17, Cook house, Chadron, NE.

Arviso, Geraldine
2004   Interview by the author. February 16, Amada's house, Mirando City, TX.

Behan, Margaret
1997   Interview by the author, February 28, Amada's house, Mirando City, TX.
Cardenas, Alan
2011   Interview by the author, February 9, Amada's house, Mirando City, TX.
Cardenas, Amada
1993   Interview by the author, November 27, Amada's house, Mirando City, TX.
1997   Interview by the author, February 2, Amada's house, Mirando City, TX.
Cardenas, Claudio
2004   Interview by the author, October 24, Amada's house, Mirando City, TX.
Cardenas, Claudio, and Melvin George
2000   Interview by the author, October 28, Amada's house, Mirando City, TX.
Garcia Cristan, Elvia
2004   Interview by the author, April 23, Cristan's Restaurant, San Antonio, TX.
Davis, Anthony
2000   Interview by the author, February 20, Amada's house, Mirando City, TX.
D'Wolf, Linda
1997   Interview by the author, February 28, Amada's house, Mirando City, TX.
Esquivel, Maria
2004   Interview by the author, April 21, Esquivel house, Mirando City, TX.
Etcitty, Jerry and Lillian
2005   Interview by the author, February 19, Amada's house, Mirando City, TX.
Geissler, Jackie
2004   Interview by the author, April 20, Geissler office, Laredo, TX.
Geissler, Richard
2004   Interview by the author, April 20, Geissler house, Laredo, TX.
Grove, Bertha
2004   Interview by the author, February 21, Amada's house, Mirando City, TX.
Guerra, Juan
2004   Interview by the author, April 22, Guerra house, Alice, TX.
Hammrick, Barry (Bear)
2004   Interview by the author, April 24, friend's house, Austin, TX.
Hammrick, Patti
2004   Interview by the author, April 25, Hammrick house, Austin, TX.
Kazen, Barbara, and Jerry Patchen
2000   Interview by the author, October 29, Amada's house, Mirando City, TX.
Innocencio, Catalina
2004   Interview by the author, April 21, Amada's house, Mirando City, TX.
Johnson, Salvador
2004   Interview by the author, April 21, S. Johnson house, Mirando City, TX.
Johnson, Teresa
2004   Interview by the author, April 10, T. Johnson house, Mirando City, TX.

Kuauhtli Vásquez, Manuel
2004 Interview by the author, February 18, Castroville Regional Park, Castroville, TX.
Lira, Guadalupe
2004 Interview by the author, April 21, Lira house, Mirando City, TX.
Lopez, Margarito
2004 Interview by the author, April 17, Lopez house, Mirando City, TX.
Martinez, Nora
2004 Interview by the author, February 25, Martinez house, Laredo, TX.
McDonald, Darrel
2004 Interview by the author, April 27, Stephen F. Austin College, Nacogdoches, TX.
Mendieta, Raquel
2004 Interview by the author, April 17, Mendieta house, Mirando City, TX.
Morales, Mauro
2004 Interview by the author, April 16, Morales house, Rio Grande City, TX.
Naranjo, Alden (Junior)
2004 Interview by the author, April 22, Amada's house, Mirando City, TX.
Patchen, Jerry
2004 Interview by the author, April 29, Patchen house, Houston, TX.
Perez, Gary
2011 Interview by the author, February 24, Bauml house, San Antonio, TX.
Sanchez, Silvester
2000 Interview by the author, February 20, Amada's house, Mirando City, TX.
Sanchez Palacios, Gloria
2004 Interview by the author, April 18, Palacios house, Laredo, TX.
Sheeran, Florinda
2004 Interview by the author, April 21, Amada's house, Mirando City, TX.
Weasel Bear, Beatrice
2005 Interview by the author, July 17, Cook house, Chadron, NE.
Zepeda, Jose
2004 Interview by the author, April 23, Zepeda House, San Antonio, TX

Index

Page numbers in italics refer to photographs.

Aberlee, David, 119
ABNDN. *See* Azee' Bee Nahaghá of Diné Nation
ACLU representation, for Takes Guns, 117
Adios to the Brushland (Longoria), 245n2
Adverse Possession in the Texas Civil Practice and Remedies Code, 51
Afraid of Bear Cook, Loreta, 115, 130, 134–35, 230
African Americans: in Mirando City, 54; Negro peyote group, 261n8
Alemán, Enrique, Jr., 254n5
Amada of the Gardens, 14, 183, 245n4, 248n1, 259n12, 274n1
American Indian Religious Coalition, 267n10
American Indian Religious Freedom Act amendment, 188–89, 267n10
Anderson, Edward, 204
Andrea (sister), 12, 58
Anglos: hippies, 123; in Mirando City, 54–56, 59–61; oil industry and, 127; vaquero traditions, 247n9
anti-drug legislation, in Texas, 99
anti-peyote laws: on BIA peyote use prohibition, 99, 265n5; Cardenas, C., Sr.'s arrest, 100–103, 236, 260n6; Catholic and Christian churches on, 98; Chávez's federal bill, 100, 257n6; Deadwood, South Dakota, 1916 ruling, 99; Department of Interior on, 98;

Oklahoma peyote use criminalization statute, 98–99; Parker on First Amendment's freedom of religion rights, 99; on peyote harvest, transportation and use, 100; state legislation on peyote as criminal offense, 99; Texas first, in 1937, on peyote transportation, 99
arrest, of Cardenas, C., Sr., 100–103, 236, 260n6
Arviso, Geraldina "Geri," 94–95, 184; on Cardenas, C., Sr.'s death, 107–8; on Navajo peyote prohibition, 97–98; on one NAC, 229; on sacred aspect of peyote harvest, 90, 230
attributes, of Cardenas, Amada: aging with dignity, 223, 224; blessings, 12, 125, 143, 164, 180, 202; charity, 169–70; compassion and service to others, 226–27; emulated, 226–28; hospitality, 8–9, 43–45, 91, 114, 125, 136, 191, 197, 217; kindness, 75, 124, 191; loving-kindness, 14, 136, 226, 232; peacekeeper, 227, 230; quiet strength, 185; religious faith, 25, 134, 172, 228; respect, 66, 69, 71, 227; signs in nature observations, 18; spirituality, 169, 193–94, 224; teacher, 224; unconditional love, 200, 225–28
Azee' Bee Nahaghá of Diné Nation (Native American Church of Navajoland) (ABNDN), 126, 185, 212, 272n9;

Azee' Bee Nahaghá of Diné Nation (*continued*)
  NAC of Oklahoma schism with, 264n2;
  Perez, G., welcome to, 216; property exodus, 214–15
Azpiazu, Jose Maria, 26

BAI. *See* Bureau of Animal Industry
Barnett, Tracy L., 272n11
Basso, Keith, 266n7
Bauml, Jim, 2, 13, 178, 205, 207–8, 267n8
Bautista Parra, Efren, 272n11
Beatrice (sister), 4
Behan, Margaret, 136
BIA. *See* Bureau of Indian Affairs; Bureau of Indian Affairs (BIA)
Bill of Rights, Navajo Tribal Council acceptance of, 35, 98
birthday meeting tradition, 5, 189–98, 218; Cardenas, Amada's, photo at, *82*, *86*; Catholic birthday mass, 3–4; ceremony, 6–7; Etcitty, J., at, 6, 7, 192, 196, 198; Etcitty, L., at, 6, 192, 196–97, 198; family at, 194–95; friends at., 6, 190–96; Lira on, 195; Vásquez on, 193–94. *See also* one hundred year birthday
Boas, Franz, 257n6
Bogue, Allan, 249n6
Border Patrol, 267n4; drone flights, 203; Tethered Aerostat Radar System and, 203; undocumented immigrants, 204
Briggs, J. R., 37
Bureau of American Ethnology, at Smithsonian Institution, 34
Bureau of Animal Industry (BAI), 246n8
Bureau of Indian Affairs (BIA), 99; on Peyotism, 265n5
Bushy, Frank D., 104, 236, 259n9
Byarlay, Patricia, 270n6

Cabeza de Vaca, Álvar Núñez, 20
Cactus Conservation Institute (CCI), 270n6

"Camp Los Ojuelos" (Ford), 253n3
Canales, A., 251n11
Cantú, Norma, 254n9, 258n11
Cardenas, Alan (grandson), *84*, 273n12; on legacy, 219–21; Perez, G., and, 219–21
Cardenas, Amada, *79*–*86*, *89*, *161*; aging health, 168, 197, 201; with author, *163*; author's first meeting with, 7–11, 176; background, 13–15; on Cardenas, C., Sr.'s, arrest, 101, 102–3; death and funeral of, 205–6, 209; education, 24–25; as healer, 133–35, 168–69, 202; home as wildlife safe haven, 20, 231; home interior wall, *159*; making of peyote chief, 131–33, *160*, *162*; Mirando City integral community member, 63–66; as mom, grandmother to others, 2, 9, 153, 164, 170–71, 176, 196, 198, 225; as Morgan's translator, 124; move to Martinez, N., home, 201–2; NAC-NA trustee, 103–4, 236, 264n2; NAC religious freedom support, 100, 115–16, 211; new construction home, 111–12, 259n1; non-Indians and, 2, 130, 148–53, 212, 216, 226; one hundred year birthday, 1–7, 197–98; open-door policy of, 171–73, 187, 212; peyote harvesters employment, 52, 73; peyote major supplier for NAC, 52; as *peyotero*, 68–76; peyote trade retirement, 128–30; on politics, 229–30; religious pilgrimages of, 25–26, 68; school activities support, 64; senior citizens' program involvement, 166; as widow, 111–15; will of, 212–16. *See also specific topics*
Cardenas, Claudio, Jr. (son), 1–2, 7, 28, 50, *88*, *89*, 208; on Cardenases' early peyote trade, 45–47; childhood, 64–65; on compassion, 226; on father's arrest, 101–2; on lack of prejudice and discrimination, 64; on Los Ojuelos, 16, 26–27; on NAC ceremonies, 95; on NAC-NA integration, 104; NAC-NA welcome by, 216;

on Native Americans, 92; on open-door policy, 172; Perez, G., conversations with, 209–10; on peyote, 30, 95–96, 110; peyote chief for, 132–33; on prayer meetings, February, 105; on religious pilgrimages, 68; on Texas Department of Agriculture permit to ship peyote, 90; on will of Cardenas, Amada, 213, 215–16

Cardenas, Claudio, Sr. (husband), 3, *78*, *79*, 245n3; arrest, 100–103, 236, 260n6; Catholic religion dedication, 65; death of, 106–8, 260n6; Mirando City clearing by, 53; Mirando City integral community member, 63–66; NAC-NA trustee, 103–4, 236, 264n2; NAC religious freedom support, 100; peyote cleaning, *79*; peyote for knee pain, 38; peyote harvesters employment, 52, 73; as *peyotero*, 43, 68–76; religious pilgrimages of, 25–26

Cardenas, David (Claudio, Sr.'s brother), *78*

Cardenas, Luis (Claudio, Sr.'s brother), 50

Cardenas, María (daughter), death at childbirth of, 27

Cardenases' peyote traders early life, 48; Cardenas, C., Sr., and, 43; eating peyote while working, 42–43; gathering peyote, 42; hospitality recollection, of Cardenas, C., Jr., 43–45; peyote meetings, Cardenas, C., Jr., on, 46–47; peyote trade routine activities, 45–46; sacred aspects of peyote harvest, 42, 45–46; Sanchez, E., and, 41

Carrizo Indians, of Coahuiltecans, 21, 34, 45

Castañeda, Carlos, 121

Catholic religion, 174, 201, 206; on anti-peyote laws, 98; birthday mass, 3–4; Cardenas, C., Sr., and Amada's dedication to, 65; feasts and celebrations, 25; in Mirando City, 57; sacramental rights, 25

CCI. *See* Cactus Conservation Institute

cedar, traditional Native incense, 6–7, 142, *162*, 193, 206, 211

ceremonial building. *See* hogan

Chadron State College: Dr. George R. Morgan Memorial Archive at, 14, 148n4; Morgan as geography professor at, 123

Chasing a Good Day to Die, 183, 267n8

Chávez, Dennis, 100, 257n6

Chavira, Juan, 263n14

Cheyenne, 43, 100, 105, 141, 145, 251n13, 259n12

Chief Special Officer of Liquor Control, 38–39

Chihuahuan Desert, 17, 31

Chiwat, 250n9

Christianity, 33, 34, 98

Christmas Eve. *See* Nochebuena

Cibecue Apaches, 266n7

City of Austin Cultural Arts Contracts, 183

Civil War, 246n7

Clark, David, 117, 118, 206, 260n6

Clinton, Sam Houston, 117, 118

Clinton, William "Bill," 188–89

Coahuiltecans, 2, 21, 173–76, 182, 266n1; area of, 173; bands of, 21; Cabeza de Vaca travel narrative on, 20; Carrizo Indians of, 21, 34, 45; indigenous hunter-gatherers, 20–21; move to San Antonio missions, 173, 266n3; NAC prayer meetings, 173; Perez, G., as, 218; peyote ceremonies, 21; warfare, 21

Collier, John, 100, 235

Comanches, 21, 34, 36, 105, 125, 253n3; Peyotism, 265n5; prayer meetings, 218

community involvement, 137–39

compadres relationships, 23

Comprehensive Drug Abuse Prevention and Control Act of 1970, 264n3

Cora indigenous peoples, peyote use by, 32

Cortinas, Frank, 39, 256n1

Cousineau, Phil, 267n10

Coyote, Peter, 267n10

Cristan, Elvia, 60, 253n4, 255n12; on Las Pastorelas, 62–63
Crow Dog, Leonard, 174
Cuatro Ciénegas, in Coahuila, Mexico, 250n9
Culture and Agriculture, 14
Curanderismo (Trotter and Chavira), 263n14
custodian term, in NAC, 120, 148, 174, 264n2, 266n2

Dale, Allen P., 47, 96, 118, 257n3; on Cardenas, C., Sr.'s arrest, 103; as NAC-US president, 100, 103; on peyote spiritual aspect, 45–46
Dale, Chris, 45, 96
Daniel, Bill, 14, 183
Danmier, Herbert F., 54
Davis, Anthony: birthday meeting tradition, 193; on peyote sacred aspects, 45–46
Davis, Bertha Grove "Red Earth Woman," 93–94, 200; on peyote theft, 184–85; on politics, 229; on respect, 227
DEA. *See* Drug Enforcement Administration, Federal
Deadwood, South Dakota, 1916 ruling on peyote, 99
de Anda, Ricardo, 13
de Anda, Rosie, 13
Dear, Sam B., 106
DeLay, Tom, 59, 254n7
Department of Agriculture, Texas: permit to ship peyote, 90; peyote degradation, 204; on peyote harvest, transportation and use, 100
Department of Interior, on anti-peyote laws, 98
Department of Public Safety (DPS), Texas: on American Indian Religious Freedom Act amendment, 189; on hippies in peyote gardens, 121; on non-Indians' peyote use, 189, 212; on peyote buttons sold 1986–2013, 249n7; peyote dealer's license and, 11, 205, 236; peyote trade regulation under, 120
Depression, 58
Dionicio Guerra, José, 23; Los Ojuelos settlement by, 22
The Doors of Perception (Huxley), 121
DPS. *See* Department of Public Safety
Dr. George R. Morgan Memorial Archive, at Chadron State College, 14, 248n4
Drug Enforcement Administration (DEA), Federal, 11, 236
Dulce Nombre de Jesús de Peyotes Spanish mission, 33

East, Robert, 74
El Bordo peyote fields, 30
Esperanza project, 272n11
Esquivel, Maria, 3, 66, 165, 177; on aging with dignity, 223; on Cardenas, C., Sr., and Amada's relationship, 110; on Mirando City, 203
Etcitty, Jerry, *81*; birthday meeting tradition, 6, 7, 192, 196, 198; NAC-US president, 264n2; tepee for prayer meeting, 186
Etcitty, Lillian: birthday meeting tradition, 6, 192, 196–97, 198; tepee for prayer meeting made by, 186; on working to resolve differences, 227

feather fan, in prayer meetings, 4, 7, 47, 142, 146, *162*, 193, 211, 268n11
Federal Controlled Substance Act, on peyote in religious ceremonies, 183
First Amendment freedom of religion rights, 99, 235, 267n10
first meeting with author, hospitality at, 8–9
First Nations in Canada, 264n2, 272n9
folk healer, Jaramillo as, 26, 247n13
Ford, John Salmon Rip, 253n3
Franco, Aida, 14, 183
Franco, Eugenia, 181

Fulbright, Bob, 40
funeral, for Cardenas, Amada: Clark speaking at, 206; Martinez, N., attention to, 205–6; mourners at, 206; Patchen, J., speaking at, 206; Perez, G., at, 209; prayer meeting, 206
Furst, Peter, 245n2

Ga'apiatañ, oral tradition of peyote origin, 34–35
Gaitán, José Manuel, 33
García, Eusebio, 53
García, José María, 53
Garza, Mario, 209, 266n3
Geissler, Jackie, 182, 224
Geissler, Richard, 204; on hippies, 122–23; on signs in nature observations, 18; on Tres Torres border crossing, 269n5
George, Melvin, 6, 9–10, 95; on NAC-NA integration, 104; on not-for-profit peyote trade, 96
George Washington holiday: celebration and parade, 258n11; NAC-NA convention, 258n10
Goddess of peyote. *See* Wuili Uwi
Gomez, Jasper, 181
Gomez, Taos, 6
Good Morning, Tellis, 190–91
Grove, Vincent, 256n2
Guadiano, Paula (mother), 23
Guerra, Ignacio (father), 23; Rancho los Ojuelos ownership, 53, 253n2
Guerra, Jorge (half brother), 4
Guerra, José Maria, 22
Guerra, Juan (half brother), 4
Gutiérrez de Castro, José Isidro (great-great-grandfather), 22

Halpern, John H., 182
Hamrick, Barry "Bear," 6, 182, 201; on birthday meeting tradition, 190–94; on peacekeeper, 230; on unconditional love, 228

Hamrick, Patti, 6, 182; birthday meeting tradition, 190–92; on spirituality, 224
Harrington, John F., 257n6
Harrington, M. R., 257n6
Harris, Nicole (great-granddaughter), 85
healer: Cardenas, Amada, as, 133–35, 168–69, 202; Jaramillo, as folk, 26, 247n13; Tejanos folk tradition of, 26
Hernandez, Danny, 266n3
Herrera, Ted, 266n3
Hinojosa, Servando, 14, 182
Hinojosa, Servando, Jr., 182
hippies, in peyote gardens, 121–23, 183–84, 261n9
Hoffman, Albert, 105, 259n12
Hoffman, Archie, 105
Hoffman, Fred, 105
hogan (ceremonial building), 188; conflict over, 186–87; covered picnic area near, 187; fence, gate and sign at, 187; inaugural peyote meeting, 186; International Convention of the NAC of, 272n11; Navajos from ABNDN building of, 185; tepee for prayer meeting, 186
Holland, Terry, 183
Hrdlička, Aleš, 257n6
Huichol Indians, 15, 218, 265n6, 267n5, 272n11; annual pilgrimage to San Luis Potosí peyote desert, 32; Cardenas, Amada's, meeting with, 179–81; peyote consumption during pregnancy, 252n15; peyote importance to, 10; peyote in religious practices, 32
"Human Peyote Interaction in South Texas" (Hinojosa), 14
Huxley, Aldous, 121

Ibarra, Cristina, 258n11
Ibarra, Lupe, 4
Improved Order of Red Men, Washington as patriotism symbol for, 258n11
Indians: federal definition of, 265; hospitality to, 43–44; mission, 21, 33, 34, 173,

Indians (*continued*)
  266n1, 266n3; one-quarter blood quantum, 120, 189, 216, 261n8, 265n5. *See also* Native Americans; *specific tribes*
Indian Territory of Oklahoma: Native Americans sent to reservations at, 22, 34; peyote diffusion by, 35
Indigenous Cultures Institute, 266n3
Inocencio, Catalina, 3, 57, 75, 136, 169, 200; on birthday meeting tradition, 195–96; on open-door policy, 172–73
Inocencio, Oscar, 3
International Convention of the Native American Church, 272n11

Jackson, Emerson, 265n5
Jacquez, Mary, *82*
Jake, Clifford, 256n2
Jamison, John, 261n8
Jaramillo, Pedrito, 26, 247n13, 263n14
John, Elizabeth A. H., 248n4
Johnson, Salvador, 174, 187, 202; on Cardenas, Amada, as teacher, 224; on Native Americans, 71; as peyote dealer, 3, 9, 73–74, 165; prayers for Cardenas, Amada, 199
Johnson, Teresa, 3, 58, 165, 168, 202; on Mirando City racial segregation, 56; on Las Pastorelas, 61–62; on peyote tonic for good health, 38
Johnson, Vicenta, 202
Johnson, W. E., 38–39
Juan Nepomuceno Cortina raids, 246n7

Karankawa Peyotism, 248n4
Kazen, Cathy, 4, 117, 182
Kazen, Drusilla Perkins, *87*
Kazen, E. James, *87, 88,* 117; on Cardenas, C., Sr.'s arrest, 103; at February prayer meeting, 182; NAC and peyote for religious purposes ruling, 4; as NAC honorary member, 118–19, 182
Kazen, Lisl, *87*

Killam, O. W., 53
Killam, Redcliff, 255n12
Kimber, Clarissa, 14; on Peyotism and peyote gardens, 182
King, Jimmie K., 103–4
"The Kiowa Peyote Rite" (Mooney), 249n6
Kiowas, 37; Carrizo Indians peyote introduction to, 34; Mooney's witness of peyote religious use by, 34; peyote gardens pilgrimage, 40–41; Peyotism, 265n5
Kroeber, A. L., 257n6

La Barre, Weston, 257n6; differential diffusion, 249n5; on Indian tribes, 33–34; on medicinal use of peyote, 263n14; on Peyotism, 251n13
Lakotas, 130, 174, 230, 232, 272n11
Lancaster, Ben "Chief Gray Horse," peyote collection and purchase, 251n13
Landes, Ruth, 251n10
La Raza Unida party, 56
Laredo: Cardenas, Amada's, move to Martinez home in, 201–2; peyote central supply point, 37; Sánchez de la Ibarrera y Garza settlement of, 21–22
The Laredo Morning Times, 24
Laredo Public Library, Special Collections at, 14
Larsen, Paul, 183
Las Marthas, 258n11
Las Pastorelas (Shepherd's Plays), 61–63, 254n8
Las Posadas celebration, 13
Laurel, Guadalupe Martínez, 253n2
legacy, of Cardenas, Amada, 207–8, 219–21
Lipan Apaches, 21, 253n16; Carrizo Indians peyote introduction to, 34; Peyotism spread by, 250n8; prayer meetings, 218
Lira, Guadalupe, 3, 65; on birthday meeting tradition, 195; on Mirando City, 203; peyote harvest, 74; on unconditional love, 225

Loneman, Rutherford, *81*, 196; NAC-US vice-president, 264n2; Patchens and, 142–46
Long Brothers Drilling Company, 58
Longoria, Arturo, 245n2
Lopez, Isabel, 174
Lopez, Margarito, 2–3; on Los Ojuelos peyote trade, 41; as vaquero, 23–24
Lophophora williamsii. See peyote
Los Mesteños (Mustang Plains), in '60s and '70s: Cardenas, Amada, as healer, 133–35; Cardenas, Amada, as widow and peyotera, 111–15; Cardenas, Amada, leaving peyote business, 128–30; hippies in, 121–23; making peyote chiefs, 130–33; Morgan and, 123–28; peyote legislation test case, in 1969, 115–21
Los Ojuelos, 17–28, 203; birthing center, 22; Cardenas, Amada's birthplace, 16; Cardenas, C., Jr., on, 26–27; Catholic priests visitation at, 25; Dionicio Guerra and Nepomuceno settlement of, 22; Gutiérrez de Castro land grant claim, 22; peyote ceremonies at, 47–48; as peyote gardens, 30; population diminished in, 54; region, Native Americans sent to reservations, 22
Los Ojuelos peyote trade: center of, 30; by Cortinas, 39; first Cadillac car, 39–40, 251n12; Johnson, W. E., first account of, 38–39; Lopez, M., on, 41; by Sanchez, E., 39
Luna, Rudy, 254n5

"Man, Plant, and Religion: Peyote Trade on the Mustang Plains of Texas" (Morgan), 13–14, 123
Martha Washington Society, 258n11
Martinez, Isidro, 202
Martinez, Nora (caretaker), 2, 3, 13, *82*, *83*, 164–68, 197, 200; Cardenas, Amada, as mom to, 170–71; Cardenas, Amada, move to home of, 201–2; on charitable actions, 169–70; funeral, for Cardenas, Amada, 205–6
Mary Attakai case, in Arizona, 116, 117
Maynard, Susan, 14, 183, 259n12, 274n1
McDonald, Darrel, 6, 14, 128; on blessings of Cardenas, Amada, 232; on Morgan, 123–24; on Peyotism and peyote gardens, 182
media, 151–52, 181
Medical Committee of the Constitutional Convention, in 1907, 99
Medical Register, 37
medicinal use, of peyote, 31; arthritis, 168; congestion, 168; for eye cataracts, 38; for fatigue, hunger, thirst, 38; headache, 37; knee pain, 38; La Barre on, 263n14; Martinez on, 168–69; during pregnancy, 252n15; therapeutic use, 263n14; tonic for good health, 38
Mendieta, Armando, 59
Mendieta, Oscar, 3, 59
Mendieta, Raquel, 3, 55, 65, 254n7, 269n1; on hippies, 121–22; on water drums, 69–70
Mercado, Leo, 270n6
Mercado, Raven, 270n6
mescal bean, 257n4; ceremonialism, 248n3
Mescalero Apaches, 34, 45, 253n16; meetings for peyote healing, 263n14; Peyotism and, 249n5
mescaline vision-producing agent, of peyote, 31, 248n2
mescalism, 248n3
Mexican Americans: discrimination and corporal punishment, 254n5; federal desegregation court case, 254n5; segregated educational system, 60–61, 254n5
Mexican-American War (1846–1848), 246n7, 247n14
Mexico, peyote transport from, 36
Mirando City: African Americans in, 54, 60; Anglos in, 54, 55; Cardenas, C., Sr.,

Mirando City (*continued*)
and Amada, as integral community members, 63–66; churches and schools, 55, 57; decline, 269n1; Depression, World War II, 58–59; development of, 53–54; Esquivel on, 203; home in, 2; house description, 51–52; Killam, O. W., as founder of, 53; Lira on, 203; Mendieta, R., on, 55; NAC-NA convention in, 258n10; people of, 3, 55–57; racial segregation, 56–57, 60–61; relocation to, 51; Tejanos in 1950s to 1970s, 60–63; in twenty-first century, 203–5; undocumented immigrants and, 204
Mirando City Record, 54
Mirando Valley area: agricultural elimination of peyote, 127, 204; peyote gathered in, 40; privatization of ranchlands, 127; ranchers' peyote access restrictions, 127
mission Indians, 21, 33, 34, 173, 266n1, 266n3
mom or grandmother to others, Cardenas, Amada as, 2, 9, 153, 164, 170–71, 176, 196, 198, 225
Montaño, Mario, 247n10
Mooney, James, 249n6; on Indian tribes, 33–34; Kiowa's peyote religious use observed by, 34; on Mescalero Apache, 249n5; NAC incorporation encouragement, 35; on Peyotism, 251n13
Mooney, James "Flaming Eagle": arrest for peyote distribution at church, 183; Oklevueha Earthwalks Native American Church of Utah, Inc., 183, 267n8
Mooney, Linda, 183
Morales, Mauro, 272n8; as licensed peyote dealer, 3, 138–39
Moran, Marly, 8, 176, 245n1
Morgan, George, 6, 13–14, 123–28, 182, 251n11, 261n9; on automobile, 251n12; at Chadron State College, in Nebraska, 123; on Cortinas, 256n1; death of, 128; on hippies, 121; NAC member at Pine Ridge Reservation, 123, 262n11; peyote chief made for, 133; on peyote gardens, 30, 124, 204; on peyote interest, 261n10; Pine Ridge Reservation burial, 262n11; on tribal tensions, 125–26
Mussato-Allen, Cristala, 209
Mustang Plains. *See* Los Mesteños
Mycoby, Ernest, 106

NAC. *See* Native American Church
NAC-NA. *See* Native American Church of North America
NAC of Oklahoma. *See* Native American Church of Oklahoma
NAC-US. *See* Native American Church of the United States
Nakum Journal, 266n3
Naranjo, Alden "Junior," 6, 9, 186, 188; at funeral, 206; on leading peyote meetings, 263n1; NAC-US and, 264n2; on peyote population decline, 270n6
Naranjo, Juanita, 6, 186
Narcotics Bureau, Texas, 100
Native American Church (NAC), 4, *81*, *156*, *157*; birthday meeting tradition, 2, 5–7; Cardenas, Amada, and, 52, 100, 115–16, 211, 228–30; Cardenas, C., Jr., on ceremonies of, 95; Cardenases and, 91–108; Coahuiltecans' prayer meetings, 173; custodian term, 120, 148, 174, 264n2, 266n2; on hippies in peyote gardens, 121; hope, love, faith and charity ways, 5, 10, 229, 230; Kazen, E., as honorary member of, 118–19, 182; legal challenges for, 265n5; Mooney, J.'s incorporation encouragement, 35; Morgan as member at Pine Ridge Reservation, 123, 262n11; NAC of Oklahoma name change to, in 1944, 235; national branch incorporation, in

1944, 100; Navajo Indians membership in, 35–36, 125–26; non-Indians involvement, 150, 183, 189, 265n5; Oklevueha Earthwalks meetings, 183, 267n8; one-quarter Indian blood quantum, 265n5; peyote as sacrament of, 3; Peyotism of, 2, 31–36; religious freedom, Navajo Tribal Council on, 35, 98, 125–26; Southern Paiute incorporation into, 256n2; water drum use in, 69–70

Native American Church of Canada, in Saskatchewan, 257n8

Native American Church of Navajoland. *See* Azee' Bee Nahaghá of Diné Nation

Native American Church of North America (NAC-NA), 212, 236, 257n8, 264n2; Cardenas, C., Jr., and, 104, 216; Cardenas, C., Sr. and Amada as trustees of, 103–4, 236, 264n2; Cardenases' home as official headquarters of Texas, 103–4; membership requirements, 272n10; Mirando City convention, 258n10; NAC-US name change, 103, 236, 257n8, 264n2; Navajos from Four Corners in, 125; on non-Indians peyote use, 265n5; one-quarter Indian blood required documentation, 216, 265n5; peyote legislation test case (1969) and, 116

Native American Church of Oklahoma (NAC of Oklahoma), 212; ABNDN schism with, 264n2; name retention, in 1949, 235

Native American Church of the Four Corners, 272n9

Native American Church of the United States (NAC-US), 100, 103, 189, 193, 257n7, 257n8; charter of 1944, 264n2; incorporation in 1950, 236; NAC-NA name change, 103, 236, 257n8, 264n2; Patchen, J., and, 257n8, 264n2; reinstatement in 1987, 264n2; Takes Gun and, 100, 264n2

Native American Church-US Texas Chapter, 146–48

Native Americans: Cardenas, C., Jr., on, 92; one-quarter Indian blood documentation lack, 261n8; respect for, 71; sent to Indian Territory of Oklahoma reservations, 22, 34. *See also* Indians; *specific tribes*

Native Americans, at Cardenas, C., Sr., and Amada's: anti-peyote laws and legal entanglement, 98–103; bonds with children, 94–95; Cardenas, C., Jr., on, 92; Cardenas, C., Sr.'s death, 106–8, 260n6; Davis, B., at, 93–94; hospitality to, 43–44, 91; Mirando City people response to, 70–72; NAC ceremonies, 103–5; not-for-profit peyote trade, 95–97; Sanchez Palacios, on prayers and meals, 92–93. *See also* prayer meetings, February

Navajo Indians, 181, 267n7; Arviso, 90, 94–95, 97–98, 107–8, 184, 230; NAC membership, 35–36, 125–26; peyote prohibition, 35, 97–98, 272n9; Peyotism arrival to, 35; tribal tensions and, 125–26. *See also* Azee' Bee Nahaghá of Diné Nation

Navajo Tribal Council: Bill of Rights acceptance, 35, 98; on NAC religious freedom, 35, 98, 125–26; peyote prohibition, 272n9; Peyotism outlawed in 1940, 35

Negrin, Yvonne, 272n11

Negro peyote group, 261n8

Nepomuceno, Juan, 22

Nickels, Anna B., Parke, Davis and Company peyote purchase from, 37

Niño Fidencio religion, 268n11

Nochebuena (Christmas Eve), 13

non-Indians: Cardenas, Amada, and, 2, 130, 148–53, 212, 216, 226; DPS prosecution of peyote use, 189, 212; NAC involvement, 150, 183, 189, 265n5;

non-Indians (*continued*)
  peyote recreational use, 265n5; at prayer meetings, 148–51, 187
Northern Navajoland Native American Church, 272n9
northwest Mexico map, 77
Nuevo Laredo, 67–68, 258n10

Oglala Sioux, 114
oil fields: Cardenas, C., Jr., on, 50; Cardenas, L., on, 50; Killam, O. W., as Mirando City founder, 53
Oklahoma: authorization of peyote use, 99–100; Indian Territory of, 22, 34, 35; peyote use criminalization statute, 98–99
Oklahoma Osage, peyote buttons and, 251n10
Oklevueha Earthwalks Native American Church of Utah, Inc., of Mooney "Flaming Eagle," 183, 267n8
Olivares, Antonio (padre), 33
one hundred year birthday, of Cardenas, Amada, 197–98; Civic Center celebration, 4–5; family present at, 1–2; Martinez planning for, 197; Mirando City longtime residents at, 3; NAC tepee birthday meeting, 2, 5–7; Tejano family members at, 1, 2–3
one-quarter Indian blood quantum: Mexican Indians problem with, 261n8; NAC-NA required documentation of, 216, 265n5; Native Americans lack of documentation for, 261n8; Negro peyote group and, 261n8; peyote sales and, 120, 189, 261n8
open-door policy, 187, 212; Cardenas, C., Jr., on, 172; Inocencio, C., on, 172–73
Opler, Morris, 33–34

Pacuache band, of Coahuiltecans, 21
Paffrath, E. A., 37
Paiute Indians, 251n13

Pappe, Alan, 14, 183
Parke, Davis and Company pharmaceuticals peyote purchase, 37
Parker, Quanah: on First Amendment's freedom of religion rights, 99; peyote chief, 262n13; peyote transport from Mexico, through Texas, 36
Pastaloca band, of Coahuiltecans, 21
Patchen, Jerry, 6, *81*, 136, 182–84, 186, 212; on February peyote meeting origin, 105–6; funeral speech, 206; Loneman and, 142–46; NAC-US Articles of Incorporation, 257n8; NAC-US resignation, 264n2; on peyote legislation test case, 116–17; on religious faith, 228; on Takes Gun, 260n5; on unconditional love, 226–27
Patchen, Linda, 6, 182; on Cardenas, Amada's death, 205; Loneman and, 142–46
Patchen, Michelle, 6
Patterson, Jody, 236
Pedro, Robert, 30
People of the Peyote: Huichol Indian History, Religion and Survival (Schaefer and Furst), 245n2
Perez, Debbie, 208
Perez, Gary, 271n7; ABNDN welcome by, 216; Cardenas, Alan, and, 219–21; Cardenas, Amada, attributes emulation, 217–18; caretaker of property, 208–9, 217; as Coahuiltecan, 218; electrical work on property, 210–11; on will of Cardenas, Amada, 213–14
Petrullo, Vicenzo, 257n6
peyote, 43, 52, *155*; ancient history of use, 32, 248n2, 250n9; benefits of, 182, 257n5; Cardenas, C., Jr., on, 30; declining populations of, 127, 128, 204, 216–17, 270n6; DPS on buttons sold 1986-2013, 249n7; drying practice, 36–37; as gift, *154*; habitat of, 17; Huichol Indians and, 10; increased demand for, 126–28, 204–5;

list of indigenous cultures use, 32; mescaline vision-producing agent of, 31, 248n2; Morgan on interest in, 261n10; as NAC sacrament, 3; Navajo Indians prohibition of, 35, 97–98, 272n9; non-Indian use of, 265n5; potency of dried, 250n9; recreational use, 265n5; as sacred plants, 230–31; sales to one-quarter Indian blood quantum, 120, 189, 261n8; Spanish clergymen negative references to, 32; spiritual experiences provoked by, 31; terms for, 31; Terry's genetics study on, 248n2; THIQ alkaloids in, 250n9. *See also* anti-peyote laws; medicinal use

peyote chief, 130, *160*, *162*, 262n12; for Cardenas, C., Jr., 132–33; healing powers of, 169, 262n13; for Native American roadmen, 133; Parker and, 262n13; in prayer meetings, 131; protective power of, 132–33, 262n13; Speck and War Eagle on, 262n13; symbolism of, 131

peyote dealers, licensed: Amada as one of first, 8, 120, 205, 236; Canales as, 251n11; DPS, Texas and, 11, 205, 236; Johnson, S., as, 3, 9, 73–74, 165; Morales as, 3, 138–39; in Rio Grande City, 10–11; Rodriguez as, 3; Tejanos increase of, 127; Texas Narcotic Law amendment for, 120

Peyote Foundation, in Arizona, 270n6

peyote gardens, 72–74, 182; Cardenas, Amada, as guardian of, 231; declining peyote populations, 127, 128, 204, 216–17, 270n6; hippies in, 121–23, 183–84, 261n9; Huichol Indians at, 179–81; Indians access to, 40; Kiowa pilgrimage to, 40–41; Los Ojuelos as, 30; Morgan on, 30, 124, 204; NAC altar, *155*; Shawnee traditions in, 40, 252n14; Tethered Aerostat Radar System and, 203; theft from, 184–85; in twenty-first century, 203–5; Vásquez on, 231

peyote harvest, *78*; Cardenas, C., Sr., and Amada, employment for, 52, 73; drying, 37, 74, 76, 91–92, 124, 129, 142–43, *156*, 251n11, 255n12; fencing of ranches, 127, 204; by Inocencio, C., 75; by Johnson, S., 73–74; by Lira, 74; overharvesting, 128, 204, 270n6; sacred aspect, 42, 45–46, 69, 76, 90, 95, 97, 230–31; shift to Lower Rio Grande Valley, 126–27; technique, 42, 76, 115, 169, 260n4; Texas Department of Agriculture and Narcotics Bureau on, 100

peyote legislation test case (1969), 115–21; Cardenas, Amada, peyote sale in, 117–18; Kazen, B., on, 118–19; Kazen, E., unconstitutionality ruling, 117–18; NAC-NA petition of Texas for exemption, 116; Patchen, J., on, 116–17; on Peyotism, 118; Takes Gun and, 116–17; Texas Dangerous Drug Act, of 1967, 116

peyote religion. *See* Peyotism

Peyote Religion (Stewart), 245n3, 248n4

"The Peyote Religion and Mescalero Apache: An Ethnohistorical View From West Texas" (Schaefer), 249n5

Peyote Road: Ancient Religion in Contemporary Crisis, 188, 267n10

peyoteros, 2; Cardenas, Amada, as, 111–16; Cardenas, C., Sr., and Amada, as, 68–76; Cardenases' early life as, 42–48; Cortinas as, 39, 256n1; Morgan on, 231; peyote harvest respect by, 42, 45–46, 69, 76, 90, 95, 97, 230

peyote trade: Briggs on, 37; Cardenas, Amada's, retirement from, 128–30; Cardenas, C., Jr., on, 110; Cardenases' early life in, 41–48; DPS, Texas regulation of, 120; federal government on peyote transport, 36; Los Ojuelos, 30, 38–41, 251n12; to one-quarter Indian blood quantum, 120, 189, 261n8; Pedro on, 30; in pre-Columbian times, 32;

peyote trade (*continued*)
    Rancho los Ojuelos and, 2; Sanchez and, 30, 39; Spanish interruption of, 32–33; transportation, 36, 37, 90, 99, 100, 246n7; weather affect on, 19
peyote trade, not-for-profit: Cardenas, C., Jr., on, 95–96; George on, 96; respectful and celebratory manner, 97
"Peyote Trade in South Texas" (Stewart and Morgan), 14
peyote use: BIA on prohibition of, 99, 265n5; Castañeda on, 121; by Cora and Tarahumara indigenous peoples, 32; Huxley on, 121; NAC-NA on non-Indians, 265n5; non-Indians, DPS on, 189, 212; Oklahoma authorization of, 99–100; Oklahoma criminalization statute, 98–99; Texas Dangerous Drug Act (1967) amendment on, 118
Peyote Way, 95
Peyotism (peyote religion), 118, 182, 248n4; BIA on, 265n5; Lipan Apaches spread of, 250n8; Mescalero Apaches and, 249n5; mescalism and, 248n3; Mooney, La Barre, and Stewart on, 251n13; of NAC, 2, 31–36; Navajo Indians arrival of, 35; peyote buttons acquisition, 251n10; spread to Canada, 236, 264n2; Stewart on, 251n13
"Peyotism in Texas" (Stewart), 248n4
Piestra, Jorge, 174
Pilar (sister), 51, 58, 111–12
Pinal County, Arizona, 270n6
Pine Ridge Reservation, South Dakota, 30, 114; Morgan as member of NAC of, 123, 262n11
Pinero, 250n8
Pitalac band, of Coahuiltecans, 21
Powwow in the Schools, of Indigenous Cultures Institute, 266n3
Pozorski, Sheila, 10
Pozorski, Tom, 10
Prairie Potawatomi, 251n10

Pratt, Steven, 181
prayer meetings, 218; Cardenas, Amada, and family members at, *86*; Cardenas, Amada, at, *81*; cedar, traditional Native incense and, 6–7, 142, *162*, 193, 206, 211; feather fan in, 4, 7, 47, 142, 146, *162*, 193, 211, 268n11; female rabbi at, 182; female role in, 47, 253n16; Indians and non-Indians at, 148–51, 187; at Los Ojuelos home, 46; men role in, 47; roadman, 5–7, 9–10, 45–46, 95, 120, 131, 133, 141–42, 145, 174, 180, 186–88, 196, 212, 253n16, 256n2, 262n12; tepee at, *158*, *159*, 186; Vásquez at, 173–75; water in, 46–48, 69, 119, 145–46, 193, 206, 253n16
prayer meetings, February, 104, 140–42, 175; after Cardenas, C., Sr.'s death, 107; author attendance at, 177; Cardenas, Amado, legacy and, 207–8; Cardenas, C., Jr., on, 105; continued, 218; Hoffman, Archie, on, 105; Kazen, E., at, 182; Naranjo, A., on, 188; Patchen, J., on, 105–6; stories on origin of, 105–6; visitors to, 181
Presidio San Juan Bautista Spanish mission, 33
Psychedelic Reflections, 262n11

racial segregation, in Mirando City, 56–57, 60–61
Rancho los Ojuelos: birthplace, 2, 23; Cardenas, Amada, and family in, *78*; female role of gardeners and domestic duties, 24; Guerra and García families ownership of, 53, 253n2; male vaquero role, 23–24; as National Historic District, 203; peyote trade birthplace, 2
Raymond, Manuel J., 117; Cardenas, C., Sr.'s attorney, 103
Raza Unida movement, 208
"Recollections of the Peyote Road" (Morgan), 262n11

Refugio mission, peyote collection permission, 33
Reyna, Amando, 11
Reyna, Jimmy, 190–91
Reyna, Roque, 11
Rhine, Gary, 267n10
Río Bravo (Rio Grande), 18; small tracts of land to farm, 21; steamboat transportation on, 246n7
Rio Grande City, peyote dealers in, 10–11
Ríos, Ray, 266n3
Rivard, Robert, 265n6
roadman, in prayer meetings, 5–7, 9–10, 45–46, 95, 120, 131, 133, 141–42, 145, 174, 180, 186–88, 196, 212, 253n16, 256n2, 262n12
Rodríguez, Lala, 55
Rodriguez, Miguel, 3
Roosevelt, Franklin D., 235

"Sacred and Profane Uses of the Cactus *Lophophora williamsii* from the South Texas Peyote Gardens" (Kimber and McDonald), 14
sacred aspect, of peyote harvest, 42, 45–46, 69, 76, 90, 95, 97, 230–31
Sanchez, Esiquio (stepfather), 3, 23, 30, 39, 41
Sánchez de la Ibarrera y Garza, Tomás, 21–22
Sanchez Palacios, Gloria (niece), 3, 12; on Cardenas, C., Sr. and Amada's relationship, 90; on Cardenas, C., Sr.'s arrest, 102; on Cardenas, C., Sr.'s death, 107; on Los Ojuelos, 16; on Mexican racial discrimination, 60–61; on peyote for knee pain, 38; values instilled in, 66
Sandoval, Danny, 274n1; on lovingkindness, 226
San Luis Potosí peyote desert: Huichol Indians annual pilgrimage to, 32; sacred peyote land of Wirikuta in, 10
Schaefer, Stacy B., 245n2, 249n5

Schultes, Richard Evans, 257n6
Severo (brother-in-law), 111–12
Shawnee peyote practices and beliefs, 40, 252n14
Sheeran, Florinda, 3, 5, 113–14
Shepherd's Plays. *See* Las Pastorelas
Shumla Cave, in West Texas peyote materials, 248n2, 250n9
Sierra, Joe T., 114, 260n2
Skishkee, Bill, 251n10
Slotkin, Sydney J., 257n7, 263n14
Smith, Elna, 257n6
Southern Arapahos, 100
Southern Paiutes, NAC incorporation of, 256n2
Southern Plains tribes, in Texas, 33
South Texas, 17; birds and wildlife in, 19; climate, 18–19; fragrances from plants in, 19; map, 77; Montaño on food traditions in, 247n10; Mustang Plains, 18, 111–35; peyote production scarcity, 216–17; Peyotism, 31–36; Spanish explorers, 18
Southwestern Historical Quarterly, 14
Spain: clergymen negative references to peyote, 32; Texas domination by, 1
Special Collections, at Laredo Public Library, 14
Speck, Frank Gouldsmith, 262n13
St. Agnes Catholic Church, birthday mass, 3–4
The State of Texas v. David Clark, 87, 118, 260n7
Sterling, W. W. "Bill," 54
Stewart, Omer, 14, 123, 245n3, 248n4, 260n2; on Grove, 256n2; on Indian tribes, 33–34; on mescalism and Peyotism, 248n3; on Peyotism, 251n13
Stolen Education, 254n5
Stonecalf, Raymond, 105
Sun Dance way, 93

Takes Gun, Frank, 81, 118, 236;

Takes Gun, Frank (*continued*)
ACLU representation, 117; Attakai and Woody cases, 116, 117; NAC-NA trustee, 103–4; as NAC-US president, 264n2; as NAC-US vice president, 100; Patchen on, 260n5
Tamaulipan thorn scrub, 17; hunter-gathers and, 31
Tamaulipas, 2
Tarahumara indigenous peoples, peyote use, 32
Tecolotes (Owls) baseball team, 255n10
Tejanos, 1, 59, 245n2; birthday mass tradition, 3–4; Christmas traditions, 254n9; folk tradition of healers, 26; Lopez, M., of, 2–3; in Mirando City, 54, 60–63; Mother's Day celebration, 25; oil field work, 56; Las Pastorelas tradition, 61–63, 254n8; peyote dealers increase, 127
Templeton, Peter, 6, 181
Teocali Quetzalcoatl, of NAC chapter, 174
tepee, for prayer meeting, *158*, *159*; made by Etcitty, L., 186; one hundred year birthday, of Cardenas, Amada, 2, 5–7; Patchen, J., donation of poles, 186
Tepehuano indigenous peoples, peyote use of, 32
Terry, Martin, 270n6; population genetics study on peyote growing, 248n2; on prehistoric specimens of peyote, 250n9
Tethered Aerostat Radar System, 203
Teton Sioux, 114
Tewa family, from Hopi pueblos, 181
Texas, 21; anti-drug legislation, 99; Cardenas, C., Sr.'s move to, 26; NAC-NA petition for church exemption, 116; as slave state, 247n14; Southern Plains tribes in, 33; Spanish domination, 1; state ratification of, 247n14; Tejano families settlers, 1. *See also* Department of Agriculture;

Department of Public Safety; South Texas
Texas Archives, in Austin, 248n4
Texas Dangerous Drug Act (1967): NAC peyote use in religious ceremony amendment, 118; peyote illegal possession, 116
Texas Foundation for the Arts, 183
Texas Historical Commission, Jaramillo historic marker by, 247n13
Texas-Mexican Railroad, dried peyote transport on, 37
Texas Narcotic Drug Act amendment, 103, 120
Texas Narcotic Law of 1969, 118
Texas State Historical Commission, 183
THIQ alkaloids, in peyote, 250n9
Tía Ana (Martinez, N.'s aunt), *88*, 197, 201, 268n11
Tonkawa Indians, 253n16
Trail of Feathers: Searching for Philip True (Rivard), 265n6
transportation, in peyote trade, 36, 37, 90, 99, 100, 246n7
Treaty of Guadalupe Hidalgo (1848), 22
Tres Torres border crossing, 269n5
Treviño, Isaac, 266n3
tribal tensions, 125–26
Trotter, Robert, 263n14
True, Philip, 265n6
twenty-first century, peyote gardens in, 203–5

Underhill, Ruth, 100
Uniendo Nuestras Organizaciones, of Indigenous Cultures Institute, 266n3
University of Texas–Pan American (UTPA), 8

vaqueros: Lopez, M., as, 23–24; male role at Rancho los Ojuelos, 23–24; Vaquero Festival, 247n9
Vásquez, Manuel Kwautli, 4, 164, 182; on

birthday meeting tradition, 193–94; on Cardenas, Amada's, unconditional love, 200; Coahuiltecan chapter of NAC and, 173–74; on peyote gardens, 231; prayer meeting attendance, 173–75; on songs and rituals, 175–76; on unconditional love, 225
Villareal, Jacinto, 73

Walker, Jim, 261n9
Walker, Mary, 124
War Eagle, on peyote chiefs, 262n13
Washington's birthday weekend celebration, 9–10, 258n10, 258n11
Washoe Indians, 251n13
Washoe roadman, on peyote chief, 262n12
water: adding peyote to, 37, 43; holy, 4, 68, 128, 180, 267n4; in prayer meeting, 46–48, 69, 119, 145–46, 193, 206, 253n16; woman, 6, 47, 220
water drums, 69–70, 200
Weasel Bear, Beatrice, 114, 133, 232, 260n3
Webb County, Texas, 21

Westlund, Derek, 270n6
wildlife laws, 20
will, of Cardenas, Amada, 212; Cardenas, C., Jr., as NAC land trust executor, 213, 216; Cardenas, C., Jr., on, 215–16; Perez, G., on, 213–14; three lots as land trust of NAC, 213
Wilson, Moonhead, 251n10
Wirikuta, 10, 272n11
Wirikuta del Norte, 179, 180
Wisdom Sits in Places (Basso), 266n7
Woody case, in California, 116, 117
World War II, 58–59, 254n6
Wuili Uwi (goddess of peyote), 180

Xinachtli Project, of Indigenous Cultures Institute, 266n3

Youngman, Bert, 106

Zepeda, José, 182
Zepeda, Zep, 182